100/-

PRICE THEORY
AND
APPLICATIONS
IN
BUSINESS
ADMINISTRATION

GOODYEAR PUBLISHING COMPANY, INC., Pacific Palisades, California

W. David Maxwell
Indiana University

PRICE THEORY AND APPLICATIONS IN BUSINESS ADMINISTRATION

**PRICE THEORY
AND
APPLICATIONS
IN
BUSINESS
ADMINISTRATION**   W. David Maxwell

© 1970 by Goodyear Publishing Company, Inc.
Pacific Palisades, California

Library of Congress Catalog Card Number 76-100076

Current printing (last digit):
10 9 8 7 6 5 4 3 2 1

Printed in the United States of America

To Ruth, Susan, and Marian

preface

This book was designed for the first (and often only) course in micro-economics required of candidates for the master's degree in business administration. In my experience most such courses are characterized by one of two attitudes. The first is that price theory is price theory irrespective of who is taking the course. But, although price theory is a well-defined subject comprised of many related parts, nothing in this characterization dictates the relative weight accorded any particular component part. The second, and opposite, attitude is that in a graduate business administration curriculum microeconomics should take the form only of applications. However, to object to this view, meaningful application of intellectual tools is unlikely in the absence of considerable familiarity with those tools.

The approach followed in this work is a compromise, determined largely by my judgment of the present and prospective relevance in business administration of the various intellectual tools and concepts under consideration. Accordingly, for example, much of the theory of consumer demand is given short shrift, while production theory is emphasized and framed in terms of assumptions closer to those with which the student works in other courses.

In the M.B.A. program at Indiana, as in many such programs these days, the students are required to take mathematics. Moreover, the profes-

sors who teach this subject in the program at Indiana are unusually coop-
erative in designing their courses so as to include the tools that other
professors desire to use in their courses. I have taken advantage of this happy
circumstance to the extent that my own feeble ability in mathematics permits,
although seldom is calculus used as other than an alternative explanation.

During the past two years I have used a rough equivalent of the present
book. I have usually been able each semester to cover only Part I plus one
of the chapters in Part II. Although on other grounds Part II should include
treatment of other topics, the knowledge that I would seldom get to discuss
them has been an adequate deterrent to their inclusion.

I have the usual apologies to family for household chores unperformed
that would probably have been unperformed even if this book had not served
as the excuse. I have also the customary debts to a number of persons who
have read parts of the manuscript and made suggestions, some of which I
have taken. Of this group I am particularly indebted to Professors Thomas
K. Kim, Robert Dorfman, and William G. Panschar. Dale Flowers, my
graduate assistant, was of great assistance in many aspects of the preparation
of the manuscript, and I am also grateful to Mrs. Gwendolyn Flowers,
Mrs. Joyce Fonner, and Miss Marilyn Shaw for typing the manuscript.

W. DAVID MAXWELL

Bloomington, Ind.
December 1968

contents

7

equilibrium of the firm and industry   142

8

factor service pricing and
economic interdependence   165

APPLICATIONS IN BUSINESS ADMINISTRATION   191

9

the pricing of motor-carrier services   193

10

production theory and production management   222

11
the marketing theory of the firm and
the balance of marketing instruments   245

PRICE THEORY
AND
APPLICATIONS
IN
BUSINESS
ADMINISTRATION

PRICE THEORY

introduction

This chapter will attempt to do three things: first, to give some indication of the basic goals and purposes of this brief treatment of price and distribution theory, second, to provide a basic understanding of some aspects of methodology, and finally, to provide an outline of what is to follow in subsequent chapters.

BASIC GOALS AND PURPOSES

Students of economic questions have been intrigued for several centuries by the fact that the economy of any country is *systematic* in nature. The activities of production, distribution, and consumption, for example, *can* occur without central direction. No central authority has to determine what quantity of the nation's land, labor, and other resources will be devoted to the production of sugar cane or to facilities for the processing of the cane into sugar. Similarly, no central authority has to decide what quantity of the nation's resources will be devoted to the transport facilities necessary to the production of sugar or to its distribution. No one has to decide how many stores will sell this sugar or at what price, nor is it necessary for any authority to indicate which persons may purchase sugar. Yet some portion of the

3

country's resources *is* devoted to the production and distribution of sugar, and this sugar ends up in the hands of particular consumers.

In some countries, of course, a great deal of central planning is used to force economic activities to conform to political goals or to yield a priority of economic goals different from that which would exist in the absence of such planning. And in all countries some degree of guidance or control of the economy is exerted by political authority. But the remarkable fact is that these highly interrelated activities do not *have* to be planned or controlled—a fact, paradoxically enough, that *permits* planning by allowing it to be partial or incomplete. No system of economic planning yet devised has attempted to encompass all economic decisions, for the attempt to plan in such detail would be self-defeating.

There is thus a mechanism or *system* at work in much of economic affairs. Further, it is an *impersonal* system. Typically, the sugar-cane farmer does not know who will consume the sugar that will be refined from his cane. Nor does the trucker or boatman who carries the cane to the mill, the miller, the refiner, the retailer, and so on. Somehow the economic system decides how much income will be distributed among the inhabitants of a nation, somehow consumers decide what portions of their incomes will be spent upon particular economic goods (such as sugar), somehow the economic system determines what portion of society's resources will be devoted to the production of which goods, and somehow the economic forces at work determine the relative prices of economic goods.

Thus the basic economic functions can be performed as a result of a host of impersonal, individual decisions and yet result in a highly interrelated system. Students of economics have long sought to understand this system. Since it is a system, it is not surprising that the explanation of its functioning—of how it works—is a highly interrelated and systematic body of thought. It is the primary purpose of this brief treatment of price and distribution theory to provide some understanding of the economic system at work.

No single book, however, could possibly treat all aspects of economic theory—all aspects of the intellectual structure that economists have created in their attempts to understand, and analyze the effects of changes in, the forces acting upon economic magnitudes. This book is designed primarily to provide some understanding of *how* the economic system operates. It makes no attempt to explain the forces that determine the *rate* at which the system operates. By analogy, we seek to explain how an automobile works. We do not attempt to explain what determines the *speed* at which an automobile operates. To understand how an automobile works one must understand its ignition system, the system by which gasoline is mixed with air and fed to the cylinders, the system by which power from the explosion of gasoline vapor is transmitted to the wheels, and so on. To understand what determines the speed at which the automobile travels, we would have to take into account other factors relating to the surface upon which the wheels move, the rate at which gasoline flows to the engine, and so on.

How the automobile works at all is one question. How fast it operates is another. Similarly one part of economic theory, called *micro*economic theory, is devoted to the question of how the economic system operates, and it is this part of economic theory with which we are concerned in this course. Another part of economic theory, *macro*economic theory, attempts to explain the determinants of the *level* of economic activity, or the rate at which the economic system operates. The sets of forces that affect the speed of the economic system or the level at which it operates are sometimes grouped under the headings of monetary theory, business-cycle theory, and income and employment theory. Still other factors that affect the *growth* of an economy through time are studied under such titles as economic development or economic growth. These aspects of economic theory we shall not treat, confining ourselves to the more basic question of the economic system itself.

Further, we shall not consider political institutions or questions of economic policy, per se. Any economic system operates within a body of man-made laws, from such basic laws as those relating to contracts to those imposing restrictions upon the individual's freedom to sell products such as narcotics. Such a framework of laws we shall take for granted. We shall also make no attempt to indicate what specific actions the political authorities *should* take concerning economic matters.

We shall not be concerned with the relationships *between* economies. We shall not deal with the theory of international trade nor with comparative economic systems.

That so much of economic theory must be put aside in order that the remainder be of manageable proportions is an indication of the depth and breadth of economic theory. Our subject is price and distribution theory—a part of microeconomics. This one part of economic theory, however, embraces questions that have occupied the lifetimes of many men, and many of these questions we can only treat briefly, if at all. This part of economic theory is the most important. Its very language permeates all other parts of economic theory, and its basic constructs are important in every area of economics. An understanding of how the economic system operates, of how it works, of its indeed being a *system* even in the absence of central direction, is basic to the pursuit of any part of the subject of economics. To provide such an understanding is the primary purpose of this book.

We also have, however, secondary goals or objectives, the pursuit of which gives this book any basic uniqueness that it may possess. It is assumed that readers, insofar as they have an interest in economic theory, are interested primarily in what economists call "the theory of the firm." This particular subdivision of price and distribution theory is therefore given greater weight (and other parts of price and distribution theory correspondingly less weight) than in many treatments of the subject. Within this emphasis, greater weight is accorded those topics and constructs thought to have more direct relevance to other subjects that deal largely with business firms. Finally, we consider several topics of particular interest to students of some of these subjects. Thus, if the book achieves its secondary goal, students of marketing, production management, transportation, and other such subjects should see more clearly the relevance of economic theory to the areas of their particular interest.

METHODOLOGY

Students often appear to be more willing to learn the *contents* of a given course than the *nature* of those contents. Typically they spend little time on such questions as "What *is* this that I am learning?" nor do they often wish to consider directly the question of what there is in what they are learning that makes it worth learning.

This is unfortunate. Such a lack of interest in basic methodological questions often leads to misconceptions concerning the degree to which what is being learned applies to reality. On the one hand, a failure to consider methodological questions can lead to unwarranted reification—that is, it can lead the student to think that the theory he is learning is more immediately applicable to reality than it actually is. From a failure to understand the nature of price theory the student may conclude that businessmen, for example, typically possess real-world counterparts of highly abstract concepts such as marginal cost and marginal revenue schedules. Thus the failure to consider the methodological nature of what he is learning may prevent the student from recognizing or appreciating the nature of the abstraction involved, so that he cannot relate properly what he is learning to reality.

On the other hand, the same failure to understand the methodological nature of what is being learned may keep the student from seeing its applicability to other areas of study. Economic theory provides a set of intellectual tools that can be fruitfully used in other areas of economics and in business administration only if the user understands the nature of these tools.

Thus an understanding of the methodological nature of price and distribution theory is necessary if one is to use the theory properly. In seeking such an understanding, let us consider two methodological questions—the question of method, narrowly construed, and the question of verification.

In our first question we are asking, "What are the methods that economists use to gain knowledge or understanding of the vast range of social phenomena in which they are interested—what are the methods of enquiry?" Our second question is that of verification. One way of putting it is to ask, "What causes economists to think that the results they obtain have any applicability to reality?"

Although the classification leaves much to be desired, we may distinguish three methods of enquiry used by economists: the statistical method, the historical method, and the deductive method. The statistical method is often used in empirical economics, the historical method in economic history,[1] and the deductive method in economic theory—although only in the latter case do we find a single method sometimes used, at least formally, to the exclusion of the other two. Let us examine the three methods in turn.

The Statistical Method

By use of the statistical method we seek regularities or patterns in economic data. We use this method in analyzing such things as economic time series in an attempt to study cycles, to find the long-term pattern that economic growth follows, and so on. In a formal sense the statistical method is used in economics in the same way as in any other discipline. For example, a historical time series comprised of economic data is analyzed by the same techniques, constructs, and intellectual tools as is an experimental time series in chemistry. A historical time series of pig-iron production in the United States is treated, formally, in exactly the same manner as is a time series showing the effect of a catalyst upon the speed of a chemical reaction.

But what features of the statistical method argue for its classification as a separate method of enquiry? First, the individual event or observation is *anonymous*. In using the statistical method you seek to generalize about a *population* of events or observations that are explicitly assumed to be homogeneous. In fact, you assume that all these events or observations would act in precisely the same manner if it were not for *random variation*. The explicit assumption of variation is the second distinguishing feature of the statistical method.

In using the statistical method, then, you are saying something like the following:

(a) I have a population comprised of homogeneous events or observations— events or observations that are just alike.

---

[1] The ranks of economic historians have included in recent years an increasing proportion of scholars whose method of inquiry is essentially that of the economic theorist or the econometrician. This classification of methods does particular violence to them, and they serve as one of the best examples of the fact that few economists employ one method to the exclusion of all others.

(b) Admittedly, however, not all of these observations behave in exactly the same manner. This seems to be inconsistent—for if they are exactly alike, why do they not all act in the same way?

(c) The answer is the concept of random variation—the idea that the generalization you are making is correct and would be true of every event or observation in the population if it were not for a host of small random influences acting upon these observations. Explicitly you assume that there exists a host of small influences that cannot be specified individually, each of which has an infinitesimal influence upon the observations, each of which is equally likely to have a positive or negative effect of the same magnitude upon the observations, and all of which are distributed randomly. This concept of random variation was truly one of the great advances in methodology—an advance whose influence has yet to have its greatest effect in many disciplines.

The *efficiency* of the statistical method can hardly be overemphasized. It permits you to arrive at generalizations that cannot be reached by any other method. It lets you use information that any other method would force you to discard. And the basis of this efficiency is a formal recognition of error—the stipulation of random or other specified form of variation. That is why the concept of random variation constituted a tremendous breakthrough in methodology.

Perhaps an illustration would clarify the point. Suppose that an astronomer is using his instruments to measure the distance from the earth to the moon. Despite every effort to standardize or hold constant the temperature, the time at which he makes his measurements, and all the other known variables that could affect his readings, he finds that he does not always get exactly the same result from successive observations. If there were no statistical method, he would have to say that he did not know how far it is from the earth to the moon, and all of his work would be for nothing. By means of the statistical method, however, he can save the results of his work and say something very useful about the distance of the earth from the moon. The concept of random variation permits him to do so. Of course, with the assistance of mathematics, the statistical method can reach much more complex generalizations than this, but the basic assumption that makes all of them possible is the assumption of variation—an explicit formal cognizance of error that is peculiar to this method of enquiry.

The Historical Method

We shall treat much more quickly the historical method, partly because the question of a method of enquiry is perhaps unfair when applied to history, and partly because historians themselves are in basic disagreement over the question of the historical method.

In contrast to the statistical method, in the historical method the individual event or observation is often *unique*. The historian wishes to explain why one Caesar crossed the Rubicon. The historian does not have a population of Caesars that he maintains to be identical, so that he must explain why only part of them crossed the Rubicon. Thus the individual event is often important and not anonymous—and there is no concept of random variation.

The economic historian may be distinguished from the general historian by the greater stress that he places upon the economic aspect of society, and he may be distinguished from the economic statistician by the fact that the individual event or observation with which he deals is often unique and not explicitly subject to random variation. Historians argue heatedly among themselves about the nature of the historical method, holding positions that vary from a contention that they think the same thoughts as Caesar to a contention that they are eclectics who make use of and reconcile the results of all methods of enquiry.

But it may be unfair to speak of a historical "method." The historian believes, and perhaps rightly so, that everything that he knows about the setting of a historical event helps him understand it.[2] And if he could use only those variables or information which he can relate in syllogistic form to the event, he would feel impoverished. Further, the lack of formal method allows the historian an efficiency of his own. Since he need not state explicitly all assumptions and need not connect all assumptions, premises, and information in formal deductive chains of reasoning, he can treat a large number of events in relatively few pages. History is thus an art and not a precisely defined discipline, and the term "historical method" may well be a misnomer.

In any case, we can perhaps say, somewhat negatively, that in the historical method, in contrast to the statistical method, the individual event is often unique and there is no concept of variation—no formal, explicit recognition of error.

The Deductive Method

The third method employed in economics is the *deductive* method. Essentially this is simply logic applied to economic questions. This method is highly developed in economics and provides a core of theory that unifies

---

[2]The economist tempted to dismiss this statement lightly should consider that intuition plays some important but poorly understood role in the advancement of economic theory. Many "breakthroughs" in economic theory have been in large part intuitive. Further, the deductive method employed in economic theory, explicit as it is about what is to be done with assumptions *once they are chosen*, provides little guidance in the *selection* of assumptions. Here again, intuition or—at best—casual empiricism plays some ill-defined role.

this discipline and gives it a cohesiveness and rigor unparalleled in the other social sciences. No other social science is sufficiently advanced to possess a central body of theory of such refinement that it can be—and has been —expressed in the language of logicians or the shorthand logic of mathematics.

Before we congratulate ourselves too highly, however, it is well to note that the greater rigor and theoretical nature of economics, relative to the other social sciences, comes from the greater simplicity of its subject matter.[3] The subject of the social sciences is man—and the most consistent of man's actions are his economic actions.

As used in economics the deductive method takes something like the following form. We begin with a fundamental assumption and an actor to whom we ascribe this assumption as a predominant attribute or character-istic. For example, we may make the fundamental assumption of rationality and ascribe this attribute to the consumer. Second, we employ a "heuristic device"—a set of subsidiary assumptions that describe the situation or arena in which our actor is assumed to act. Thus we may assume that our rational consumer has a fixed money income and that he faces a market in which there are goods whose prices he knows. Such terms as "monopoly," "perfect competition," "oligopoly," and so on are merely designations or convenient names for particular heuristic devices or assumed situations in which the "rational producer" is assumed to act. Third, we "figure out" or deduce the actions of the type of actor we have assumed in the situation we have posed. In other words, we conjoin our assumptions and find the logical implications of the conjuncture.

Basically that is all there is to it. Pose the actor and the attribute ascribed to him, pose the situation, deduce the conclusions. In practice, of course, the situation posed may be quite complex and the deductive chains quite lengthy. Hence geometry and other forms of mathematics are quite useful in stating the assumptions and the heuristic device precisely and compactly and also in checking and adding to the deductions made.

This method has the significant advantage of dividing arguments into (1) arguments over the assumptions and (2) arguments over the conclusions that may be drawn from those assumptions. By contrast with the statistical method, in the deductive method there is no explicit assumption of variation —no formal cognizance of error. Formally an actor with the attributes ascribed must, in the situation posed, act in the manner deduced. A profit-maximizing firm must produce the output at which marginal cost equals marginal revenue. This is the only conclusion that can be deduced. A firm

---

[3]"Simplicity" in this context is a necessary condition for analytical rigor. The sim-plicity or regularity of behavior of the phenomena with which they deal allows some of the natural sciences to be more rigorous than any social science.

producing any other output, in the situation assumed, could not be a profit-maximizing firm.

The fact that the conclusions in economic theory follow inexorably as deductions from the assumptions has led to misunderstandings about this method by friend and foe alike. Even fellow social scientists sometimes construe the assumption of rationality—of economic man—to mean that economists believe man to be completely selfish and every producer to have desk drawers labeled "marginal cost" and "marginal revenue." Economists, however, realize that their assumptions are not completely accurate and that the abstraction that yields the heuristic device does not reproduce reality. *Within* the process, however, there is no cognizance of error—no concept of variation—and hence the conclusions follow inexorably as a matter of logic. *Validity* is complete—*applicability* is a separate question.

While the deductive method resembles the historical method in that there is no concept of random variation, it is unlike the historical method in that the individual event is not unique. Any actor possessing exactly the attribute assumed (to a degree such as to more than offset the concerted opposing influence of all other attributes) and acting in the exact situation posed would have to act in the manner deduced. But both actor and situation are abstractions. It is not claimed that any specific empirical counterpart of the actor has only the attribute ascribed or that the empirical situation in which he acts is completely described by the heuristic device. Thus the deductive method is used to explain *the* consumer or *the* firm, and does not claim to explain all of the actions of a specific consumer or a specific firm.

The frequent use of abstractions of a high order has also led to criticism and misunderstanding among even fellow social scientists. This is not the occasion to *defend* the methods we are attempting to explain, but perhaps it should be pointed out that the use of abstraction is an attempt to *secure* reality, not escape it, and that the use of abstraction is not to be scorned because it is abstraction. This is as true in economics as it is in engineering. There is no such thing as a straight line, or a circle, or a square, but these abstractions are very useful in building bridges.

The Choice of Methods

In economics, as in all of the social sciences, one never has the choice of fact versus theory, despite the frequency with which this supposed choice is voiced. The idea that because we have a formal choice of the statistical method or the deductive method, we have thus a choice between subjective theory and objective fact, is a naive notion in the social sciences. It is more nearly true that in the social sciences we have a choice of theories—not a choice of theory versus fact.

You will recall our earlier example of a historical time series. Formally we treat a historical time series in exactly the same way that we treat an experimental time series in the natural sciences. This means that we use ideal constructs. Thus we treat our observation of the pig-iron production of 1890 as though the year in which it was produced were irrelevant—yet we know that a host of forces acting in 1890 affected that observation. Nonetheless we treat this observation as though it were equivalent to an observation in an experimental time series that could be duplicated again and again under controlled conditions.

Also we treat this observation for 1890 as though it were independent of the observation that we have for the year 1889. Obviously, the amount of pig-iron produced in one year could not be entirely independent of that produced in a subsequent, or preceding, year. And formal tests for such things as autocorrelation and serial correlation are themselves deductions from assumptions that are not completely met in reality. Thus, data in the social sciences are always forced into mental constructs into which they do not completely fit, and much work remains to be done in developing statistical theory so that we can judge the consequences of the failure of our data to fit the molds. Stated somewhat differently, statistics is a theory that provides ideal constructs for our use. We use these constructs in the social sciences, but always under conditions that violate the assumptions of the theory. An important, often neglected, question is how to allow for this violation. Quite often the use of the statistical method is accompanied by a quite spurious sense of reality, but theory is not only not being avoided—the most relevant theory (that devoted to the question of the preceding sentence) is so complex that it is seldom enunciated.

Thus in economics we have a choice of theories. Seldom, however, is a blanket choice of methods really necessary. Both the statistical and deductive methods are imperfect in their applications in the social sciences and both can usually shed some light on the subject of enquiry. No matter which method is used, we do not have the controlled laboratory conditions of the natural scientist, and thus to call any social science a science is, in a sense, misleading.

VERIFICATION

As indicated above, our classification of the methods of enquiry used by economists is by no means completely satisfactory. The statistical and historical methods employ deduction, and deduction must have some empirical reference. In economics deduction cannot proceed in a complete vacuum, owing nothing to empirical reality. Thus the methods used by economists are not completely independent, although our classification suggests that they are. Nonetheless, let us proceed to the second of our questions—the question of verification.

Put broadly, by verification we mean the following:

(a) We have indicated that three methods are used by economists to secure an understanding of economic phenomena.

(b) What makes us think that these methods provide such an understanding?

Put somewhat more narrowly, by the use of these methods we arrive at certain conclusions. What causes us to think that these conclusions have any applicability to reality? Note that we say "applicability" rather than "validity." In the present context "validity" is the formal, logical property that a conclusion can be deduced from the conjoining of assumptions. "Applicability" is the coincidence of the conclusion with reality. Thus many conclusions are valid but of little applicability.

We must readily grant that there can be no verification in an ultimate sense. It is always possible that an alternative hypothesis is actually the correct one and could yield the same conclusion as one that we regard as coming from a true explanation. A hypothesis or theory can therefore never be *confirmed* by coincidence of its conclusions with reality. Coincidence, even in the natural sciences, merely means that the hypothesis or theory has not yet been *disconfirmed*. But in the social sciences we have the further (or, at least greater) problems that establishing coincidence of conclusions with reality is itself not a completely neutral process, and that the process of choosing one theory or hypothesis over another cannot be done as systematically as in some of the natural sciences. Thus, to say that a hypothesis or theory pertaining to the social sciences can be verified is too absolute a statement, if we use "verify" in the sense in which it can be used in the natural sciences. Since verification is always a matter of degree, however, we can say—somewhat loosely—that an economic theory or hypothesis is verified if it is valid (that is, internally consistent) and if it appears to be supported by more evidence than any other valid alternative.

Verification and the Statistical Method

In a sense the statistical method is the frankest and clearest on the question of verification, but this frankness and this clarity are, in some respects, more apparent than real. The statistical method makes such formal statements as: "On the assumption that all independent variables *not* contained in the model act in a random manner upon the dependent variable, the hypothesis is valid."[4] Note, however, that "valid" is used here in the same sense in which it was used above.[5] It means, in this context, that we have assumptions from which we can logically deduce this hypothesis as a conclusion. Thus, if *all* of the assumptions of the model were met completely, the hypothesis would apply *in reality*. If the assumptions (including the assumption of random variation) are completely true (that is, coincide with reality completely), it is inconceivable that the hypothesis could be false.

The distracting thing about conclusions arrived at by the statistical method is the peculiar way in which they are phrased, if phrased formally. The concept of random variation, having been introduced as an assumption, determines the nature of the conclusion.

What we wish to do, of course, is to establish the truth of our assumptions so that we can say incontrovertibly that our hypothesis is applicable. But consider, for example, the assumption of random variation. There is no independent way of establishing the truth of this assumption. For examples such as we have suggested, only by making the assumption of random variation can you account for your findings. Thus, if you *assume* that your findings are correct, you can deduce random variation as a logical necessity. But what we want to do is to determine whether or not our hypothesis is correct.

Thus we find that the assumption of random variation is an a priori assumption not capable of direct verification. Similarly, such statistical concepts as tests of significance are internal tests (internal to statistical theory) that actually describe the applicability of a statistical generalization only if all of the assumptions of the statistical model coincide completely with reality. Since we know this is not the case in the social sciences, we ascribe little significance in reality to a statistically significant association between the butterfat content of yak milk and freight-car loadings in Newark.

---

[4]Actually this is an example of what might be termed the "strong" statistical method, in which a unique hypothesis is the mechanical result of the conjoining of assumptions. The hypothesis in this case corresponds to the conclusions in the deductive method. A second, somewhat less strong type of statistical method is that in which more than one valid hypothesis can be deduced from the same set of assumptions. A third type of statistical method is that in which the hypothesis or hypotheses are tentatively accepted as not obviously inconsistent with the assumptions. In this weakest form the validity of the hypothesis is not determined prior to attempts to determine its applicability. The decision to accept or reject the hypothesis in this case rests almost solely upon the evaluation of its applicability. The discussion in the text is phrased in terms of the "strong" statistical method. The necessary extensions and modifications needed to encompass the weaker versions should be apparent. I am indebted to Professor Donald L. Harnett for this classification of the statistical method.

[5]As Morris Cohen has observed [*Reason and Nature* (New York: Harcourt, Brace & World, Inc., 1931), p. 116],

If an inductive inference is valid it must conform to the condition of all valid inference. If the latter is called deduction, induction is not its antithesis but a special form of it.

Thus statistical theory is essentially tautological, as is all theory.[6] No hypothesis can be deduced that was not implicit in the premises, and at least one of these premises or assumptions is incapable of direct verification.

But one might well contend that *predictability* is a sufficient test of applicability. We can predict, for example, that 95 per cent of the confidence intervals generated by random samples will contain the population parameter. If 95 per cent of the limits do include the population parameter, however, we can only trust that this is not a consequence of the *in*correctness of our assumptions. Thus, ultimately we have to accept on faith the truthfulness of our assumptions—or rather, we have to have faith that the extent of their lack of complete coincidence with reality is not sufficient to render our conclusions inapplicable. And since what we seek is understanding, predictability alone is insufficient.[7]

We may thus summarize the problem of verification of the results yielded by the statistical method as follows:

    (a) Given the assumption of random variation (or some other basic assumption of a probabilistic nature), and given other assumptions concerning homogeneity and independence of observations, and so on, we can deduce a hypothesis (the process of deduction being greatly aided by the use of mathematics).

    (b) The hypothesis is also of a probabilistic nature. If one or more of the independent variables were assumed to be subject to random variation, the conclusion is stated as being subject to this same disturbing influence.

    (c) Formally the hypothesis is valid as a logical deduction from given assumptions or premises.

---

[6] As T. W. Hutchison has aptly pointed out in discussing economic theory [*Significance and Basic Postulates of Economic Theory* (London: Collier-Macmillan Ltd., 1938), p. 28],

> People sneer at tautologies, but because the proposition $2 \times 2 = 4$ is to most people "self evident" while the proposition $17 \times 37 = 629$ is probably not, this does not imply that they are of different logical types.

Or, as Hutchison also said (idem, p. 36),

> Long deductive chains lose their trivial, but not their analytical-tautological character. The *applicability* of the assumptions of a piece of theory may be criticized; this has nothing to do with the *form* of a proposition of pure theory which must necessarily be "tautological," "circular," and "assume what it proves."

[7] I may be able to predict quite accurately that my hand placed near the antenna of my radio receiver will change its volume, but this, *per se*, does not tell me why it does so. If I have some knowledge of the relevant aspects of physics, my action may strengthen my confidence in the explanation physics provides. This explanation, however, may subsequently be superseded as its assumptions are found to be incorrect, but they would prove to have been incorrect in such a way as to reconcile the earlier coincidence of the conclusions of the outmoded theory with the change in volume resulting from the proximity of my hand to the antenna. If I have *no* theory of why my hand in proximity to the antenna affects the receiver's volume, this occurrence is—so far as I am concerned—witchcraft, regardless of its predictability. Thus prediction must be coupled with a theory to constitute verification—contingent though the verification may be.

(d) The hypothesis deduced is subjected to a formal test of its applicability. In other words, it is confronted by what are presumed (for the purposes of the test) to be the empirical counterparts of elements to which it refers. As we have seen, this is not a completely neutral process, and the hypothesis would be completely applicable if, and only if, the assumptions were completely true. Nonetheless, verification is partially formalized.

(e) The assumption of random or other variation cannot be independently verified, and many of the other assumptions employed do not completely hold for economic data.

(f) We thus ascribe applicability to the hypothesis to the extent that we believe the assumptions to be correct.

Verification and the Historical Method

For the reasons given earlier, we shall again treat the historical method only briefly.

Historians make inferences on the basis of written evidence. Ordinarily, however, the process by which conclusions are reached is not made explicit or formalized. Similarly, the question of verification is perhaps not so often treated explicitly by historians as by economists. Often it appears that the historian who constructs the hypothesis that appeals most to fellow historians is the one whose explanation is accepted. This initial explanation or thesis is often disputed by other historians, however, until—in a somewhat Hegelian manner—the initial hypothesis is tempered, qualified, or moderated.

This process is very similar to what occurs in the literature relating to economic theory—except that in history the process is lengthened and confused because rigor is lacking and there is less awareness of the process. As noted earlier, however, lack of rigor in history allows efficient coverage of events, and historians may be well advised not to be too concerned with methodology.

Verification and the Deductive Method

Most of what we have said about verification with respect to the statistical method holds for the deductive method. If the assumptions are true and the logic correct, the conclusions are not only valid but also fully applicable.

Again, however, we know that the assumptions are not completely true. Although it may be true, for example, that men are more nearly rational than irrational, they certainly are not completely rational in economic matters. Much of their action is habitual and blindly repetitive. In recognition of this limitation the generalizations of economic theorists refer to direction of effect rather than magnitude. Such limited generalizations require only, for example, rationality at the margin—that is, the element of rationality need only be stronger than the concerted opposing force of the elements of irrationality.

Perhaps the most vulnerable step in the deductive process is the heuristic device. These sets of subsidiary assumptions describing the situation in which the actor is presumed to act are heroic abstractions, which greatly simplify reality and fail to describe it completely. Further, the question of which heuristic device describes best an actual situation often cannot be answered except as a matter of judgment. Finally, the number of heuristic devices is, of course, far more limited than the number of situations that exist in reality. The many oligopolistic situations that we have constructed, for example, are few relative to the number of forms in which oligopoly exists in reality.

Limitations of the deductive method, other than those pertaining to the heuristic device, also cause us to ascribe only partial applicability to its results. Characteristics of the actor other than those assumed cannot be directly taken into account when we judge the value of the results of the analysis. Further, the deductive method finds perhaps its most important use in the analysis of the results of alterations in the subsidiary assumptions comprising the heuristic device, but usually we can analyze such changes only by mentally holding all other variables constant—a condition that we know would not hold for such changes in reality.

Thus, in using the deductive method we again force reality into mental constructs that it does not completely fit. And despite the limited nature of the generalizations we reach, we cannot verify them in the sense of demonstrating their complete applicability to reality. This method does not include a formal test of even partial applicability. The best that we can hope for, from even the most elegant theorizing, is a sense of understanding that we cannot so readily achieve in any other way. Putting this in a somewhat more complicated way, all of us interpret reality or information about reality in terms of a mental screen or framework. We cannot approach reality with a tabula rasa. A knowledge of economic theory permits us to perceive regularities and interrelationships in reality that we might otherwise overlook; it permits us, in a sense, to order the information that we perceive. Because verification is so primitive, however, we must be constantly on guard to distinguish understanding from mere coincidence of conclusions with previously acquired prejudices.

Thus, in economics verification is incomplete whatever method of enquiry is used, and its incompleteness is apparent at a far lower level of abstraction than that at which verification is incomplete even in the natural sciences. Whatever method of enquiry is used, verification of the conclusions reached thereby is not a completely neutral process in the social sciences. No system of testing altogether avoids abstraction from reality, and "facts" in the social sciences are not completely inert entities independent of our way of looking at or ordering them. In this book we shall employ primarily the deductive method. This method, like any of the others that economists may use, can lead to an increased understanding of the interrelated activities that characterize the economy of any nation—if it is used with an appreciation of its nature and limitations.

AN OUTLINE OF WHAT IS TO FOLLOW

The Fundamental Problem of Economics

The fundamental problem of economics arises from the fact that man's wants exceed the ability of his resources to satisfy those wants. The economic system is the mechanism that man has erected to deal with this problem, and microeconomic theory is the economists' explanation of this system.

It follows from this problem that only a portion of man's economic wants can be satisfied and that only a part of society's resources can be devoted to the satisfaction of any particular want. To explain how some of man's economic wants come to be expressed in the marketplace and how economic resources are guided by these wants and come also to the marketplace in a form suitable to fulfill them is a basic goal of price and distribution theory.

Derivation of the Market Demand Curve

The explanation of how some wants come to be expressed in the marketplace while others do not and of the form their expression takes constitutes the derivation of the market demand curve. In subsequent chapters we shall pose a rational consumer whose wants far exceed his income and who thus faces the problem of allocating or rationing that income among the economic goods he desires. In treating this problem we shall derive the individual consumer's demand curve, and from the individual consumer's demand curve we shall arrive at the market demand curve. At this point we shall have provided an explanation of how some of man's economic wants come to be expressed in the market while others do not.

Derivation of the Market Supply Curve

There would be little point in the expression of some of man's wants in the market if there were not in the market the means of satisfying them. Economic actors other than the consumer convert resources into the final goods that consumers desire, and offer them in the market. To explain what determines the conditions under which goods are offered we shall also, in subsequent chapters, derive the market supply curve. To explain this curve we shall need to consider the revenue and cost functions of the firm, and to understand the nature of the firm's cost functions we shall have to consider the firm's production function and the conditions under which the services of the factors of production are supplied. At this point we shall have provided an explanation of the process by which the services of the factors of production are combined to yield economic goods, which are then offered for sale in the marketplace.

Distribution Theory

When factor services are sold, income accrues to the owners of those services. Thus, in explaining what determines the payments that firms make for factor services we are also explaining what determines the income earned by owners of the factors of production. At this point we have, in essence, closed the circle, for we have explained the origin of the income that— together with the consumer's wants—permitted us to derive the individual consumer's demand curve.

We shall not go deeply into distribution theory, chiefly because in this area the relevant theory is of greater complexity and yields less satisfactory explanations than does price theory per se. There is, for example, no single theory of interest to which all economists subscribe, and the determinants of the monetary return to the owners of labor services are too numerous and complex to be embraced in a single simple model.

Distribution theory will be treated only to the extent required for a relatively simple explanation of the workings of the economic system. The fact that resources are scarce gives rise to the income received by the owners of resources, and this same scarcity means that only some of the consumer's wants can be satisfied. *Which* wants will be satisfied depends upon the priority assigned to those wants by the consumer and upon the consumer's income, the limitation on his income stemming basically also from the scarcity of resources. Paradoxically, if resources were not limited, no income would arise from owning them, but—by the same token—if resources were not limited, all wants could be satisfied and the concept of a limited income would be nonsensical.

Part I: A Diagrammatic Outline

Figure 1.1 is a diagrammatic outline of what is to follow in Part I of this book. Like any outline, it is necessarily incomplete, and each single diagram represents a great deal of discussion that will follow in subsequent chapters. Further, it is not expected that this outline will be of great immediate assistance. If the reader understood all of its ramifications at this point, he would not need to read most of the remaining chapters. None-

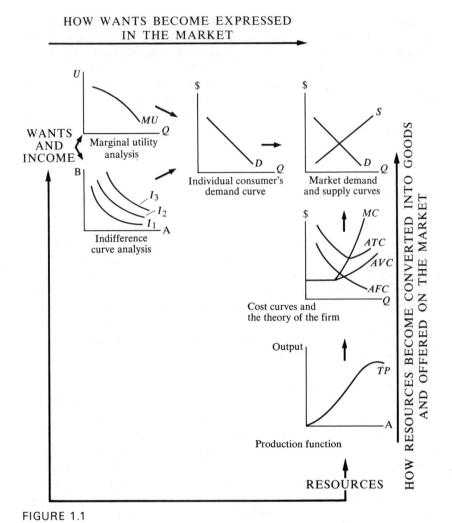

FIGURE 1.1

theless, the outline does present in capsule form the essence of what is to be discussed in Part I; it will become clearer as the discussion progresses, and frequent references back to it will enable the reader to "position" himself from time to time in the total argument of Part I.

Part II: Applications in Business Administration

The first eight chapters comprising Part I are designed primarily to give the reader a basic understanding of the functioning of the economic system. In Part II certain tools and concepts introduced in Part I are developed in greater depth, and they are used to analyze topics of particular interest to students of business administration. Thus, the theory of price discrimination is developed more fully and applied to the pricing of transportation services, and the production theory of Part I is reviewed in terms of some aspects of "production" as a field within business administration. By such means the second part of the book seeks to help the student gain further understanding of the relevance of microeconomic theory.

SELECTED REFERENCES

COHEN, MORRIS, *Reason and Nature* (New York: Harcourt, Brace & World, Inc., 1931).

HUTCHISON, T. W., *Significance and Basic Postulates of Economic Theory* (London: Collier-Macmillan, Ltd., 1938).

KAUFMANN, FELIX, *Methodology of the Social Sciences* (New York: Oxford University Press, 1944).

KEYNES, JOHN NEVILLE, *Scope and Method of Political Economy* (London: Collier-Macmillan, Ltd., 1891).

ROBBINS, LIONEL, *An Essay on the Nature and Significance of Economic Science*, 2nd rev. ed. (London: Collier-Macmillan, Ltd., 1952).

the derivation of the individual consumer's demand curve

The basic purpose of this chapter is to derive the individual consumer's demand curve. We employ the term "derive," however, in a rather special sense. For our purposes, the most important property or characteristic of the individual consumer's demand curve is that, in general, it is downward sloping—that is, this demand curve possesses a negative slope. Thus, what we wish to be able to conclude is that, *ceteris paribus* (holding all other variables constant), the quantity demanded of an economic good by the individual consumer tends to vary inversely with the price of that good.[1] Although the analysis yields other important points, this is the primary conclusion to be established, and establishing this property or characteristic of the individual consumer's demand curve is what we mean by "deriving" it.

In terms of the methodological discussion of the previous chapter, our basic assumption is that of rationality, and the actor to whom this assumed rationality is attributed is an abstraction called the consumer. It is also assumed that the consumer has an income that is limited relative to his desire for economic goods and that he faces markets in which there are

---

[1] As we shall see, the *Giffen* good is an exception to the general law of demand.

goods the prices of which he knows but cannot affect by his purchases. This actor and this situation are common to all analyses.

We shall thus be interested in determining what can be deduced, given this kind of actor and the situation posed. We shall be particularly interested in two questions: (a) How does a rational consumer apportion or allocate his limited income among the various goods he purchases? (b) How does a rational consumer react to price changes? In answering the first question we shall develop the *principle of rational consumer's expenditure*, and in answering the second we shall derive the *individual consumer's demand curve*.[2]

THE PRINCIPLE OF DIMINISHING MARGINAL UTILITY

Consumers regard economic goods as desirable. Indeed, if they were not desirable—if consumers did not want them—they would not be economic goods. The quality or characteristic of economic goods that causes them to be desired is what economists call "utility."

That an economic good possesses "utility" does not mean that it is necessarily *useful* in any sense other than that it satisfies the consumer's desire for it. If a consumer wants it, it possesses—by definition—"utility." The fact that a consumer chooses between economic goods implies that they do possess the common characteristic of utility, for in the absence of this common characteristic, economic goods could not be compared.

In the marginal-utility approach, however, much more than this is assumed about utility. It is assumed also—at least for the possible quantities of economic goods that the consumer's limited income and wealth permit him to purchase—that more goods are preferable to less. The consumer's *total* utility, in other words, increases as a function of the number of economic goods he possesses. But what about the *quantity* of any *particular* economic good? It would appear reasonable that, although the consumer might prefer more goods to fewer goods, the range over which he would prefer a larger quantity of a given good to a smaller quantity would be much more limited. Thus a given consumer's total utility might be expected to be greater if he possessed three oranges rather than two, but it is not at all apparent that he would necessarily prefer thirty-four oranges to thirty-three (omitting the possibility of his acting as a seller).

Economists, in using this approach, therefore make the further assumption that the consumer's desire for any particular economic good can be

---

[2] A number of approaches may be used to derive the individual consumer's demand curve. We shall first use one of the older marginal-utility approaches and then an indifference-curve approach that retains the concept of a unique (though no longer cardinal) utility function. Finally, we shall sketch an indifference-curve approach employing the preference relationship and utility indices.

satiated by his possessing a sufficiently large quantity of that economic good, and that such a point of satiety could be reached—for some economic goods—even within the limits imposed upon the consumer by his ability to purchase those goods. But if the possession of three oranges rather than two increases the consumer's total utility, why need it not be also true that the possession of thirty-four oranges is preferable to the possession of thirty-three?

The answer lies in the manner in which total utility is assumed to vary as a function of the quantity of a particular good. It is assumed that as successively greater quantities of a given economic good are acquired, total utility increases *at a decreasing rate*, until a point is reached at which total utility will actually decline if the quantity of the particular good is increased further. This assumption—that possession of each additional unit of the commodity *adds* to total utility a lesser amount—is called *the principle of diminishing marginal utility*. More precisely, *marginal utility* is the rate of change of *total utility* relative to variation in the quantity of one good, the quantity of all other goods being unchanged. This rate of change is assumed to decrease as quantity increases, and this assumption is called *the principle of diminishing marginal utility*.

The definition of the marginal utility of one good under conditions of a given quantity of all other goods reflects a realization (except in the earliest versions of the marginal-utility approach) that the utilities received from possession of more than one good are not independent and additive. In other words, if we pose some fictitious unit of utility (such as a "util"), the number of utils of satisfaction that a consumer receives from oranges may be affected by the number of grapefruit he has. We cannot simply sum the utils received from oranges and then those received from grapefruit, because the two are not independent. Thus the principle of diminishing marginal utility is an assumption concerning the utility received from various quantities of one good, for given quantities of all other goods.

Figure 2.1 expresses geometrically the assumptions we have made concerning utility. It portrays several sections of a utility "surface," a three-dimensional representation of how utility (the vertical axis) varies with the quantities of two goods, A and B. The planes or sections of the utility surface are taken for the specific quantities B_1, B_2, and B_3 of good B and show how utility changes as the quantity of good A is changed while the quantity of B is held constant. The fact that the planes or sections become higher as one moves away from the origin reflects the assumption that total utility increases as more of both goods are acquired. The fact that each plane or section possesses a maximum reflects the assumption of satiety. The fact that the height of each plane increases at a decreasing rate, as A increases, reflects the assumption of diminishing marginal utility. Although Figure 2.1 portrays sections for given values of B, sections of the same nature would

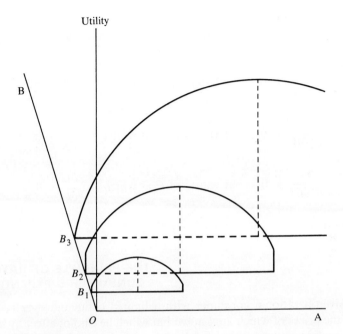

FIGURE 2.1

result if we depicted variation of B for given values of A. Thus geometry can be used to portray quickly and accurately the assumptions that we have made about utility.

Finally, the same assumptions can be expressed in terms of calculus. The assumption that utility is a function of the number and quantity of goods can be expressed as

$$U = f(A, B, C, \ldots),$$

where U represents utility, and $A, B, C, \ldots$ represent quantities of the various goods under consideration. The *marginal* utilities of $A, B, C, \ldots$ would thus be

$$\frac{\partial U}{\partial A}, \quad \frac{\partial U}{\partial B}, \quad \frac{\partial U}{\partial C}, \quad \ldots$$

The assumption of diminishing marginal utility would be expressed as

$$\frac{\partial^2 U}{\partial A^2} < 0, \quad \frac{\partial^2 U}{\partial B^2} < 0, \quad \frac{\partial^2 U}{\partial C^2} < 0, \quad \ldots$$

And the assumption that the consumer can reach a point of satiety with respect to the quantity acquired of any one economic good can be expressed as

$$\frac{\partial^2 U}{\partial A^2} < 0 \quad \text{at values of } A \text{ at which} \quad \frac{\partial U}{\partial A} = 0,$$

$$\frac{\partial^2 U}{\partial B^2} < 0 \quad \text{at values of } B \text{ at which} \quad \frac{\partial U}{\partial B} = 0,$$

$$\frac{\partial^2 U}{\partial C^2} < 0 \quad \text{at values of } C \text{ at which} \quad \frac{\partial U}{\partial C} = 0,$$

and so on.

THE PRINCIPLE OF RATIONAL CONSUMER'S EXPENDITURE

Given a rational consumer with a limited command over economic goods, the prices of which are known but which he cannot affect by his purchases, and given the principle of diminishing marginal utility, how will the consumer allocate his expenditures among economic goods? In the language of Chapter 1, what can be deduced about his pattern of expenditures from the conjoining of these assumptions?

From the assumption of rationality and the definition of utility it follows that the rational consumer would act so as to maximize utility. He would wish his pattern of expenditures to yield a larger total utility than any alternative. If there were no limitation upon his income and wealth, we could conclude—because of the principle of diminishing marginal utility— that he would allocate his expenditures in such a way that the marginal utility of each good became zero. In other words, he would purchase that quantity of each good beyond which any greater quantity would yield a smaller total utility. His total utility would thus be maximized by the acquisition of quantities of the various goods such that their marginal utilities were equal to each other and also equal to zero.

But the assumption of a limited command over economic goods (which we shall henceforth call simply a limited "income") requires that the maximum that the consumer seeks be subject to this constraint. In other words, the consumer will seek that pattern of expenditures, *consistent with the limitation upon his income*, which will maximize his total utility. Given the prices of goods, and given his limited income, there are a number of patterns his expenditures *can* take. Of these possibilities he will choose the pattern that yields the highest total utility. If the quantities in which goods are purchased were perfectly divisible and if the prices of all economic goods were the same, the consumer would so allocate his expenditures that the marginal utility of any one good was equal to that of any other good. Thus if the prices of all economic goods were one dollar, the consumer would so allocate his income that the marginal utility of good A was equal to the marginal utility of good B, and so on, and a dollar spent upon any economic good would yield the same marginal utility. Since the prices of economic goods differ, however, the consumer, in allocating his expenditures in such a way that a dollar spent upon any good would yield the same marginal utility, so allocates his income that the marginal utilities of goods are proportional to their prices. If one good costs twice as much as another, the consumer would so allocate his expenditures that the marginal utility of the first good was twice as great as that of the less expensive good.

This, then, is the principle of rational consumer's expenditure—that a consumer will so allocate his expenditures as to make the marginal utilities of goods proportional to their prices. Stated symbolically, the consumer will so allocate his expenditures that

$$\frac{MU_A}{MU_B} = \frac{P_A}{P_B}.$$

When we rearrange the expression and expand it, the principle of rational consumer's expenditure becomes

$$\frac{MU_A}{P_A} = \frac{MU_B}{P_B} = \frac{MU_C}{P_C} = \cdots$$

Geometrically the process can be illustrated as shown in Figure 2.2. Figure 2.2 is the same as Figure 2.1 except for the addition of the plane the base of which is A_2B_3. If the consumer were to spend all of his income upon good A, it is assumed that—given the price of A—he could buy the quantity A_2, whereas if he were to spend all of his income upon good B—at the present price of B—he could purchase the quantity B_3. The line A_2B_3 thus constitutes a locus of points showing those combinations of A and B which the consumer *can* buy (if he spends all of his income), and the ratio OB_3/OA_2 equals the ratio of the price of A to the price of B.

The total utility yielded by any of the combinations represented by points lying along A_2B_3 is the distance from that point to be utility surface. These distances are represented by the dotted portions of the vertical lines rising from the line A_2B_3. In other words, a vertical plane is erected, its base being A_2B_3 with its upper edge above the utility surface. The highest point common to the plane and the surface would represent that combina-

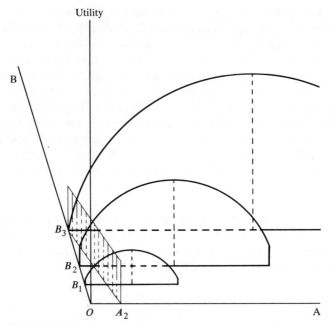

FIGURE 2.2

tion of the two goods which, of all combinations that the consumer could purchase, would yield the greatest total utility.

Mathematically, we can derive the principle of rational consumer's expenditure (for the two-good case) by the method of the Lagrangian multiplier in the following way:

Let the consumer's utility function be given by

$$U = f(A, B)$$

and his income constraint by

$$Y = P_A A + P_B B.$$

The problem is to maximize the consumer's utility subject to his income constraint. In order to do so, construct the function

$$Z = f(A, B) - \lambda(P_A A + P_B B - Y),$$

where λ is a Lagrangian multiplier. Thus (for a given Y) the first-order conditions for a maximum are that

$$\frac{\partial Z}{\partial A} = \frac{\partial U}{\partial A} - \lambda P_A = 0 \quad \text{or} \quad \frac{\dfrac{\partial U}{\partial A}}{P_A} = \lambda,$$

$$\frac{\partial Z}{\partial B} = \frac{\partial U}{\partial B} - \lambda P_B = 0 \quad \text{or} \quad \frac{\dfrac{\partial U}{\partial B}}{P_B} = \lambda.$$

Consequently, the condition for the maximum (assuming second-order conditions to be met) is that

$$\frac{\dfrac{\partial U}{\partial A}}{P_A} = \frac{\dfrac{\partial U}{\partial B}}{P_B}.$$

The Individual Consumer's Demand Curve

From the principle of rational consumer's expenditure to the individual consumer's demand curve is a relatively short step. Given that the consumer is so allocating his income that a dollar yields the same marginal utility regardless of the good upon which it is spent, there is only one condition under which the consumer could be persuaded to alter his allocation of a given money income so as to purchase more of a given good—namely, if the price of the good fell. Put otherwise, if the price of a good fell, the ratio of marginal utility to price would increase for this commodity, upsetting the equality of this ratio to all similar ones that defines the principle of rational consumer's expenditure. The consumer would consequently increase his purchases of the good whose price has fallen, thus lowering its marginal utility, decreasing the ratio of marginal utility to price, and reallocating his expenditures until the principle of rational consumer's expenditure was reestablished.

Ordinarily the reduction in price will cause the consumer to purchase more of the good—for two reasons: (1) Because this good has become cheaper relative to others, the consumer will wish to purchase more of it and curtail his purchases of other goods[3] (thus raising the ratio of their marginal utility to price). Second, because of the reduction of the price of the one good, the consumer's real income is increased, causing him—in

---

[3] While any particular other good could be a complement of the good the price of which has changed, all other goods taken as a whole would have to be a substitute for this good. See J. R. Hicks, *Value and Capital*, 2nd ed. (Oxford: Clarendon Press, 1946), pp. 46–47.

general—to purchase more of this good as well as others. Thus at lower prices for a given good the consumer tends to purchase greater quantities of that good—that is, the individual consumer's demand curve tends to be downward sloping.

In terms of Figure 2.2, a fall in the price of A would cause the plane whose base is A_2B_3 to be replaced by a similar plane whose base possessed a larger value of A as its intercept on the A axis but the same B-axis intercept. In effect, the plane would swing outward from the origin, pivoting on B_3, until the new price relationship was reached. The new highest point common to plane and surface would ordinarily possess a larger value of A as a coordinate. Thus the lowering of the price of A tends to increase the quantity of it purchased.

The Utility Function and Indifference Curves

In Figure 2.3, points C and D lie on the utility surface at the same height (as do all other points on the curved line on which they lie). Thus the combination of A and B represented by C' yields the total utility $C\text{-}C'$, and the combination of A and B represented by D yields the equal total utility $D\text{-}D'$. In effect, a plane horizontal to the AB plane has been passed through the utility surface at the level $C'C = D'D$. Projection of the intersection of

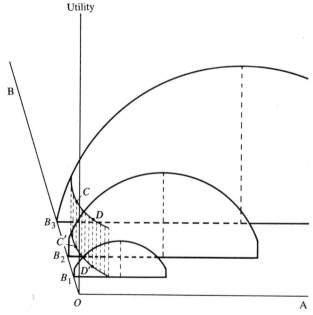

FIGURE 2.3

the plane with the utility surface down to the AB plane indicates the combinations of A and B that yield this level of total utility. Repeating the procedure at a higher level of total utility would yield another curved dotted line in the AB plane similar to that on which C' and D' occur but to the right of it. The same procedure at a lower level of utility would yield a curved dotted line to the left of that on which C' and D' occur.

Curves such as that on which C' and D' occur are called *indifference curves*, because they indicate the various combinations of the two goods that yield the same utility—so that the consumer would therefore be indifferent between these combinations. The consumer would prefer any combination on a higher indifference curve to any combination on a lower indifference curve, but he would be indifferent between the combinations on the same indifference curve.

Figure 2.4 portrays the *indifference map* of the consumer, showing a few of the (theoretically) infinite number of indifference curves that exist, each representing a different level of utility. It is assumed, for the relevant range of consumer choices, that economic goods possess positive marginal utility (they are desired by consumers) and, further, that a larger quantity of a good is preferred to a small quantity of that good.[4] From this assumption it follows that an indifference curve must be downward sloping, for if the indifference curve were upward sloping the consumer would be indifferent between a given combination and another that contained more of both goods. Put otherwise, if the indifference curve were upward sloping, loss of some units of one of the two commodities could be compensated for by *taking* from the consumer some units of the other. But if this were the case, the units taken from him could not possess a positive utility. Thus the assumption that economic goods possess a positive marginal utility precludes the possibility of upward-sloping indifference curves.

Similarly, the same assumption precludes horizontal or vertical indifference curves, for the consumer would then be indifferent between a given combination and another that possessed more of one of the two goods and the same quantity of the other. If an indifference curve were horizontal or

---

[4]Alternatively, the utility surface can be viewed as cone-shaped, its base lying in the *AB* plane and its vertex representing absolute satiety. The indifference curves, in such a case, would be represented as concentric circles enclosing a point that represents the top of the cone. In the first quadrant (first 90 degrees) both "goods" would be "nuisance" goods (possess negative marginal utility), since possession of a lesser quantity of either or both goods would place the consumer on a higher indifference curve. Similarly, in the fourth quadrant the "good" on the horizontal axis would be a "nuisance" good, and in the second quadrant the "good" on the vertical axis would have a negative marginal utility. Thus, only in the third quadrant would it be true that neither good is a nuisance (both possess positive marginal utility).

Since, for most analyses, both commodities are desired by the consumer, the third quadrant constitutes the relevant range of choice. In this quadrant indifference curves are downward sloping and convex, and higher indifference curves lie to the right.

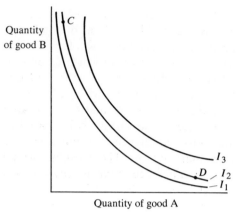

FIGURE 2.4

vertical, loss of some units of one good would not decrease the consumer's total utility even though the quantity of the other good was unchanged. Thus from the assumption that economic goods possess positive marginal utility it follows that indifference curves must be downward sloping.

From the same assumption it also follows that indifference curves depicting higher levels of satisfaction lie to the right of those depicting lower levels of satisfaction. If either or both of the quantities comprising a combination on a given indifference curve were increased, the consumer would experience a higher level of satisfaction. Since other combinations could yield this same (higher) level of satisfaction, the altered combination would lie on a different indifference curve. Since any combination on the indifference curve representing the higher level of satisfaction that contained the same quantity of one of the goods as a less preferable combination would have to contain a greater quantity of the other good, the indifference curve representing the higher level of satisfaction would have to lie to the right of that representing equally less-preferred combinations. Thus I_2 in Figure 2.4 represents combinations that, although equally desired, are all more desirable than the combinations represented by I_1.

By definition, indifference curves cannot intersect. Every point on an indifference curve represents a combination yielding the same satisfaction as every other combination represented on that indifference curve. Every point on a higher indifference curve represents combinations preferable to any of those represented on the lower indifference curve. Intersection would yield a point common to both curves, which would mean that the consumer was indifferent between combinations depicted on the higher indifference curve and those on the lower indifference curve. But, by definition, all combinations between which he is indifferent comprise a single indifference curve. Thus there could have been only one indifference curve to begin with, and no intersection. Higher indifference curves therefore cannot intersect lower indifference curves, since every point on the former represents a combination preferable to any of those on the latter.

Finally, indifference curves are convex to the origin. This is *consistent with* the principle of diminishing marginal utility but does not rest upon it. The characteristic of convexity means that, as any indifference curve is extended, combinations are being substituted that contain less and less of one good and more and more of the other. If, for example, we consider a combination comprised of a relatively large amount of B and small amount of A (point *C* in Figure 2.4), loss of a unit of B could be compensated for by the addition of a very small amount of A, returning the consumer to this same indifference curve. This *could* be due to the relatively large marginal utility of A when there is a relatively small quantity of it and the relatively small marginal utility of B when there is a relatively large quantity of it—if one wishes to assume diminishing marginal utility. Similarly, the relatively large quantity of A necessary to compensate for the loss of a unit of B at a combination comprised of very little B and a large quantity of A (point *D* in Figure 2.4) *could* be due to the relatively small marginal utility of A and large marginal utility of B—if one wishes to assume diminishing marginal utility. All that it is *necessary* to assume at this point, however, is that the *ratio* of the marginal utility of A to the marginal utility of B decreases as one moves along the indifference curve from *C* to *D*. This ratio could, of course, decrease even though its numerator (MU_A) became larger or its denominator (MU_B) became smaller as one moved along the curve from *C* toward *D*. Thus the assumption of convexity is, at this point, an assumption that the *ratio* MU_A/MU_B decreases as movement occurs down an indifference curve. This is not the same as an assumption of diminishing marginal utility with respect to the two goods—an assumption that would yield a decreasing ratio but that is not the only possible source of a decreasing ratio. Thus the principle of diminishing marginal utility is consistent with, but not necessary to, an assumption of convexity.

The switch to indifference curves also permits us to drop another assumption and substitute a weaker one. We need no longer assume utility to be *cardinally measurable*. All we need assume is an *ordinal* measure of utility. It is only necessary, for example, that the combinations on higher indifference curves be preferred to those on lower indifference curves. It is *not* necessary for us to be able to stipulate, in some units such as utils, the *amount by which* combinations on a higher indifference curve are preferred to those on a lower indifference curve. As we shall see, these alterations in our assumptions do not prevent our reaching the principle of rational consumer's expenditure, nor do they hamper us in deriving the individual consumer's demand curve.

If the consumer *could* substitute the combinations comprising an indifference curve, he would, having done so, be equally well off. The consumer's *ability* to substitute one combination for another, however, is limited by his income and the relative prices of the two goods. Because of these limitations, there are only certain substitutions that he can make. The consumer's equilibrium occurs when one of any combinations, the acquisition of which would leave him equally well off, is a combination that his income and the relative prices of the two goods permit him to acquire.

In Figure 2.5 it is again assumed that if the consumer were to spend all of his income on good A he could purchase A_2 units of A, whereas if he were to spend all of his income on good B he could purchase B_3 units of

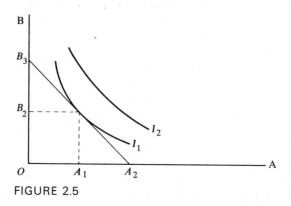

FIGURE 2.5

B—given the prices of the two goods. The line connecting A_2 and B_3 indicates all of the other combinations that he *could* buy, assuming that he spent all of his income. (Alternatively, if the consumer desires savings, this could be one of the two goods.) This line connecting A_2 and B_3 is called the *budget line* or *line of attainable combinations*.[5] Of those combinations that the consumer *can* buy, one will yield more satisfaction than any other—namely, that combination at which the budget line is tangent to the indifference curve. This, then, is the combination the consumer would purchase in equilibrium (the combination A_1, B_2). His income does not permit him to reach any higher indifference curve, and he would not be making a rational choice if he chose a combination on any lower indifference curve.

If, at a point on the indifference curve, a very small amount of B is withdrawn, this loss to the consumer of $-\Delta B \times MU_B$ can be compensated for (returning us to the indifference curve) by the addition of ΔA of A. This gain of utility, $\Delta A \times MU_A$, equals the loss of utility $-\Delta B \times MU_B$. Since the gain equals the loss,

---

[5] Note that the slope of the budget line equals the ratio of the price of A to the price of B, not the converse.

$$\Delta A \times MU_A = -\Delta B \times MU_B$$

or

$$\frac{MU_A}{MU_B} = -\frac{\Delta B}{\Delta A}.$$

The ratio of the marginal utility of A to the marginal utility of B is called the *marginal rate of substitution* of A for B. For very small movements it indicates the number of units of A that must be added per unit of B withdrawn, if the consumer is to maintain a constant level of utility. The ratio $-\Delta B/\Delta A$ is the slope of the indifference curve and is also equal, of course, to the marginal rate of substitution of A for B. At the point of tangency of the budget line and the indifference curve, the slope of the budget line OB_3/OA_2 equals that of the indifference curve. The slope of the budget line also equals the ratio of the price of A to the price of B. Consequently, at the consumer's equilibrium,

$$MRS = -\frac{\Delta B}{\Delta A} = \frac{MU_A}{MU_B} = \frac{P_A}{P_B}.$$

Rearranging the last equality,

$$\frac{MU_A}{P_A} = \frac{MU_B}{P_B},$$ the principle of rational consumer's expenditure.

The consumer's equilibrium may also be expressed in the following way. Let the utility function be $U = f(A, B)$ so that an indifference curve is $U = f(A, B) = h$, where h is a constant. Taking the total derivative of the equation of the indifference curve, we find

$$\frac{\partial U}{\partial A} dA + \frac{\partial U}{\partial B} dB = 0,$$

$$\frac{\partial U}{\partial B} dB = -\frac{\partial U}{\partial A} dA,$$

$$-\frac{dB}{dA} = \frac{\frac{\partial U}{\partial A}}{\frac{\partial U}{\partial B}}.$$

Since, in equilibrium, $-dB/dA = P_A/P_B$,

$$\frac{\dfrac{\partial U}{\partial A}}{\dfrac{\partial U}{\partial B}} = \frac{P_A}{P_B} \quad \text{or} \quad \frac{\dfrac{\partial U}{\partial A}}{P_A} = \frac{\dfrac{\partial U}{\partial B}}{P_B}.$$

Having established the principle of rational consumer expenditure, we could proceed from this point to derive the individual consumer's demand curve just as we did earlier. It could be quickly deduced from this principle, and the assumptions previously made, that the individual consumer's demand curve is, in general, downward sloping.[6]

Although this property of the individual consumer's demand curve is all that actually need be demonstrated, it is perhaps instructive to show how the particular points comprising the demand curve could be calculated if the consumer's utility function were known to us. More accurately, we would actually need to know only the *ranking* ascribed by the consumer to all possible combinations of the two goods. We would not need to know *by*

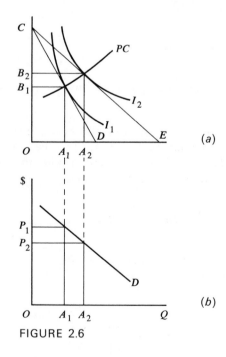

FIGURE 2.6

---

[6]Again with the exception (to be discussed subsequently) of the Giffen good.

how much the combinations on a higher indifference curve were preferred to those on a lower one.

Figure 2.6(a) depicts the result of a decrease in the price of A upon the quantity of A (and B) purchased by the consumer. Before the reduction in price, the price of A (in terms of B) is OC/OD and the consumer buys OA_1 of A and OB_1 of B. With the fall in the price of A the consumer purchases OA_2 of A and OB_2 of B. A graph such as that shown in Figure 2.6(b) could therefore be constructed indicating the specific quantities that would be demanded by the consumer at various prices. The points of tangency resulting from the various prices of A comprise a locus of points entitled the *price-consumption curve*, indicating how the consumption of A would vary with variations in its price. Note that despite the name, prices, as such, are not coordinates of points on the price-consumption curve.[7]

The Preference Relationship and Indifference-Curve Analysis

Development of the analytical tool of the indifference curve, as we have just seen, permits us to make two alterations in our assumptions. First, we no longer need the assumption of diminishing marginal utility. All that is necessary is that the *ratio* of the marginal utility of A to that of B decreases for movements down the indifference curve. Second, we find that we no longer need to conceive of utility as *cardinal*. We need pose no fictitious unit such as the util, for we don't need to know the magnitude, in terms of utility, of the satisfaction yielded by the combinations comprising a particular indifference curve, nor do we need to know *by how much* the combinations on a higher indifference curve are preferred to those on a lower indifference curve.

Other alterations or weakening of our assumptions can be made, however, without affecting adversely our ability to arrive at the principle of rational consumer's expenditure or the individual consumer's demand curve. Here we shall merely summarize some of these alterations, leaving to advanced treatments of the subject the task of deriving them more rigorously.[8]

Pose a hypothetical consumer who is requested to express his preferences concerning alternative combinations of two goods, these being the only two goods of which he is aware. His statements concerning these alter-

---

[7] Nor is *price* either axis of the indifference-curve diagram. The vertical axis of Fig. 2.8 can be conceived of as all goods other than good A (the good on the horizontal axis) and thus as an approximation of income or money—in some analyses. In *no* analysis, however, can the vertical axis (or the horizontal axis) of an *indifference-curve* diagram be considered price.

[8] This section is largely a condensation of D. W. Bushaw and R. W. Clower, *Introduction to Mathematical Economics* (Homewood, Ill.: Richard D. Irwin, Inc., 1957), pp. 103–116.

natives do not employ any such terms as "utils" or "utility" and are made without consideration of the prices of the goods or his income. Letting *x* and *y* represent any two combinations, we assume his statements to be such that one of the following is clear:

1. He prefers *x* to *y*.
2. He prefers *y* to *x*.
3. He is indifferent between *x* and *y*.

Further, it is assumed that for our consumer and with respect to any three combinations *x*, *y*, and *z*:

1. *x* is indifferent to *x*. (In technical terms, the preference relationship is *reflexive*.)
2. If *x* is indifferent to *y*, then *y* is indifferent to *x*. (The preference relationship is symmetrical.)
3. If *x* is indifferent to *y*, and *y* indifferent to *z*, then *x* is indifferent to *z*. (The preference relationship is *transitive*.)
4. If *y* is preferable to *x*, and *y'* and *x'* are any combinations indifferent, respectively, to *y* and *x*, then *y'* is preferable to *x'*. (The preference relationship is *invariant* when substitution of indifferents is made.)

Conceptually, if the two sets of conditions posed above were met, we could, starting with a given combination, determine all those combinations indifferent to it (and to each other). Repeating the procedure first for combinations preferred to, and then less preferable than, the original combination, we could conceptually identify a family of indifference curves. It is assumed that the consumer always (within the relevant range) prefers to get more of one commodity if he can do so without getting less of another, so that we can represent combinations between which the consumer is indifferent but that are preferred to those on our initial indifference curve as comprising a higher indifference curve. Finally, if we assume our indifference curves to be smooth, downward sloping, and convex (to the origin), we have an indifference map such as that represented in Figure 2.5.

The budget line would retain the same meaning as before, the marginal rate of substitution would continue to show the rate at which the consumer was willing to substitute good A for good B (that is, the MRS would still equal the negative of the slope of the indifference curve), and the consumer's equilibrium could be portrayed, as before, by tangency of the budget line with the indifference curve. But all of this would have occurred without overt reference to utility.

Mathematically, we could also proceed as before, except that we would need only a utility *index* rather than the utility function itself. The utility index is merely a way of representing the *order* in which the consumer places alternative combinations. If the consumer preferred combination *y* to combination *x*, the value of the index would have to be lower for *x* than for y. Similarly, if the consumer were indifferent between x and y, each would be represented by the same value of the index. No unique index is required; any index that met these conditions would suffice. Letting $U = f(A, B)$ now represent the utility *index*, we could secure the principle of rational consumer's expenditure, as before, by maximizing $f(A, B)$ subject to the income constraint.

Applications of Indifference-Curve Analysis

Figure 2.7 indicates the effect of changes in the consumer's money income upon the combination of the two goods that is selected. Since the prices of the two goods have not changed, the higher budget line is parallel to the lower one. As a result of the increase in income the consumer selects combination F rather than E, and the locus of points representing the combinations selected at various income levels is called the *income consumption curve* (*IC* in Figure 2.7).

SUPERIOR AND INFERIOR GOODS.   For most goods it will be true that increases in income (prices remaining constant) lead to purchases of a greater quantity of that good. Thus in Figure 2.7 a greater quantity of A and B comprise combination F than combination E. Such goods are termed *superior goods*, and indifference-curve diagrams depicting two superior goods always yield upward-sloping income-consumption curves. For some goods in some situations, however, smaller quantities will be purchased as income increases (prices remaining constant). It might well be, for example, that less corn meal would be purchased at higher income levels, consumers preferring at these higher levels to purchase bread made from

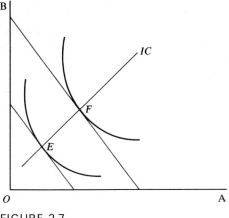

FIGURE 2.7

wheat rather than to make cornbread. Economic goods of which the consumer would purchase less at higher income levels (prices remaining constant) are called *inferior goods*. If A in Figure 2.7 were an inferior good, the income-consumption curve would have a negative slope, rising toward the "northwest" as income increased. If B were an inferior good, the income-consumption curve would again have a negative slope and the curve would fall toward the "southeast" as income increased. If the consumer has only two goods to consider, both cannot be inferior.

INCOME AND SUBSTITUTION EFFECTS OF A PRICE CHANGE.   Although in the preceding discussion prices were held constant as income changed, it is also true that changes in price give rise to changes in income. The money income of the consumer can change, in other words, without there being a change in price, but a change in the price of any good that a consumer buys constitutes a change in his *real* income. At a lower price the consumer would be better off even if he did not increase his purchases of the good the price of which has fallen, for he could then purchase the same quantity by giving up a smaller portion of his total money income. Thus at the lower price his total utility would be greater. The consumer thus, in effect, moves to a different indifference curve as a result of a change in price, because the change in price changes his real income, causing his total utility either to increase or decrease depending upon the direction of the price change involved. Thus one effect of a price change is its *income effect,* and this effect, when it is that of an increase in real income, may cause the consumer to purchase either a greater or lesser quantity of the good, depending upon whether the good is, respectively, a superior or an inferior good. If it is a *superior* good, the income effect is said to be *positive*; if it is an *inferior* good, the income effect of the price change is said to be *negative.*

Paradoxically enough, however, the consumer would *have* to change the quantity he purchased of a good when its price changed if there were no income effect of the price change. If the price of a good falls but the consumer's real income somehow is not permitted to change, more of this good must be substituted for those which have now become relatively more expensive. This effect of the price change, conceptually distinct from the income effect, is called the *substitution effect.*

A graphical division of the two effects of a price change may help to make the distinction between them more apparent. In Figure 2.8, as a result of a decrease in the price of A, the consumer's purchases of A change from A_1 to A_2. He is, of course, better off as a result of the price decrease, as reflected in his selection of a combination on a higher indifference curve, I_2, rather than the lower indifference curve, I_1. The relevant question thus becomes that of distinguishing the portion of the increase $(A_2 - A_1)$ in A that is attributable to the substitution effect of the price change from that which is due to the income effect of the price change.

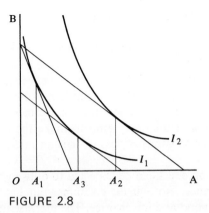

FIGURE 2.8

To accomplish the separation we assume a hypothetical reduction in the consumer's income (perhaps, for example, an income tax) that prevents any increase in utility from occurring as a result of the decrease in the price of A. We permit the altered price, in other words, but prevent the alteration in price from making the consumer any better off than he was before the price change.[9] If he were to be no better off as a result of the price change, then he would have to choose a combination not preferable to that of which A_1 is a component. Consequently we construct a hypothetical budget line parallel to the higher budget line (thus giving him the price reduction) but tangent to the lower indifference curve (thus not permitting him to choose a combination preferable to that of which A_1 is a component).

If such a hypothetical experiment were performed, the consumer would choose the combination of which A_3 is a component. This new combination at the new price yields the same total utility as did the combination of which A_1 is a component at the old price. Thus that portion of the increase $(A_2 - A_1)$ in A attributable to the substitution effect of the price

---

[9]Alternatively, we can separate the income and substitution effects of a price change by—in effect—*not* permitting the price change but giving the consumer a subsidy such that he is as well off as if we had permitted the price change (but had given no subsidy). The magnitude of the subsidy would be such as to shift the original budget line to the right (without changing its slope) until it became tangent to the higher indifference curve I_2. Under this method the rightward movement on the A axis from A_1 to the value of A corresponding to the tangency of the new budget line with I_2 would be considered as due to the income effect. The movement along I_2 from the tangency of the new budget line to the point of tangency of which A_2 is a coordinate would be attributed to the substitution effect.

Interestingly enough, there is no *economic* reason to assume the essentially mathematical conditions under which the two methods would yield the same results (in terms of A).

A third method, useful in some analyses, of separating the income and substitution effects of a price change is to permit the price change but reduce the income of the consumer by an amount such that at the new price he can purchase the original combination (that of which A_1 is a component) if he wishes. This method has the conceptual shortcoming that, given the new price, the consumer may well be better off, despite his reduction in income. Again there is no reason to assume that this method would yield the same result as either of the other two.

change is $A_3 - A_1$, and the remainder of the increase $A_2 - A_3$ is due to the income effect of the price change.[10]

If A is an inferior good, the income effect will be negative and A_2 will lie to the left of A_3. Figure 2.8 thus shows A to be a superior good. Because indifference curves are convex, the *substitution* effect must always be positive: the substitution effect will always tend to make the consumer purchase more at a lower price. The income effect, as we have seen, may be either positive or negative and thus may tend to make the consumer buy either more (if it is a superior good) or less (if it is an inferior good) at a lower price.

The substitution effect can be expected to outweigh a negative income effect, in most instances, so that the consumer purchases a larger quantity of even an inferior good at a lower price. The increase in real income that a consumer experiences from a decrease in the price of one of the goods he buys will affect his purchases of all goods, so that the magnitude of the income effect upon the quantity purchased of any one good (including the good the price of which has fallen) may be expected to be small. In the exceptional case of "Giffen's paradox," however, the income effect is not only negative but also stronger than the substitution effect. In Figure 2.8 such a case would cause A_2 to lie to the left of A_1 and the consumer would purchase *less* of A at a lower price. Such a case is a valid exception to the generalization that individual consumers' demand curves are downward sloping.

CONSUMER'S SURPLUS. Figure 2.9 permits us to analyze *consumer's surplus*, a concept that will prove to be of some analytical usefulness in subsequent chapters. On the vertical axis we shall measure income itself (not price), so that the consumer is assumed to possess an income of OM_1. On the horizontal axis various quantities of the economic good A are measured, A_2 being the quantity of A that the consumer could purchase if he were to spend all of his income on this good, A_2M_1 being the budget line, and A_1 representing the quantity of A that the consumer does purchase.

Consumer's surplus may be defined as the difference between the amount that a consumer would be willing to pay for a given quantity of a good, rather than do without it, and the amount that he actually does pay for that quantity of the good. Such a "surplus" arises because the consumer pays the same price for each unit of the good that he purchases, even though he would be willing to pay a higher price if he could only purchase a lesser

---

[10]In some analyses we wish to derive a demand curve in which there is no income effect—a "compensated" demand curve. One way of deriving a compensated demand curve is by removing the income effect of each successive price change by the method indicated in the text and then plotting the change in quantity demanded that is attributable only to the substitution effect of the price change.

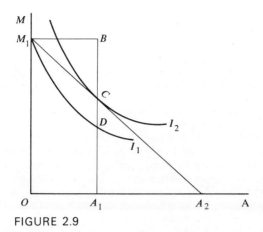

FIGURE 2.9

quantity. Since any lesser quantity is included within the quantity that he purchases at the given price, he is paying a lower price for these lesser quantities than he would be willing to pay in order to get them. Thus he pays less in total for A_1 rather than do without it.

Since with money one can always acquire more A, there must be some quantity of money, alone, that is of equal utility to the consumer as any combination of money and A.[11] Hence there must be an indifference curve intersecting the vertical axis at M_1, indicating the combinations of money and A that are indifferent to the combination of M_1 money and no A. This indifference curve is labelled I_1 in Figure 2.9.

To secure the combination shown at C in Figure 2.9, the consumer gives up BC of money. The combination C is preferable to the combination M_1 of money and no A, and thus there exists a consumer's surplus. If the consumer had been forced to pay BD in order to secure A_1 of A, however, there would be no excess of what he is willing to pay for A_1 over what he does pay for A_1. The sum CD, therefore, is a measure of the consumer's surplus.

SUMMARY AND CONCLUSIONS

The individual consumer's demand curve can be expected (in all instances except that of Giffen's paradox) to be downward sloping. If we assume a rational consumer with given tastes who confronts a market on which there are goods the prices of which he knows but cannot affect by his purchases, and if we further assume the income constraint and either the principle of diminishing marginal utility or convexity of indifference curves, we can deduce the principle of rational consumer expenditure. This latter principle, together

---

[11] Assuming A not to be a complete necessity.

with assumed changes in price, yields (except for the Giffen good) a downward-sloping demand curve for the individual consumer.

The quantity that a consumer purchases of a good is, of course, affected by factors other than the price of the good. How changes in income affect the quantity purchased can be readily analyzed, using the indifference-curve technique. Throughout the discussion, however, the consumer's tastes or preferences have been assumed constant, or given. Although it is obvious that changes in the consumer's tastes or preferences would cause changes in the quantity demanded of a particular good, there is little that economics can tell us about the nature or causes of such changes. It is apparent that the consumer's utility function and indifference curves would be altered by each change in his preferences, but we can only state a utility function, a utility index, or a set of indifference curves for a given set of these preferences.

Similarly, we have assumed rationality even though there may be a great deal of irrationality in the behavior of the typical consumer. There is no theory of irrational economic behavior, and the element of rationality need only be greater than the concerted opposing effect of the elements of irrationality in order for the assumption of rationality to be preferable to an assumption of irrationality. Nonetheless, it is true that we have analyzed the behavior of an abstraction called "the consumer." This analysis should permit us to see order in many of the actions of actual consumers, but it does not provide us with a complete description of their behavior. Wherever economic and noneconomic factors are involved, economic theory permits us to isolate and put into comprehensible form only the economic variables. This is both a virtue and a shortcoming.

SELECTED REFERENCES

BUSHAW, D. W., and R. W. CLOWER, *Introduction to Mathematical Economics* (Homewood, Ill.: Richard D. Irwin, Inc., 1957), chap. 5.

DUE, JOHN F., and R. W. CLOWER, *Intermediate Economic Analysis*, 4th ed. (Homewood, Ill.: Richard D. Irwin, Inc., 1961), chap. 5.

FERGUSON, C. E., *Microeconomic Theory* (Homewood, Ill.: Richard D. Irwin, Inc., 1966), chaps. 1 and 2.

HICKS, J. R., *Value and Capital*, 2nd ed. (Oxford: Clarendon Press, 1946), chaps. 1 and 2.

HICKS, J. R., *A Revision of Demand Theory* (Oxford: Clarendon Press, 1956), chap. 2.

LEFTWICH, R. H., *The Price System and Resource Allocation*, 3rd ed. (New York: Holt, Rinehart and Winston, Inc., 1966), chaps. 4 and 5.

LIEBHAFSKY, H. H., *The Nature of Price Theory* (Homewood, Ill.: The Dorsey Press, 1963), chap. 4.

STIGLER, G. J., *The Theory of Price*, rev. ed. (New York: The Macmillan Company, 1959), chaps. 4 and 5.

from the demand curve of the individual consumer to the market

INTRODUCTION

In the present chapter we shall do three things. First, we shall review the concept of the individual consumer's demand curve and take the relatively short step from this demand curve to the market demand curve. Second, we shall introduce the concept of elasticity and the more specific concepts of price elasticity of demand, income elasticity of demand, and cross elasticity of demand – relating these concepts back to indifference-curve analysis. Finally, we shall introduce the concept of market equilibrium, seeking to explain why – in a competitive market – a single price tends to rule. At this point we shall have provided an explanation of the process by which wants come to be expressed in the market and—temporarily taking the supply curve as given—an explanation of how individual prices are determined.

THE INDIVIDUAL CONSUMER'S DEMAND CURVE
AND THE MARKET DEMAND CURVE

The Individual Consumer's Demand Curve

In Chapter 2 it was argued that the individual consumer's demand curve is downward sloping. Given the assumptions of rationality, limited income, a set of preferences, and diminishing marginal utility (or, alternatively, convex downward-sloping indifference curves), a consumer would purchase a greater quantity at a lower price, with the exception of Giffen's paradox.[1]

This, then, is the *law of demand*—that, *ceteris paribus*, quantity demanded varies inversely with price. It is recognized that changes in tastes, in income, or in the prices of other goods also affect the quantity demanded of any good, but these variables are treated as *parametric constants* in the concept of the consumer's demand curve. As such, these variables can occasion shifts in the level of a demand curve by changes in their values, and any demand curve is drawn for a given set of variables other than price.

Thus D_1 in Figure 3.1 indicates how quantity demanded varies with price, assuming a given set of values for all variables other than price. If one of the parametric constants, such as income, should change, this causes a shift in the demand curve such as the movement from D_1 to D_2. A shift

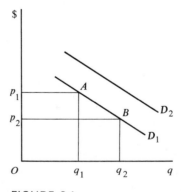

FIGURE 3.1

---

[1]Of some goods that are not Giffen goods it may also be true that a smaller quantity would be demanded at a lower price, these particular "snob" goods being valued, in part, *because of* their relatively high prices. Such cases are not regarded as true exceptions to the law of demand because they violate the implicit assumption that the consumer's preferences must be independent of prices.

in a demand curve is referred to as a *change in demand*, whereas a movement along a given demand curve is referred to as a change in *quantity
demanded*. Thus the shift from D_1 to D_2 is an increase in *demand*, showing
that there is a greater *quantity demanded* at every price. The movement from
A to B on D_1 is a movement along a single demand curve showing an
increase in the *quantity demanded* from q_1 at the price p_1 to q_2 at the price p_2.
The distinction between a change *in demand* and a change in the *quantity
demanded* is an important one, because the latter refers to the effect of
changes in the price of a good upon the quantity demanded of that good,
whereas the former refers to the effect of changes in variables *other than* the
price of the good upon the quantity demanded.

Mathematically, a general expression for the demand curve of the
individual consumer (which does *not* treat variables other than the price of
the good as parametric constants) would be

$$Q_A = f(P_A, P_B, P_C, \ldots, Y),$$

where Q_A is the quantity demanded, P_A is the price of the good in question,
P_B, P_C, and so on are the prices of other goods, and Y is the consumer's
income. While changes in the consumer's preferences would also affect the
quantity demanded of A, this factor is not conceptually quantifiable in the
derivation of the consumer's demand curve and is generally assumed as
given throughout. If we assume that P_B, P_C, $\ldots$, and Y are given parameters, we may then write

$$Q_A = f(P_A).$$

The Market Demand Curve

Given a set of individual consumer demand curves, we can add these
curves horizontally so as to secure the market demand curve. We can, in
other words, at each price add together all the quantities demanded by the
individual consumers. Thus in Figure 3.2 at a price of $1 the quantity
demanded by one consumer is six and the quantity demanded by another
is eight, so that the total quantity demanded by the two consumers, at a
price of $1, is fourteen. Similarly, the total quantity demanded by the two
consumers at a price of $0.50 is twenty. In a like manner, the demand curves
of all individual consumers could be summed so as to yield the market
demand curve.

Put otherwise, the market demand curve is the horizontal summation
of the individual consumer demand curves. Since the process of summation
does not affect this characteristic, we know from the fact that the individual

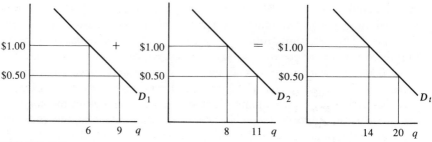

FIGURE 3.2

consumer's demand curve is negatively sloped that the market demand curve is also downward sloping.

Put mathematically, if the demand of the ith consumer for the good is

$$Q_i = f_i(P),$$

the market demand curve will be the result of a summation at each price:

$$Q = \sum_{i=1}^{n} f_i(P) = f(P) \qquad (i = 1, 2, 3, \ldots, n).$$

Thus the market demand curve is a horizontal summation of individual consumer demand curves and represents the effective expression of the collective wants of the consumers in a given market. Many wants are blocked from the market by the income constraint, but those consumer wants that survive this obstacle do become expressed in the market. The market demand curve is a geometrical device portraying quickly and concisely the part that consumers' wants play in determining price.

ELASTICITY OF DEMAND

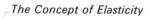

The Concept of Elasticity

The concept of elasticity has many applications throughout all of economics, and few other concepts are so central to price and distribution theory. Elasticity is a perfectly general concept, however, and is not specific to economics.

We may define *elasticity* as *a ratio of relative changes in variables that are thought to be related.* Suppose, for example, we have good reason to believe that the yearly growth of bamboo shoots depends upon the amount of rainfall. Clearly, the bamboo cannot grow at all without some rain, and some amounts of rainfall benefit its growth more than others. Thus annual rainfall and annual growth of bamboo shoots are related variables. But we may wish to find out more about the *way* in which these two variables are related. We may wish to know the effect of *changes* in one of these variables upon the other. Not only is annual rainfall related to annual growth, but *changes* in annual rainfall may be expected to be related to *changes* in annual growth. We therefore desire an expression of the *responsiveness* of annual growth to changes in rainfall.

Finally, we wish the *changes* involved to be relative, or *percentage*, changes. A variation of two inches in rainfall might not be very important in a year in which there was a great deal of rain, but in a year of little rain this same absolute change might be crucial. The use of relative changes also permits derivation of a measure that is independent of units of measurement. Thus if we divide the relative change in growth by the relative change in rainfall, we shall have a comparable measure of the responsiveness of annual growth or its *elasticity*, irrespective of the units in which growth and rainfall are measured.

To use a more familiar example, the length of a rubber string is related to the force with which its two ends are pulled apart. We may wish to know whether the length of the string changes by 10 per cent, by more than 10 per cent, or by less than 10 per cent when we change the force applied to it by 10 per cent. Thus we may wish to relate relative changes in the two variables involved. Because (under most conditions) the physical dimensions of rubber change readily with changes in the force applied, we refer to rubber as possessing greater elasticity than other substances. Although no one speaks of the elasticity of annual growth of plants, the basic concept involved is the same.

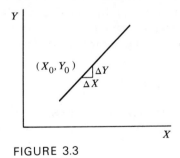

FIGURE 3.3

Figure 3.3 depicts a relationship between the two variables X and Y. The elasticity of the function would be the relative change in X divided by the relative change in Y. We can express elasticity as

$$\frac{\frac{\Delta X}{X}}{\frac{\Delta Y}{Y}} = \frac{Y \Delta X}{X \Delta Y} = \frac{Y}{X} \frac{1}{\frac{\Delta Y}{\Delta X}}.$$

It should be carefully noted (from the final expression above) that the elasticity of a function is *not* its slope. $\Delta Y/\Delta X$ is the slope of the function. Elasticity is the result of multiplying the ratio of Y to X by the inverse of the slope. Thus, while slope is related to elasticity, it is by no means the same thing. In Figure 3.3 the elasticity at the point shown would be the ratio of the coordinates of this point (X_0, Y_0) multiplied by the inverse of the slope $(\Delta Y/\Delta X)$.

Mathematically we may express elasticity as

$$\frac{E_y}{E_x} = \frac{x}{y} \frac{dy}{dx}.$$

Alternatively,

$$\frac{E_y}{E_x} = \frac{d \log y}{d \log x}.$$

Price Elasticity of Demand at a Point

We have previously concluded that price and quantity demanded are related variables. In fact we have concluded that, other variables remaining constant, price and quantity demanded are inversely related—that is, the demand curve is downward sloping. We shall find of great analytical usefulness, however, a measure of the relative responsiveness of quantity demanded to price. Such a measure is the *price elasticity of demand*, which may be expressed in any of the following forms:[2]

$$\eta_p = -\frac{\frac{\Delta q}{q}}{\frac{\Delta p}{p}} = -\frac{p}{q} \frac{\Delta q}{\Delta p} = -\frac{p}{q} \frac{1}{\frac{\Delta p}{\Delta q}}.$$

If the quantity demanded is very responsive to price changes, a given relative change in price will occasion a more than proportionate change in

---

[2]The reason for the negative sign in this definition will become apparent in subsequent discussion.

quantity demanded, and the price elasticity of demand will be greater than unity. If, for example, a 10 per cent change in price causes a 20 per cent change in quantity demanded, the price elasticity of demand will be 2. If, on the other hand, a 10 per cent change in price causes only a 5 per cent change in quantity demanded, the price elasticity of demand will be $\frac{1}{2}$. Thus the numerical value of price elasticity of demand indicates the relative responsiveness of quantity demanded to changes in price. If price elasticity of demand exceeds unity, the demand curve is referred to as being *elastic* at the point or over the range for which this is true. If this elasticity is less than unity, the demand curve is referred to as being *inelastic* at the point or over the range for which this is true. And, if this elasticity has a value of 1, the demand curve is referred to as being *unitarily elastic* at the point or over the range for which this is true.

Some sharp-eyed readers will have noted the negative sign that precedes each of the expressions given above for price elasticity of demand. Figure 3.4 will help make apparent the need for the negative sign. Since changes in price are associated with opposite changes in quantity, the ratio $\Delta p/\Delta q$ will be negative for all downward-sloping demand curves. Or, in terms of the first expression given above for price elasticity of demand, since a relative change in price is always accompanied by a relative change in quantity of the opposite sign, the ratio of the two relative changes is always negative. Thus, if there were no negative sign preceding our expressions for price elasticity of demand, these expressions would always be negative. Such a state of affairs would lead to ambiguity, for while -3 is smaller than -2, an elasticity with the absolute value of 3 indicates greater responsiveness of quantity demanded than does an elasticity with the absolute value of 2. To avoid this difficulty we customarily preface each of the expressions with a negative sign, so that the number yielded for elasticity will always be positive. Then a greater responsiveness of quantity demanded to relative changes in price results in a larger numerical value for price elasticity of demand.

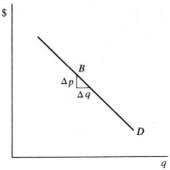

FIGURE 3.4

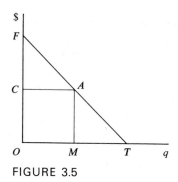

FIGURE 3.5

The fact that the expression for price elasticity of demand *includes* the slope of the demand curve permits us to derive easily three geometrical ratios whose value would be that of this elasticity at any given point on the demand curve. In Figure 3.5 the demand curve has been extended to its price and quantity intercepts, and we seek three geometrical ratios, any one of which would give us the value of price elasticity of demand at the point A.

Since we have drawn a straight-line demand curve (thus possessing only one slope), we know that the ratio AM/MT is an expression of the (negative) slope of this curve. Thus, when we substitute in the expression

$$\eta_p = -\frac{p}{q}\frac{1}{\dfrac{\Delta p}{\Delta q}},$$

this elasticity becomes

$$\eta_p = \frac{MA}{OM}\frac{1}{\dfrac{MA}{MT}} = \frac{MT}{OM}.$$

Similarly, since CF/CA is another expression for the (negative) slope, we can also substitute in the same expression for elasticity so as to yield

$$\eta_p = \frac{OC}{CA}\frac{1}{\dfrac{CF}{CA}} = \frac{OC}{CF}.$$

Since triangle ACF is similar to triangle TMA,

$$\frac{MT}{AC} = \frac{MA}{CF} = \frac{TA}{AF},$$

$$\frac{MT}{AC} = \frac{MT}{OM} = \eta_p,$$

and

$$\frac{MA}{CF} = \frac{OC}{CF} = \eta_p.$$

Therefore

$$\frac{TA}{AF} = \eta_p.$$

Thus we have three geometrical ratios, each of which is the value of price elasticity of demand at a given point on the demand curve. But our proof employs a straight-line demand curve. Can it be generalized to curvilinear demand curves?

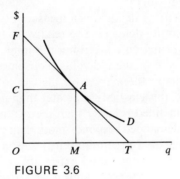

FIGURE 3.6

Figure 3.6 depicts a curvilinear demand curve and a point at which we wish to measure the price elasticity of demand. Since a tangent to the curve at this point has the same slope as the curve itself, it is evident that we can find geometrical ratios that provide measures of price elasticity of demand at this point.

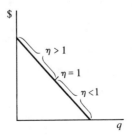

FIGURE 3.7

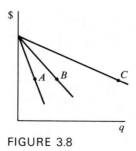

FIGURE 3.8

It should again be emphasized that while slope is a component part of price elasticity of demand, it is not synonymous therewith. As indicated in Figure 3.7, a downward-sloping straight line—while possessing only one slope—has a different elasticity at every point. Figure 3.8 shows a number of points, all of which have the same elasticity but different slopes. And Figure 3.9 indicates a demand curve every point on which has unitary elasticity but a different slope.[3]

Since price elasticity of demand is a measure of the responsiveness of relative changes in quantity demanded to relative changes in price, it automatically provides information concerning the total expenditure made by the consumer (in the case of the individual consumer's demand curve) or the group of consumers in the market (in the case of the market demand curve). If, for example, this elasticity is greater than unity, then the relative change in quantity demanded is larger than the relative change in price. In this case the quantity demanded responds more than proportionately to the change in price, so that total expenditure increases if price is lowered and decreases if price is raised (since total expenditure is the result of multiplying price by quantity demanded). Thus if we know that this elasticity is greater than unity, we know automatically that total expenditure is greater

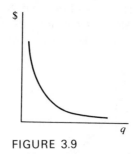

FIGURE 3.9

[3] If drawn correctly, this demand curve is a rectangular hyperbola—that is, the product of the coordinates is the same at every point on the curve. Thus the total expenditure (price multiplied by quantity) is the same for every quantity.

at lower prices and smaller at higher prices. Similarly, if price elasticity of demand is unity, the total expenditure by the consumer or consumers is the same at every price, and if this elasticity is less than unity, total expenditure increases with increases in price and decreases with reductions in price.

We can express these relationships mathematically. If p = price and q = quantity demanded, then pq = total expenditure. If pq is increasing (decreasing) as q increases (decreases),

$$\frac{d(pq)}{dq} > 0,$$

$$p + q\frac{dp}{dq} > 0,$$

$$p > -q\frac{dp}{dq},$$

$$\eta_p = -\frac{p}{q}\frac{1}{\dfrac{dp}{dq}} > 1.$$

Similarly, if pq is decreasing (increasing) as q increases (decreases),

$$\eta_p = -\frac{p}{q}\frac{1}{\dfrac{dp}{dq}} < 1.$$

And, if pq is constant as q increases (decreases),

$$\eta_p = -\frac{p}{q}\frac{1}{\dfrac{dp}{dq}} = 1.$$

Arc Price Elasticity of Demand

We have previously referred to elasticity as the result of multiplying the ratio of the coordinates of a point by the inverse of the slope of the function at that point. We have also previously defined price elasticity of demand as the ratio of a relative change in quantity demanded to a relative change in price. So long as infinitesimal changes are involved, there is no

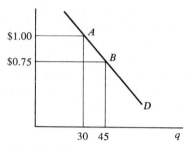

FIGURE 3.10

problem, but if finite changes in price and quantity demanded are involved, we have not one but two points on the demand curve to consider.

To treat the case involving discrete or finite changes in price and quantity demanded, economists have developed the concept of *arc* price elasticity of demand. What is envisaged is a movement along the demand curve from one point to another, and what is sought is a single estimate of elasticity for the whole range of points over which the movement occurs. Thus in Figure 3.10 we desire a single estimate of elasticity for the range of points bounded by *A* and *B*.

While there is no difficulty in determining the values of Δp and Δq ($\$0.25$ and 15, respectively, in Figure 3.10), there *is* difficulty in converting these absolute changes into the relative changes $\Delta p/p$ and $\Delta q/q$ in order that they may be used in the expression

$$\eta_p = -\frac{\dfrac{\Delta q}{q}}{\dfrac{\Delta p}{p}}.$$

There are two prices and two quantities, so it is possible to secure four different numerical values for the elasticity. To get a result that lies between the extreme possible values, many economists—by convention—select the low price and the lesser quantity in computing arc elasticity.[4] Following this convention, the arc elasticity of demand in Figure 3.10 would be

$$\eta_p = \frac{\dfrac{15}{30}}{\dfrac{0.25}{0.75}} = \tfrac{1}{2} \cdot 3 = 1.5.$$

---

[4]Another convention is to use the midpoints over the arc for both price and quantity. In this method the ratio of the change in quantity to the *sum* of the two quantities is divided by the ratio of the change in price to the *sum* of the two prices. In essence this method makes

Arc price elasticity of demand can be related to total expenditure in essentially the same manner that point price elasticity of demand was related to total expenditure. Thus, in the schedule presented here, total expenditure increases (decreases) for price decreases (increases) when the arc elasticity between the points is greater than unity; total expenditure decreases (increases) for price decreases (increases) when the arc elasticity between the points is less than unity; and total expenditure is the same at points between which arc elasticity is unitary.

Price	Quantity Demanded	Total Expenditure
$10	1	$10
9	2	18
8	3	24
7	4	28
6	5	30
5	6	30
4	7	28
3	8	24
2	9	18
1	10	10

Determinants of Price Elasticity of Demand

Among the factors that affect price elasticity of demand are (1) availability of substitutes for the good, (2) proportion of total income spent for a unit of good, (3) durability of the good, (4) proportion of the total cost of some other good of which the cost of this good is a component part, and (5) habit.

If substitutes for the good in question are readily available, changes in its price will affect greatly the quantity demanded of it, customers curtailing their purchases of substitutes and increasing their purchases of this good when its price declines and deserting this good quickly when its price increases. Thus the greater the availability of substitutes, the more elastic the price elasticity of demand tends to be.

Similarly, if a good is very expensive relative to the incomes of the consumers in the market, the quantity demanded may tend to be very responsive to price changes. Even a small percentage change in the price of

---

use of the *average* price and the *average* quantity, even though the averages themselves are not computed (there would be no point in a separate step that divided numerator and denominator by 2).

such a good may cause a large percentage change in quantity demanded, because the remaining income that the consumer is free to spend is affected significantly by a change in the quantity purchased of this good. The relatively large elasticity of market demand may well be due, however, not to a correspondingly high elasticity of individual consumers' demand curves but to changes in the number of consumers who purchase the good. Thus a fall in the price of color TV sets may result in a relatively large increase in quantity demanded, owing not so much to the purchase of greater quantities by the existing customers as to an increase in the number of consumers in the market.

If a good is durable, the consumer enjoys some discretion with respect to the time of its replacement; thus the demand for the good may possess greater price elasticity than it would if it were not durable. On the other hand, if the good is a relatively unimportant part of a collection of goods that together meet some single want, the demand for this one good may tend to be relatively inelastic. The cost of lubricating oil, for example, is a relatively small proportion of the cost of owning and operating an automobile, and thus the demand for such oil may have relatively low price elasticity. Finally, an item that a customer habitually buys (such as cigarettes) will generally also possess a relatively low price elasticity of demand.

Income Elasticity of Demand

The quantity demanded of an economic good depends upon the price of the good and also upon the income of the consumer. Changes in the income of the consumer can be expected to cause changes in quantity demanded, even though the price of the good has not changed. The *income elasticity of demand* is a measure of the responsiveness of quantity demanded to a relative change in income. As a point elasticity, it may be expressed as

$$\eta_y = \frac{\dfrac{\Delta q}{q}}{\dfrac{\Delta y}{y}},$$

where y = income.

For most goods this elasticity is positive, since consumers will purchase more of most goods when their incomes rise. Goods possessing a positive income elasticity are referred to as *superior* goods. Of some goods it is true, however, that consumers will purchase less of them as income increases. Such *inferior* goods possess a negative income elasticity, arising usually because there are higher-priced but more desirable substitutes for them to which the consumers transfer their allegiance as their incomes rise. Thus, as incomes rise, fewer pork chops may be bought because the consumers are purchasing more steak. Pork chops in such an instance would be inferior goods and would possess a negative income elasticity of demand.

Relatively little is known about the determinants of income elasticity of demand. It is probably true, however, that most "luxury" items possess a greater income elasticity than do "necessities." Empirical evidence also suggests that changes in expenditure patterns tend to lag behind changes in income, suggesting that income elasticity tends to be greater over longer periods of time.

Cross Elasticity of Demand

While conceptually the quantity demanded of any economic good is affected by the prices of all other goods, it is usually true that only the prices of those goods which are *related* to the first good exert a significant effect upon the volume of it purchased. *Cross elasticity of demand* is a measure of the responsiveness of the quantity demanded of one good to relative changes in the price of another. As a point elasticity, it may be expressed as

$$\eta_{ab} = \frac{\dfrac{\Delta q_a}{q_a}}{\dfrac{\Delta p_b}{p_b}}.$$

As noted in Chapter 2, the total effect of a change in price upon quantity demanded may be divided into the substitution effect of the price change and the income effect.[5] If the price of a good increases, one of the effects is a tendency to substitute for it other goods that have not risen in price and are, relatively, less expensive. Goods that meet wants similar to those met by the good that has risen in price tend to be substituted for it. Thus if A is a substitute for B, it would tend to have a positive cross elasticity in terms of B—that is, its quantity demanded would tend to increase with increases in the price of B and decrease with decreases in the price of B. If, for example, the price of one soft drink were to increase, the quantity demanded of another (whose price had not changed) would tend to increase. Similarly, if the relationship between goods is that of *complementarity*, cross elasticity tends to be negative. If the price of automobiles increases, the quantity demanded of automobile radios tends to decrease.

---

[5] The relatedness of goods is defined in terms of the substitution effect of a price change. Cf. J. R. Hicks, *Value and Capital*, 2nd ed. (Oxford: Clarendon Press, 1946), chap. 3.

Because of the presence of the income effect, however, one cannot always conclude from a positive cross elasticity that the goods involved are necessarily substitutes in the sense of meeting similar wants, nor can one always conclude from a negative cross elasticity that the goods are necessarily complements in the sense that they share in meeting a single want. If, for example, the price elasticity of demand for B is greater than unity, less will be spent upon B at a higher price, and more will be spent on other goods—perhaps including A. Thus the increase in quantity demanded of A may not be due to A's ability to meet a want similar to that met by B, despite the positive cross elasticity of demand for A in terms of the price of B. Similarly, a *price* elasticity of demand for B of less than unity may yield a negative cross elasticity of demand for A in terms of the price of B even though A and B are not complements. Despite this shortcoming, cross elasticity of demand is often used empirically as a measure of the relatedness of goods, for lack of a better alternative. Because the income effect of a price change can usually be expected to have only a very small effect upon the quantity demanded of any particular good, this shortcoming is not a major one.

Relationship of Demand Elasticity to Indifference-Curve Analysis

Figure 3.11 indicates how the price elasticity of demand may be determined from the slope of the price-consumption curve. In order to secure A_1 of A the consumer, at the higher price of A, gives up DE of his income (measured in terms of B). Thus his total expenditure for the quantity A_1 is DE (in terms of B). With the fall in the price of A the consumer increases his quantity demanded to A_2, his total expenditure, however, declining to FG. From the fact that his total expenditure is less at the lower price we know that if we proceed to the actual construction

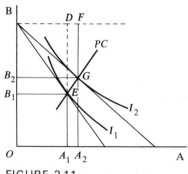

FIGURE 3.11

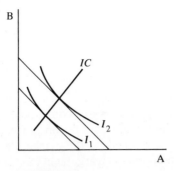

FIGURE 3.12

of his demand curve it will have a price elasticity of less than unity over the quantity range A_1–A_2.[6] Similarly, if the price-consumption curve is downward sloping we know that the demand curve has a price elasticity of greater than unity over this range of quantity demanded, and that it possesses unitary elasticity for any range over which the price-consumption curve is horizontal.

The quantity of B demanded at a lower price of A will increase when the price-consumption curve is upward sloping, will remain the same when the price-consumption curve is horizontal, and will decrease when the price-consumption curve is downward sloping. Thus the *cross* elasticity of demand for B will be negative for changes in the price of A when the *price* elasticity of demand for A is less than unity, will be positive when the *price* elasticity of demand for A is greater than unity, and will be zero when the *price* elasticity of demand for A is unitary.

The nature of the *income* elasticity of demand may be judged from the *income* consumption curve. Figure 3.12 indicates that as the consumer's income increases, the quantities demanded of both goods increase, indicating that both are superior goods (that they both have positive income elasticities of demand). If the income-consumption curve sloped downward to the right, this would indicate positive income elasticity of demand for A but negative for B, whereas an income-consumption curve sloping upward to the left would indicate the opposite. Vertical income-consumption curves indicate zero income elasticity of demand for A and greater than unity for B, and horizontal income-consumption curves indicate the opposite for A and B. For any good (when depicted on the horizontal axis) the price-consumption curve will lie to the right of the income-consumption curve. For any inferior good the *income*-consumption curve will be negatively sloped. For a *Giffen* good both the price-consumption and income-consumption curves will be negatively sloped.

---

[6] Assuming the same relationships to be true for intermediate points.

MARKET EQUILIBRIUM

The Buyers

Earlier in this chapter the market demand curve was derived from the demand curves of individual consumers. Thus the explanation of the process by which some of the consumer's wants come to be expressed in the market has been completed. The explanation, begun in Chapter 2, yields as a final result a downward-sloping function, the market demand curve, geometrically portraying the conclusion of an argument based on certain assumptions, including the assumption of diminishing marginal utility or, alternatively, downward-sloping convex indifference curves.

Put otherwise, we have reached a general conclusion concerning the behavior of buyers in a market. We have concluded that, *ceteris paribus* (other variables being constant), buyers will desire lesser quantities at higher prices. This is our conclusion regarding their response to changes in *price*, assuming that there are no changes in the other variables that affect quantity demanded. This conclusion is expressed geometrically by the device of the market demand curve.

We shall assume now that the buyers or customers in the market are *purely competitive*—that is, while any buyer would purchase a greater quantity at a lower price than he would at a higher price, the quantity purchased by any one consumer is so small relative to the quantity bought by all consumers that the individual consumer has no realization of the effect upon price of changes in the quantity he purchases. Thus each consumer, so far as he is concerned, has no influence upon the market price and simply adjusts his purchases to the price. While, as we shall see, the reactions of all the consumers taken as a whole (as reflected in the market demand curve) help to determine price, the part played by any one consumer is so small that he takes no cognizance of it.

For example, there is a market demand for toothpaste, and this market demand plays a crucial role in the determination of the price of toothpaste, but the individual consumer does not typically recognize the very small influence that his purchases exert upon price. Conceptually the market demand for toothpaste is a horizontal summation of individual consumer demands and is downward sloping because they are downward sloping, but the summation involves so large a number of individual consumer demand curves that the demand of an individual consumer has very little effect.

The Sellers

A *market* consists of a group of buyers and sellers in sufficiently close contact with one another that the actions of buying and selling can occur. Thus, depending upon the good and the question being analyzed, markets may be national, regional, or local in scope. Whatever their nature, markets include sellers as well as buyers. We have reached some strong conclusions with respect to the behavior of buyers, but as yet we have said nothing about the behavior of sellers.

In subsequent chapters we shall have a great deal to say about the behavior of sellers in various market situations. At present, however, we are primarily interested in the determination of market price, and for this reason we shall make certain assumptions concerning the behavior of sellers without defending these assumptions or indicating the arguments from which they are derived.

We shall thus assume that our sellers, like our buyers, are purely competitive—that no seller recognizes the influence that changes in the quantity he sells has upon price. We shall also assume, however, that the individual seller would be willing to sell a greater quantity at a higher price than at a lower price and that this is true also of the sellers as a whole. Thus, geometrically, we shall assume an upward-sloping market *supply curve*, such as that depicted in Figure 3.13, indicating that sellers will react to higher prices by increasing the quantity that they are willing to supply. As in the case of the market demand curve, variables other than the present price affect the quantity supplied, but these variables are assumed constant in relating the price of the good to the quantity supplied. Also, as in the case of the purely competitive buyer, the collective action of all purely competitive sellers (as reflected in the market supply curve) plays a crucial role in the determination of market price, but the number of sellers is so large and the quantity supplied by any one of them so small relative to the total quantity in the market that no individual seller recognizes the influence upon price of changes in the quantity he supplies to the market.

The Determination of Market Price

Given a market comprised of purely competitive buyers and sellers— that is, given a purely competitive market—and given the other assumptions we have made about buyers (as reflected in the market demand curve) and

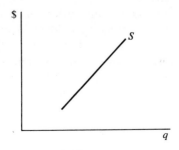

FIGURE 3.13

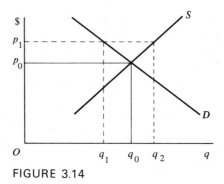

FIGURE 3.14

sellers (as reflected in the market supply curve), how is price determined? Figure 3.14 portrays geometrically the assumptions we have made concerning buyers and sellers and assists us in drawing the conclusions yielded by the conjoining of these assumptions.

Let us pose initially the price p_1 in order to determine whether or not this price is consistent with the assumptions we have made concerning buyers and sellers. At the price p_1 the quantity demanded by buyers is q_1, while the quantity that sellers are willing to sell is q_2. Sellers are thus willing to sell at this price a larger quantity than the buyers are willing to purchase. Since our sellers are competitive, they tend to bid down the price in an effort to dispose of the excess supply $q_2 - q_1$. Thus an excess of quantity supplied over quantity demanded tends to lower price. Similarly, if we pose a price lower than p_0, the quantity demanded will exceed the quantity supplied, and competitive buyers will tend to bid up the price. Thus in a purely competitive market that price at which quantity demanded equals quantity supplied tends to be established in the market. Such a price is termed a *stable equilibrium price*,[7] since any departure from it would set into action forces tending to restore it. The price in the market can, of course, change as a result of changes in the consumers' incomes, in their tastes, in the prices of other goods, or in any of the determinants of the supply curve other than the price of the good. *Given these parameters*, however, only one price can rule in a competitive market.

Thus the market, in establishing a price, reconciles the strength of the consumers' desire for a good (relative to their incomes and the prices of other goods) with the willingness of sellers to supply that good. The market demand curve is the expression of the effective wants of the consumers for this good, indicating the quantities they would purchase at various prices. The market supply curve indicates the quantities sellers are willing to sell

---

[7] Technically, what is depicted in Figure 3.14 is a *stable* equilibrium price. For a discussion of stability see Hicks, *Value and Capital*, chap. 5.

at various prices. The market or equilibrium price is that price at which the quantity that consumers desire is equal to the quantity that sellers are willing to sell.

The Effect of Changes in Demand and in Supply upon Market Price

As indicated previously, the market demand curve is an expression, in the market, of consumers' wants. Implicitly it is also an order or challenge to producers to convert resources into a form that can satisfy those wants and bring them to the market. The supply curve is an expression of the conditions under which sellers will meet the challenge. Changes in the incomes of the consumers, in their tastes, or in the prices of other goods, however, cause changes in the strength of the consumers' desire for the good, thus producing changes or shifts in the market demand curve. Similarly, changes in costs or in other factors may cause changes in the conditions under which sellers are willing to supply the good, thus occasioning changes in supply.

Figure 3.15 indicates the effect upon price of changes in demand. An increase in demand such as that indicated by the replacement of D_1 by D_2

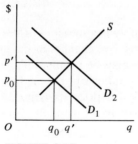

FIGURE 3.15

tends to increase the market or equilibrium price and increase the equilibrium quantity. A decrease in demand would tend to have the opposite effect. Similarly, an increase in supply, indicated in Figure 3.16 by the replacement of S_1 by S_2, would tend to cause a fall in market price and an increase in the equilibrium quantity. A decrease in supply would tend to have the opposite effect upon the equilibrium price and quantity. In Figure 3.15 the relative responsiveness of the quantity supplied to the change in price would depend upon the price elasticity of demand.

Mathematically, changes in demand and in supply are simply changes in the values of variables, other than the price of the good, that also affect the quantity demanded or supplied. Thus, if

$$Q_A = f(P_A, P_B, P_C, \ldots),$$

a shift in the demand function could be indicated by

$$Q_A = f(P_A, P'_B, P_C, \ldots),$$

the shift in this instance arising from a change in the price of good B.

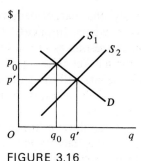

FIGURE 3.16

PRICE ELASTICITY OF SUPPLY

The price elasticity of supply is a measure of the relative responsiveness of the quantity supplied to relative changes in the price of the good. Since the slope of the supply curve may be positive, there is no need for a negative sign. With this exception (and except for the fact that q refers to the quantity supplied), the formula for price elasticity of supply (at a point) is the same as that for price elasticity of demand. Thus

$$\eta_s = \frac{\dfrac{\Delta q}{q}}{\dfrac{\Delta p}{p}} = \frac{p}{q}\frac{\Delta q}{\Delta p} = \frac{p}{q}\frac{1}{\dfrac{\Delta p}{\Delta q}}.$$

Geometrical measures for the price elasticity of supply (at a point) can be derived by the same procedure as that followed in arriving at such measures for point price elasticity of demand. Thus in Figure 3.17

$$\eta_s = \frac{BX}{OB}\frac{1}{\dfrac{BX}{OB}} = 1.$$

Any straight-line supply curve passing through the origin, or any point on

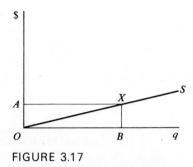

FIGURE 3.17

a curvilinear supply curve the tangent of which passes through the origin, will have a price elasticity of supply of unity.

Figure 3.18 depicts a straight-line supply curve with a positive price intercept. One geometrical measure of the price elasticity of supply at the point X would be

$$\eta_s = \frac{CX}{OC} \frac{1}{\dfrac{CX}{CD}} = \frac{CD}{OC}.$$

Similarly, other geometrical measures of the price elasticity of supply at the point X would be OB/AB and DX/AX. Note that this elasticity is necessarily greater than unity. Hence any point on a straight-line supply curve possessing a positive price intercept, or any point on a curvilinear supply curve the tangent to which has a positive price intercept, will have a price elasticity of supply greater than unity. Finally, it can be shown in the same way that a negative price intercept necessarily implies a supply price elasticity less than unity and that there exist three geometrical measures of its magnitude.

Attempts to measure the *arc* elasticity of supply encounter difficulties

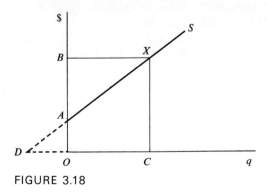

FIGURE 3.18

similar to those arising with the arc elasticity of demand. We cannot, at this stage in the development of our total argument, treat in depth the question of the determinants of the price elasticity of supply, for we have not yet derived the supply curve itself. Subsequently the supply curve will be related to the cost curves of the firm, making apparent some of the factors that may be expected to influence its price elasticity.

SUMMARY AND CONCLUSIONS

In the present chapter we have derived the market demand curve from the demand curves of individual consumers, and we have introduced the concepts of elasticity and market equilibrium. While such concepts serve as useful guides to empirical economists, they are perhaps best regarded as tools in the economist's analytical kit. Their expression in geometrical or mathematical form is largely for convenience in exposition and analysis.

The reader should not imagine that in most markets there is some caretaker of market demand and supply curves who keeps them up to date as new data are supplied to him. Useful as they are to economists in explaining the behavior and reaction to change of buyers, sellers, and markets, these concepts are, nonetheless, abstractions rather than the empirical counterparts that they help us to understand. Many aspects of the behavior of consumers, of sellers, and of markets are not encompassed by these concepts. Only by looking at selected aspects of reality, however, can we understand it. Therein lies the strength and weakness of abstraction.

SELECTED REFERENCES

(Most of the references cited at the end of Chapter 2 also cover some of the topics treated in this chapter. Additional references are cited below.)

BAUMOL, WILLIAM J., *Economic Theory and Operations Analysis*, 2nd ed. (Englewood Cliffs, N.J.: Prentice-Hall, Inc., 1965), chap. 9.

BRENNAN, MICHAEL J., *Theory of Economic Statics* (Englewood Cliffs, N.J.: Prentice-Hall, Inc., 1965), chap. 4.

STONIER, ALFRED W., and DOUGLAS C. HAGUE, *A Textbook of Economic Theory*, 2nd ed. (London: Longmans, Green & Co., Ltd., 1957), chaps. 1 and 3.

4

demand as seen by the individual firm

INTRODUCTION

Referring back to Figure 1.1, we have now completed most of the subject matter encompassed by the horizontal arrow at the top of the diagram. Accepting as given the consumer's income constraint and set of preferences, we have derived the individual consumer's demand curve by marginal-utility and indifference-curve analysis, and from the demand curve we have derived the market demand curve. Thus we have provided an explanation of how some of the wants of the consumer come to be expressed in the market.

In the present chapter we shall, in terms of the schematic outline, pause for a bit in order to consider the relationship of the individual firm's demand curve to the market demand curve. We shall find that the individual firm's demand curve may have any one of a number of different relationships to the market demand curve, depending primarily upon the manner in which the firms in the industry are organized. And we shall find that the demand curve of the individual firm is *not* related to the market demand curve in the simple way that the individual consumer's demand curve is related to the market demand curve. Instead, we shall find the concept of price elasticity of demand essential to our understanding of the relationship of the market demand curve to that of the individual firm.

In terms of the methodological discussion in Chapter 1 we shall discuss the individual firm's demand curve in six different "situations" or "arenas of action." Since the nature of the individual firm's demand curve depends upon the set of assumptions used to describe the situation in which the firm is presumed to act, we shall consider firms in terms of the "heuristic devices" or logical situations known as pure competition, monopoly, monopolistic competition, oligopoly, price discrimination, and joint production. We shall also discuss the construction of marginal-revenue curves and relate the concepts of average revenue and marginal revenue to the concept of price elasticity of demand.

THE DEMAND CURVE OF THE INDIVIDUAL FIRM

The nature of the demand for the output of the individual firm depends primarily upon the competitive relationship of this particular seller to other sellers of the same good or closely related goods. Put otherwise, the demand for the output of the individual firm differs from the demand for the output of the industry as a whole, the extent of the difference depending primarily upon the competitive relationship between the individual sellers. If there are many competitive sellers of the same good, the demand for the output of any one seller will be very different from the demand for the output of the industry; whereas if there is only one seller of the good, the two demand curves will be the same.[1]

The demand curve for the output of the industry shows, as we have seen, the reactions of consumers to changes in price. As such, it is the horizontal summation of the demand curves of individual consumers. From another point of view, however, the industry or market demand curve indicates the various quantities that could be sold to consumers at a corresponding schedule of prices. At higher prices this industry, or this group of firms, could only sell less to consumers, whereas at lower prices it could sell more. Since the individual seller—in all instances save that of monopoly—sells only a portion of the industry's output, his demand curve will reflect the effect of changes in the allocation of any given total output of the industry among the firms comprising it, as well as changes in the total itself.

Thus the demand curve for the output of the individual firm indicates the various quantities that this firm could sell at a corresponding schedule of prices. If its output is a sufficiently small part of the total output of all the firms in the industry, variations in its output will have no appreciable

---

[1]For a qualification of the latter part of this statement see the discussion in this chapter of the demand for the output of the monopolist.

effect upon market price, and there will be no sense of rivalry among sellers. If, however, there are only a few sellers in the market, changes in the output or price of any one of them may be expected to alter significantly the conditions under which others can sell, and there may be a high degree of rivalry among sellers—each seller reacting to changes in the price or output of other sellers.

Just as the price elasticity of the individual consumer's demand curve is affected by the availability of substitute goods, the price elasticity of the individual *seller's* demand curve is affected by the relative ease with which this firm's output can replace or be replaced by that of others. If there are no other firms in the industry—if this firm is a monopolist—there are no other sellers whose output can replace or be replaced by that of this firm. In such a case the demand curve of this firm has the same elasticity as that for the output of the industry, for the two demand curves are one.[2] In all other instances, however, the price elasticity of the demand of the individual seller will be different from that of the industry or market demand, reflecting the relative ease with which the output of other firms can replace or be replaced by that of the individual firm. If the number of firms is very large and the output of each firm is a very small part of total output, a reduction in the output of any one firm could easily be compensated for by minute changes in the outputs of the remaining firms. Similarly, an increase in the output of the individual firm would have little effect upon total output and so little effect upon the output of any one of the other firms comprising the industry that it would hardly be noticed. By the same token, the quantity sold by the individual firm, in this case, could vary greatly without appreciable effect upon market price. What would constitute, to the individual firm, a large relative change in output would be—in terms of the industry's output—an inconsequential change.

Thus, in general, the price elasticity of the demand for the output of the individual firm will be greater than that of the industry or market demand curve. If the individual firm raises its price, the relative change in the quantity that it can sell will be greater than the relative change in the quantity sold by the industry as a whole, both because a given absolute change in quantity sold is a greater relative change for the individual firm than it is for the industry as a whole (in all cases except that of monopoly) and also because some part of the decrease in the quantity that the individual firm can sell will be due to increases in output by the remaining firms. Similarly, a reduction in price by the individual firm will cause a greater relative increase in quantity sold for the individual firm than for the industry, both because a given absolute change will constitute a greater relative change in output for the individual firm than for the industry and also

---

[2]See footnote 1.

because some part of the increase in the quantity sold by the individual firm will be at the expense of the other firms in the industry.

Paradoxically, if the output of one firm is so small a proportion of the total industry output that this firm *could* pursue an independent price policy—secure in the knowledge that changes in its price would not provoke retaliation from other firms—there would be no point in its doing so. For, in such an instance, there would be no reason for the individual firm to charge a price lower than the market price. At this price it can sell any quantity it is willing to produce. If, on the other hand, the individual firm charged a price above the market price, it could sell no quantity at all. The output that it formerly contributed would be compensated for by minute increases in output by the other firms in the industry, and its increase in price would provoke no change in price by the other firms. In this case the price elasticity of the demand for the output of the individual firm would be infinite.

Thus the demand for the output of the individual firm is related in no simple way to that of the industry. If there is only one seller, the industry and individual-firm demand curves coincide,[3] their elasticities are—of course —the same, there can be no sense of rivalry among firms in the industry (since there is only one firm in the industry), and the firm can—of course— pursue a price policy independent of that of other firms in the industry (since—again—there is only one firm). If there are so many competing firms that the output of any one firm can have no appreciable effect upon market price, the price elasticities of the industry and individual firm's demand curves are completely independent, there is again no sense of rivalry among firms, and the individual firms again could—but will not—pursue a completely independent price policy. In all other cases the individual firm's demand curve will be of greater price elasticity than that of the industry but will not be independent of it, there will be some sense of rivalry among sellers, and no individual firm will be able to pursue a completely independent price policy.

The individual firm's demand curve is thus a *distortion* of the industry or market demand curve, the extent of the distortion being reflected in the difference between the elasticities of the two demand curves. In the case of the monopolist there is no distortion and the two elasticities are the same.[4] At the opposite extreme, when the output of one firm can have no appreciable effect upon market price, the distortion is complete, and the differences between the two elasticities is infinite. In the cases that lie between these extremes there will be, in general, finite differences between the two elasticities (that of the individual firm being greater than that of the indus-

---

[3] See footnote 1.

[4] See footnote 1.

try), the magnitude of the difference in elasticities corresponding to the degree of dissimilarity in the two demand curves.

The magnitude of the difference in the two elasticities is a measure of the degree of actual, or potential, competition among the firms comprising the industry. In the limiting case of pure competition this difference is infinite. In the limiting case of monopoly, it is zero.

THE DEMAND CURVE OF THE PURE COMPETITOR

As the preceding discussion has amply illustrated, one cannot speak of the demand for the output of the individual firm without stipulating what type of firm it is. Put otherwise, the nature of the demand for the output of the individual firm depends upon the type of market organization of the industry. Economists have a limited number of "heuristic devices" or sets of assumptions that are used to describe various forms of market organization or various situations or arenas of action in which a firm might conceptually find itself.

These situations are, of course, abstractions, and none of them would describe completely any actual market situation in which a firm might be operating. Some of the most analytically useful, in fact, are situations that we know do not exist in reality; rather, they are sets of assumptions describing situations that logically mark the ends or limits of a continuum of logically possible situations, even though only a few possibilities are defined.

One such situation is that of *pure competition*. This term refers to a particular set of assumptions defining a situation in which a firm might be conceived to find itself. "Pure competition" describes a benchmark situation —one that, although it might never occur in reality, permits us to orient other sets of assumptions partially describing actual market situations of more frequent occurrence. The distinction is a tricky but important one. No heuristic device describes reality completely. Thus no set of assumptions describes completely the market situation confronting an individual firm. Some heuristic devices or sets of assumptions, however, *purposely* do not describe reality but provide references, benchmarks, or ends of continuums comprised of logical situations—many of which are not defined. The heuristic device of pure competition is one such set of assumptions. It is no more to be derided because it does not exist than is the concept of a perfect circle or a straight line. And, just as these latter concepts may be usefully employed in a vast range of applications despite their lack of complete coincidence with reality, the concept of pure competition is of great analytical usefulness in treating a large range of economic phenomena.

One of the assumptions comprising the set of assumptions known as "pure competition" is that the output of the individual firm comprises so small a proportion of the total output of all firms in the industry that changes in the output of the individual firm have no appreciable effect upon market price.[5] A related assumption is that of product homogeneity—that in the eyes of consumers all firms in the industry sell the same product, so that the purchaser is indifferent to which firm meets his needs. The initial assumption implies a large number of sellers and marks the end of a continuum of fewer and fewer sellers possessing more and more influence over market price. The second assumption similarly distinguishes a point of departure, from which it is possible to treat firms selling differentiated products or each selling more than one product. The immediate question is that of the nature of the demand for the output of the individual firm in this type of situation.

Average Revenue, Marginal Revenue, and Total Revenue for the Pure Competitor

Since, in the situation of pure competition, the output of the individual firm can have no appreciable effect upon market price, market price is to the individual firm a given datum. Regardless of the number of units sold, the individual firm receives for each unit the given market price. Thus the firm's revenue per unit, or *average revenue*, equals the price. Consequently the total receipts of the firm, or *total revenue*, is a constant multiple of the quantity sold, being determined for any quantity by multiplying that quantity by the given price. If the market price is $1 and the quantity sold is 100, the total revenue is $100 and the average revenue is $1. If the firm chooses to sell 50 units rather than 100, the total revenue is $50 and the average revenue remains $1.

Since the total revenue is a constant multiple of the quantity sold, the rate of change of total revenue relative to changes in the quantity sold, or *marginal revenue*, is also constant and equals average revenue or price. Total revenue changes in direct proportion to changes in quantity, so that the rate of change of the former relative to the latter is constant. Put more crudely, the absolute *change* in total revenue resulting from a unit change in output is constant and equal to the average revenue or price. If the firm sells one unit more or less, its total revenue will change by the amount of the price, since price is unaffected by changes in the quantity sold by the firm.

The situation is portrayed geometrically in Figure 4.1. Since the individual firm cannot affect the market price by changes in its output, the demand for the output of the individual firm is a horizontal line of infinite

---

[5]More accurately, it is assumed that the individual firm does not take account of any effect upon price of changes in its output.

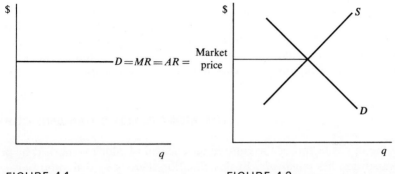

FIGURE 4.1   FIGURE 4.2

elasticity (and zero slope) at the market price. The price, in this situation, equals the firm's average revenue and marginal revenue. Figure 4.2 depicts the market demand and supply curves, establishing by their intersection the market price that the firm takes as given. It should, perhaps, be reemphasized that the difference in the elasticities of the two demand curves is infinite and that *the market demand curve cannot be derived by summation of the individual firms' demand curves.*

Mathematically, if p is price and q is the quantity sold by the firm,

$$p = \text{average revenue,}$$

$$pq = \text{total revenue}$$

$$\frac{d(pq)}{dq} = \text{marginal revenue} = p + q\frac{dp}{dq}.$$

Since, in pure competition,

$$p = k \qquad \text{(some constant),}$$

$$\frac{dp}{dq} = 0,$$

hence marginal revenue $= p$, or average revenue.

While pure competition is most usefully conceived of as a logically limiting case, it could be used, without a great deal of inaccuracy, to portray the individual producer of agricultural products in an economy in which the producers of agricultural products were not singled out for particular governmental attention. Thus the individual wheat producer would expect to receive the same average and marginal revenue for each bushel of wheat sold, would not expect changes in his output to affect the market price, and would feel no sense of rivalry toward his neighbor. In fairness it should be noted that a major element in the argument for particular governmental treatment of agricultural producers is the high degree of coincidence of their form of market organization with that of pure competition.

THE MONOPOLIST'S DEMAND CURVE

At the opposite end of the continuum one end of which is marked by pure competition lies *monopoly*. In this situation there is by definition only one seller of the product in question, so that the market demand for the product becomes the demand for the output of the firm. In order for this to hold, however, it must also be true that for the period for which the market demand is given there is no fear on the part of the monopolist that other firms will enter the industry—regardless of the price selected. Otherwise, the monopolist might reasonably fear that at a relatively high price he could not sell the quantity indicated by the market demand curve, because other firms would enter the industry at such a price. Similarly, since any market demand curve is derived by assuming the prices of other goods to be given, it must also be true that the monopolist sells a product not closely related to any other product. If this were not the case, he could not pursue an independent price policy, and any change in his price would evoke changes in the prices of related goods, thus altering the market demand for his own product.

Just as in the case of pure competition, the heuristic device of monopoly serves primarily as a logical benchmark. For no product would it be true that the market demand for it is entirely unrelated to that for any other good. Nonetheless, as the case in which market demand and the firm's demand coincide it is analytically useful.

Average Revenue, Marginal Revenue, and Total Revenue for the Monopolist

The distinction between average revenue and marginal revenue is an important one in the case of the monopolist. Since the market demand curve is downward sloping, the coincident demand for the output of the monopolist has the same downward or negative slope. Consequently the price received by the monopolist varies inversely with the quantity he sells and is not, as in the case of pure competition, independent of the output of the firm. Average revenue remains the revenue per unit or price, but it is different for every different quantity selected. Similarly, total revenue remains the result of multiplying price by quantity, but total revenue differs for every quantity not only because of the change in quantity but also because of the change in price that accompanies every change in quantity. In this situation the *marginal revenue*, or rate of change of total revenue relative to changes in the quantity sold, is not constant, because price does not remain the same as quantity changes. Put more crudely, the absolute change in total revenue resulting from a unit change in output is not constant and is not equal to the price. A decision to sell one unit more, or one unit less, is a decision not only to change output but also to accept a different price for the new output than that for which the old output could be sold. Thus the marginal revenue for a unit change in output is the difference between the total revenue received if a given quantity is sold (at the initial price) and the total revenue received if a new quantity, differing by one unit, is sold (at the new price).

Since the demand curve of the monopolist is downward sloping, the marginal revenue for any given quantity will be less than the price, or the average revenue. The decision to sell a given quantity rather than a quantity one unit less is a decision to accept for all units of the given quantity a lower price than that at which the smaller quantity could be sold. Consequently the sale of an additional unit increases the firm's total revenue not by an amount equal to price but by an amount less than price. Similarly, a decision to sell a quantity smaller by one unit does not result in a decrease in total revenue equal to price, because the price at which the smaller quantity can be sold is higher than that at which the larger quantity can be sold. Marginal revenue must, therefore, be less than average revenue, or price, for the monopolist.

The situation of the monopolist is portrayed geometrically in Figure 4.3, and the relationship between average revenue, marginal revenue, and total revenue is shown in Table 4.1.

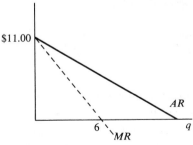

FIGURE 4.3

Mathematically, if p is price or average revenue and q is the quantity sold by the firm,

$$p = f(q).$$

TABLE 4.1

Average Revenue or Price	Quantity	Total Revenue	Marginal Revenue
$10	1	$10	—
9	2	18	$8
8	3	24	6
7	4	28	4
6	5	30	2
5	6	30	0
4	7	28	−2
3	8	24	−4
2	9	18	−6
1	10	10	−8

Since the demand curve is downward sloping,

$$\frac{dp}{dq} < 0,$$

$$pq = \text{total revenue} = qf(q),$$

$$\frac{d(pq)}{dq} = \text{marginal revenue} = qf'(q) + f(q) = p + q\frac{dp}{dq}.$$

Since $dp/dq < 0, p > 0, q > 0,$

$$p + q\frac{dp}{dq} < p,$$

or marginal revenue is less than price.

While monopoly, in its purest form, is not likely to occur in reality, it should be apparent that almost every firm in reality has some of the attributes of monopoly and that there exists, conceptually, a continuum of situations stretching from monopoly in its purest form to pure competition. For almost every firm it is true that the price received is affected to some extent by the quantity sold, but this would be much more the case in some market situations than in others.

THE CONSTRUCTION OF MARGINAL-REVENUE
CURVES AND THE RELATIONSHIP OF AVERAGE
REVENUE, MARGINAL REVENUE, AND ELASTICITY

Before proceeding to other market situations in which the demand for the output of the individual firm (and its relationship to the demand for the output of all firms in the industry) differs from pure competition or monopoly, it is helpful to understand the geometrical relationship between the marginal revenue and average revenue curves and to understand, also, the mathematical relationship of average revenue, marginal revenue, and price elasticity of demand.

The Geometry of Marginal-Revenue Curves

Careful inspection of Figure 4.3 reveals that in this case the marginal-revenue curve bisects any horizontal line drawn from the vertical axis to the average-revenue or demand curve. This occurs in any instance of *straight-line* demand curves and provides the key to the construction of marginal-revenue curves. Put otherwise, the slope of the marginal-revenue curve is twice that of the average-revenue curve in all cases in which the average-revenue curve is a *straight line*.

Mathematically, any straight-line demand curve may be represented by the equation

$$p = a - bq,$$

where a is the price intercept (the value of p when $q = 0$) and $-b$ is the slope. Total revenue would then be price multiplied by quantity, or

$$pq = aq - bq^2.$$

The rate of change of total revenue relative to quantity, or marginal revenue, would thus be, in the *straight-line case*,

$$\frac{d(pq)}{dq} = a - 2bq.$$

The slope of the marginal-revenue curve in the straight-line case $(-2b)$ is thus twice that of the demand or average-revenue curve. From this (and the common intercept a) it follows that the marginal-revenue curve, in the straight-line case, bisects any horizontal line drawn from the price axis to the demand or average-revenue curve.

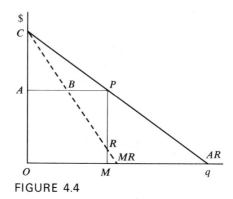

FIGURE 4.4

Thus in Figure 4.4 the marginal-revenue curve could have been constructed by locating the midpoint (B) of AP, joining B and C, and extending BC through R to ascertain that at the quantity OM the value of marginal revenue is MR. In the straight-line case the points comprising the line CR constitute the values of the marginal-revenue curve.

Alternatively, since the triangles ABC and PBR are congruent, $AC = PR$, so that the marginal revenue corresponding to any price can be located by moving down from that price the vertical distance from the price to the price intercept. As we shall see, this method is perhaps more useful in the construction of nonlinear marginal-revenue curves.

In the case of curvilinear demand curves essentially the same methods may be used to construct the marginal revenue curve with the important exception that the exercise must be repeated for every different price. In Figure 4.5 we are interested in determining, first of all, the value of marginal revenue at the price EP. We therefore construct a *tangent* to the demand curve at that price. Using either of the methods previously described, we determine that EF is the value of marginal revenue, *at the quantity OE*.

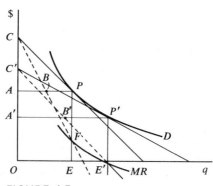

FIGURE 4.5

The dotted line passing through F is now merely a construction line determining the value of marginal revenue *only for the quantity OE*. Then moving to other quantities, such as OE', we repeat the operation until sufficient values of marginal revenue have been determined to permit us to sketch the remainder of the curve. Note that the marginal-revenue curve does not pass through B and B'.

Mathematically,

$$p = f(q),$$

$$pq = qf(q),$$

$$\frac{d(pq)}{dq} = p + q\frac{dp}{dq}.$$

In the special case in which $p = a - bq$

$$\frac{d(pq)}{dq} = a - bq + q(-b)$$

$$= a - 2bq.$$

The Relationship of Marginal Revenue, Average Revenue, and Price of Elasticity of Demand

A crude idea of the relationship among marginal revenue, average revenue, and elasticity is provided by Figure 4.6 and Table 4.2. Since we

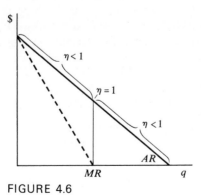

FIGURE 4.6

know that, for price decreases, total revenue increases when elasticity is greater than unity, we know that marginal revenue is positive, or greater

TABLE 4.2

MR	η	AR
> 0	> 1	> 0
0	1	> 0
< 0	< 1	> 0

than zero, over the range for which total revenue is increasing and elasticity is greater than unity. Similarly we know that when total revenue is constant, elasticity is unitary and marginal revenue is zero. Finally, when elasticity is less than unity, total revenue is declining for price decreases and marginal revenue is negative.

One method of deriving the precise relationship of marginal revenue, average revenue, and elasticity makes use of the geometrical ratios that are

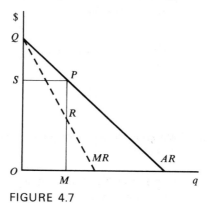

FIGURE 4.7

measures of price elasticity of demand at a point. Thus, in Figure 4.7 we know that one measure of the price elasticity at point P is OS/SQ. Since

$$\eta = \frac{OS}{SQ} = \frac{MP}{SQ} = \frac{MP}{RP} = \frac{MP}{MP - MR},$$

$$\eta = \frac{\text{price}}{\text{price} - \text{marginal revenue}}.$$

Cross-multiplying and solving for marginal revenue yields

$$\text{marginal revenue} = \text{price} \left(1 - \frac{1}{\eta}\right),$$

or

$$MR = AR\left(1 - \frac{1}{\eta}\right).$$

Mathematically,

$$\eta = -\frac{p}{q}\frac{dq}{dp},$$

$$MR = \frac{d(pq)}{dq} = p + q\frac{dp}{dq},$$

$$MR = p\left(1 + \frac{q}{p}\frac{dp}{dq}\right).$$

Since $(q/p)(dp/dq) = -1/\eta$,

$$MR = p\left(1 - \frac{1}{\eta}\right),$$

or

$$MR = AR\left(1 - \frac{1}{\eta}\right).$$

However derived, the relationship is an extremely important one, relating as it does three of the most fundamental concepts of economic theory.

THE DEMAND CURVE OF THE MONOPOLISTIC COMPETITOR

A third logical situation posed for the firm by economists is *monopolistic competition*. To some the juxtaposition of terms might seem incongruous, but to economists this particular heuristic device reflects an awareness of market situations in which both monopolistic and competitive forces are present. As in pure competition, it is assumed that there are many firms in the industry, each so small relative to the market that the individual firm need fear no retaliation from other firms as a result of changes in its output or price. It is also assumed that the product or service sold is *differentiated*— that each seller is able, by packaging, brand name, trademark, location, or in some other way to distinguish himself to customers so that at least some of them do not regard other sellers' products or services as perfect substitutes for his own. Nonetheless, the goods of all sellers in the industry are close substitutes, the cross elasticities of demand are high, and the ability of any one seller to distinguish himself from his fellows is quite limited.

While each firm in pursuing its price policy need not fear retaliation from any other firm, its freedom to vary price is severely limited by the high price elasticity of the demand for its output, this high price elasticity arising from the fact that the products produced by all firms are similar. Thus any change in price can be expected to cause a relatively large change in quantity demanded, not because some other firm reacts sharply to the change in price but because customers readily change their allegiance. Thus a small reduction in price will cause a large increase in output, relative to the maximum quantity the firm can sell, but the change in quantity is small relative to total industry output and any reduction in the quantity sold by any one of the other firms is so small as to provoke no reaction. Similarly, even a small increase in the firm's price will cause a relatively large (to the firm) reduction in the quantity it can sell and an increase in the quantity sold by other firms in the industry. But the many small firms comprising the remainder of the industry share this increase among them, and it constitutes a negligible increase for any one of them.

Product differentiation is the door through which the element of monopoly enters. By product differentiation the monopolistic competitor seeks to raise the level of his demand curve (increase his "share of the market") and render it less elastic (increase the allegiance of his present customers so that they will not so readily leave him or decrease their purchases if he raises the price slightly). Though the demand curve may be so portrayed geometrically, it is not necessarily true that the price elasticity of demand will be the same for price decreases as for increases.

The demand curve for the output of the monopolistic competitor is, of course, far more elastic (at a given price) than that for the output of the industry as a whole. The difference of elasticities, while very great, is not infinite, however, as in the case of pure competition. The small range of prices that the monopolistic competitor can charge is, in general, the range of prices that other sellers in the industry can charge for their very similar products. The level of this range of prices is determined by the demand for the output of the industry relative to the total output of the firms comprising the industry.

Average Revenue, Marginal Revenue, and Total Revenue
for the Monopolistic Competitor

Geometrically the demand for the output of the monopolistic competitor (or his average revenue) may be represented, as in Figure 4.8, as a curve possessing a very small downward or negative slope. Since it has a

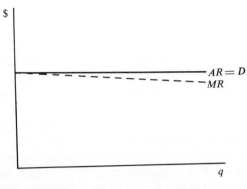

FIGURE 4.8

slope other than zero, marginal revenue and average revenue will differ, though not nearly so greatly (for a given quantity) as in the case of monopoly, and marginal revenue will, of course, be less than price (for a given quantity). Total revenue remains the product of price and quantity, both changing when either changes. Mathematically this situation is treated like the case of monopoly.

It is usually assumed to be relatively easy for new firms to enter an industry that is monopolistically competitive. Indeed, this is one of the factors accounting for the high price elasticity of the demand for the output of the individual firm. New firms may not sell the identical product or service but may duplicate it as closely as possible. Thus one producer of a particular brand of canned peas may find at any time a new rival selling almost the same product but under a different brand name, and one dry-cleaning establishment may find that it has a new rival almost or equally as well located to serve the neighborhood custom. The situation of monopolistic competition is thought by economists to have widespread applicability, especially in the production of services in large cities and of many commodities for national or regional markets.

THE DEMAND CURVE OF THE OLIGOPOLIST

A fourth market situation posed by economists is that of *oligopoly*. In this situation it is assumed that there are only a few sellers in the industry and that the output of each is so large a proportion of total output that any change in the output or price of one firm is bound to change the output of rival firms by a noticeable amount. Further, there is no difficulty in identifying the firm making the initial change, so that any firm so doing may expect retaliation by its rivals.

While any one oligopolist may expect any action that he may take to provoke a reaction, there is great uncertainty as to the precise form and extent of the reaction to be expected. Further, firms in reacting may realize that there may be reaction to their reaction, and this may condition their first reaction (and the initial change may well have been conditioned by the reaction expected). Since there are a wide range of possible interactions and various degrees of perception of these interactions by the individual oligopolist, there is no unique set of assumptions that can describe the many situations that may be expected to occur under oligopoly. The individual oligopolist may see the demand for his output in very different ways, depending upon how he evaluates such factors as the probable type and magnitude of the reaction to changes in price or output. Rivalry is intense (so long as there is no collusion), but its manifestations may well be varied and uncertain with regard to the individual firm.

Since there is no unique demand for the output of the oligopolist, there can be no one geometrical representation of his demand curve. One situation in which an oligopolist might find himself, however, is depicted geometrically in Figure 4.9. In this situation there is some customary price (occurring at the abrupt bend or "kink" in the demand curve) established by custom, tacit collusion, or some other factor. The oligopolist expects that if he were to lower his price from its customary value, his rivals would quickly react by also lowering price. On the other hand, he expects that if he were to raise his price his rivals would not raise theirs. Consequently, lowering the price would permit him only to share in the increased total quantity sold by the industry as all firms reduced their prices. Raising his price would occasion a drastic reduction in sales, since his price increase would not be followed by his rivals and much of his custom would be lost to them. Thus the demand curve of the oligopolist, in this situation, possesses for price decreases the same elasticity as that of the market demand curve (assuming his share of the market not to change), but it has a much greater elasticity for price increases.

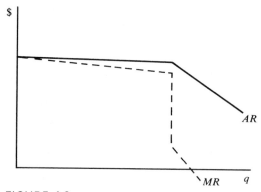

FIGURE 4.9

Average Revenue, Marginal Revenue, and Total
Revenue in One Oligopoly Situation

Restating the situation somewhat differently, Figure 4.9 portrays an oligopolist who expects only small increases in total revenue to accompany reductions in his price below its customary value. Hence for prices below the "kink," marginal revenue is very low, or even negative. The oligopolist also expects much larger decreases in total revenue to accompany increases in his price above its customary level. In such a situation he may be understandably reluctant to "rock the boat" by initiating a price or output change unless some form of collusion causes him to change his expectations. Even so, a set of expectations similar to those held initially may reassert itself at the new price, once agreement has been reached on the new price.

Characteristically, oligopolists employ product differentiation so that the price at which the "kink" occurs (if the oligopoly situation is characterized by a kink) is not necessarily the same for each oligopolist. Instances in which there may well be a single customary price for each oligopolist (and a kink) include local bottlers of soft drinks or producers of candy bars. Oligopoly in all its forms is characteristic of a large part of the manufacturing sector of the American economy. In some instances the output of the entire industry is produced by a dozen or fewer large firms. In others a few large firms predominate, while a considerable number of small firms account for only a minute part of the total output of the industry. Oligopoly characterizes the production of a number of basic metals such as steel and aluminum, industrial products such as sulfur and alcohol, and consumer products such as soap and automobiles.

THE DEMAND CURVES OF THE PRICE DISCRIMINATOR

It should be apparent that between the extremes of pure competition and monopoly there exist a host of market situations possessing some of the characteristics of both. Moreover, some of these situations have characteristics, alien to both extremes, that themselves may be present in varying degrees in the intermediate market situations. While monopoly may be conceived of as both an absence and ultimate form of product differentiation, the degree of product differentiation need not coincide with the closeness of a given market situation to monopoly. Thus in some oligopolistic situations there is little if any product differentiation despite a high degree of monopolistic influence, while in the much more competitive situation of monopolistic competition product differentiation is an essential characteristic. Similarly, a sense of rivalry is absent in pure competition, monopoly, and (in any directed way) monopolistic competition, but may be present in varying degrees in other market situations.

In all of the discussion of individual-firm demand curves thus far, however, it has been assumed that, whatever its nature, the individual firm possesses only one demand curve. In other words, it has been assumed that all firms sell their products or services in a single unfragmented market and receive a single price for their output. Price and average revenue are thus synonomous. Implicitly we have assumed, then, up to this point, either that the customers of the individual firm are homogeneous in the eyes of the seller or that the seller cannot take advantage of any lack of homogeneity of which he is aware. Thus any customer must be treated as is any other customer and a single price charged to all.

Quite obviously, this is not always the case. Though a more complete treatment of price discrimination must wait for the development of other analytical tools, it is immediately apparent that a seller in some instances is able to distinguish between different groups of customers and charge them different prices.

In such a situation the individual seller has a *total* demand curve and a number of separate demand curves corresponding to the different classes into which he can separate his customers (and comprising his total demand curve).[6] In terms of his total demand curve he may be a monopolistic competitor, an oligopolist, a monopolist, or any kind of seller other than a pure competitor. Moreover, he may employ product differentiation as a basis for separation of his customers. Thus his total demand curve may bear any of the relationships previously described to the market demand curve (except that of the pure competitor).

Average Revenue, Marginal Revenue, and Total
Revenue for the Price Discriminator

In its simplest form price discrimination is a situation in which the individual firm sells the identical product to two separate groups of customers at different prices. In essence such a situation may occur because some factor (such as geographical location) permits one group of customers to be distinguished from another and because the respective price elasticities of demand of the two groups are not the same (perhaps because the number of rival sellers and thus the number of substitute sources of supply is not the same for the two groups of customers).

Assuming the cost of serving the two groups to be the same, it is clear

---

[6]This way of putting the matter is slightly misleading, since the total quantity sold by a price discriminator may be affected by his decision to engage in this form of pricing, rather than to follow a single-price policy.

that a rational price discriminator in this situation would so allocate any quantity sold that the *marginal* revenue would be the same in each submarket, even though he would have to charge two different prices to accomplish this result. If, for a given output, the marginal revenue received from sales to one group was higher than that received from a second group, output would be diverted from the latter to the former (since the decrease in total revenue accompanying a decrease in the quantity sold in the second market would be less than the increase in total revenue accompanying an increase in the quantity sold in the first market).

Figure 4.10 shows the two demand curves in the submarkets served by the price discriminator. A common price axis is used for both demand curves; an increase in quantity in the first market constitutes a rightward

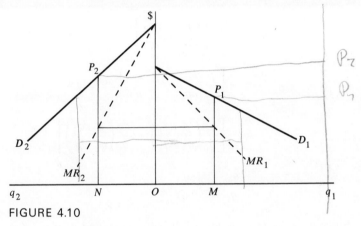

FIGURE 4.10

movement away from O, whereas an increase in quantity in the second market constitutes a leftward movement away from O. The arbitrarily chosen quantity NM is divided in such a way that marginal revenue is equal in each market. If this were the total quantity sold, OM would be sold in the first submarket, at a price of MP_1, whereas ON would be sold in the second submarket, at a price of NP_2. The *average revenue* received for this quantity would be the *sum* of the total revenues received in each submarket divided by the total quantity sold, and it would not be equal to either price.

Mathematically, if AR is average revenue and q_1, p_1 and q_2, p_2 are the respective prices and quantities sold in the two submarkets,

$$AR = \frac{p_1 q_1 + p_2 q_2}{q_1 + q_2}.$$

If η_1, η_2, and η_t are the price elasticities of demand (at a given price) in the two submarkets and the total market, then

$$\eta_t = -\frac{p}{q_t}\frac{dq_t}{dp},$$

$$\eta_1 = -\frac{p}{q_1}\frac{dq_1}{dp},$$

and

$$\eta_2 = -\frac{p}{q_2}\frac{dq_2}{dp}.$$

Since $dq_t/dp = dq_1/dp + dq_2/dp$,

$$\eta_t = -\frac{p}{q_t}\left[\frac{dq_1}{dp} + \frac{dq_2}{dp}\right]$$

$$= -\left[\frac{p}{q_t}\frac{dq_1}{dp} + \frac{p}{q_t}\frac{dq_2}{dp}\right]$$

$$= -\left[\frac{q_1}{q_t}\left(\frac{p}{q_1}\frac{dq_1}{dp}\right) + \frac{q_2}{q_t}\left(\frac{p}{q_2}\frac{dq_2}{dp}\right)\right]$$

$$= \frac{q_1}{q_t}\eta_1 + \frac{q_2}{q_t}\eta_2.$$

Since $q_1 + q_2 = q_t$, η_t must fall between η_1 and η_2 if $\eta_1 \neq \eta_2$.

Since the firm so allocates output as to equate the marginal revenues in the two submarkets,

$$p_1\left(1 - \frac{1}{\eta_1}\right) = p_2\left(1 - \frac{1}{\eta_2}\right).$$

Thus the prices will be different in the two submarkets if the price elasticities of demand are different.

The preceding analysis has been confined to the simplest case of price discrimination and is, even for this case, incomplete. In reality there are a large number of market situations in which some form of price discrimination constitutes an element. Further, it is perhaps apparent even at this point that price discrimination employing product differentiation shades off into the analysis appropriate to a firm selling more than one product. Thus the analysis of the multiproduct firm is a logical extension of price discrimination.

THE DEMAND CURVES OF THE PRODUCER OF
JOINT PRODUCTS

It is probably true that most real-world firms produce more than one product. In many such cases the costs of producing the two or more products are interrelated—that is, the cost of producing a given quantity of one of the products depends upon the respective quantities of other products that the firm is also simultaneously producing. Further complicating matters is the fact that there may be various degrees of interrelatedness of costs. The highest degree of interrelatedness of cost, and the easiest to analyze, is the case in which products are produced in fixed proportions. This case is known as *joint cost*.

The analysis of joint cost is related to that of price discrimination, being the logical limit of a series of analyses that begins with the simple price discriminator selling a single product in separate submarkets and progresses to a seller of more than one product the costs of which are not related, to cases in which the costs of the several products are related to some degree, to the case of joint costs or joint production. Like the price discriminator, the producer of joint products may be, in terms of the demand for each product, a monopolist, oligopolist, monopolistic competitor, or any type of seller other than a pure competitor. Thus each of his demand curves may bear to the market demand for that product any of the relationships previously described except that of the pure competitor. As in the simple case of price discrimination discussed earlier, the producer of joint products may well charge different prices for his products.

Average Revenue, Marginal Revenue, and Total Revenue
for the Producer of Joint Products

Figure 4.11 depicts the case of joint cost, or joint production, in which two products are produced in a fixed ratio of one to one. The classical illustration employed by economists is that of the steer and his hide. Every steer comes equipped with one carcass and one hide and these two products are sold in essentially two separate markets. While over time scientists may be able to alter the proportion of meat to uncured leather, this consideration need not trouble us in our analysis. More broadly, the analysis would have relevance for a large number of instances in which by-products are produced in a fixed proportion to the major product.

Basically the analysis is quite similar to that of the preceding section, except that output cannot be so allocated to the two markets as to equate marginal revenue at any output. A decision to produce a given number of

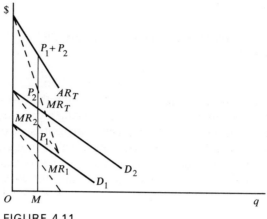

FIGURE 4.11

carcasses is also a decision to produce that same number of hides, although a decision to *sell* a given quantity of one of the two products does not necessarily mean that the same quantity of the other product will be *sold*. In some instances it will be more profitable to destroy or even pay for the disposal of a portion of the by-product while selling only part of it.

In Figure 4.11 the respective demands for the by-product and the major product are shown as D_1 and D_2, respectively. Since the two products are produced in a ratio of one to one, the horizontal axis is expressed in composite units, one unit representing one steer *with hide,* two units two steers with their two hides, and so on. If the firm were to sell the quantity OM steers (with hides), the price received for the hides would be MP_1 and for the steers (more accurately, their carcasses) MP_2. AR_T, the vertical summation of the two prices, would constitute the average revenue received for OM steers and hides. AR_T, MR_1, MR_2, and MR_T cannot be drawn beyond the point shown until other elements of the situation (for example, what to do about excess hides) are stipulated.

Mathematically,

$$\text{total revenue} = p_1 q + p_2 q,$$

$$\text{average revenue} = \frac{p_1 q + p_2 q}{q} = p_1 + p_2.$$

In a subsequent chapter we shall return to the case of joint cost and analyze it more fully. It is sufficient at this point to establish that in this instance the firm has more than one demand curve and average revenue is not equal to a single price. A producer of joint products might also, of course, engage in product differentiation and/or price discrimination in selling one or more of his products.

SUMMARY AND CONCLUSIONS

The first chapter identified three basic steps in the deductive method as used in economic theory. First, rationality is assumed as a basic attribute of some specified "actor." Second, a set of assumptions is used to specify the "situation" or "arena of action" in which the actor is presumed to act. Third, the assumptions are conjoined and the logical results of their conjuncture are deduced.

The present chapter has partially described six situations in which the firm (the "actor") might find itself. We have attempted to ascertain the nature of the demand for the output of the firm in these situations and to relate this demand to the demand for the output of the industry. The six "situations" or "heuristic devices" by no means exhaust the possibilities, and, quite obviously, some market situations could best be analyzed as combinations of two or more of the cases discussed. Most of the six cases will be discussed in greater detail in subsequent chapters.

The present chapter has served the more general purpose of completing our treatment of demand theory as a separate topic. Earlier chapters derived the individual consumer's demand curve and the market demand curve. There remained for this chapter the task of explaining the nature of the demand for the output of the individual firm (which can only be done in terms of the particular market situation posed for the firm). In order to facilitate understanding of the six cases, we defined the concepts of average revenue, marginal revenue, and total revenue and developed the relationship of average revenue, marginal revenue, and price elasticity of demand.

Before we can draw further deductions concerning the actions of firms in the situations posed, we have to describe these situations more fully. Specifically, we have to describe the cost conditions under which the firm operates. To explain what factors determine these conditions, we must first develop the theory of production.

SELECTED REFERENCES

BAIN, JOE S., *Price Theory*, rev. ed. (New York: Holt, Rinehart and Winston, Inc., 1952), chap. 2.

DUE, JOHN F., and ROBERT W. CLOWER, *Intermediate Economic Analysis*, 4th ed. (Homewood, Ill.: Richard D. Irwin, 1962), chap. 4.

LEFTWICH, RICHARD H., *The Price System and Resource Allocation*, 3rd ed. (New York: Holt, Rinehart and Winston, Inc., 1966), chap. 6.

the theory of production

In terms of Figure 1.1, we begin in this chapter the long trek from resources to the supply curve. Thus we begin the explanation of how, why, and under what conditions resources are changed into products and services to meet the consumer wants that are expressed in the market. The theory of production underlies the theory of costs, and the theory of costs underlies the supply curve.

Provided automatically by the theory of production is a description or explanation of a great deal of the firm's behavior relating to the production process. Just as derivation of the individual consumer's demand curve automatically provides a description or explanation of consumer behavior, the theory of production automatically provides a description of the behavior of the individual firm in converting resources into products and services. The theory of production also provides the basis for explanations of the demand for and allocation of resources themselves, and for the distribution of any given level of national income into wages, interest, rent, and so forth. Last, but not least, the theory of production provides fundamental concepts and relationships that are used—in one form or another—in almost all areas of economics, upon occasion even spilling over into common parlance.

As usual, we shall assume rationality and we shall ascribe this characteristic to the firm. As usual, also, we shall construct various sets of assumptions constituting different "situations" in which the firm might be presumed to act. These "situations," however, will not be those of the preceding chapters but will relate instead to such questions as the number of inputs that can be varied, the quantity of a given input available to the firm, and the nature of the quantitative relationship between input and output. Finally, we shall again pose only a few of many possible situations—hopefully, enough to give the reader some perception of the full range of possibilities.

The body of the present chapter is divided into five major sections. The first makes fundamental distinctions between factors of production and factor services and between divisibility in acquisition and divisibility in use. The second section is devoted to the production function. The remaining three sections describe the output-expansion path on the production surface in, respectively, the market period, the short run, and the long run. In the market period it is assumed that the quantities of all factor services are fixed in acquisition. In the short-run situation it is assumed that the quantities of the services of one or more (but not all) factors of production are variable in acquisition, whereas it is assumed in the long run that the respective quantities of all factor services are variable in acquisition.

TWO FUNDAMENTAL DISTINCTIONS

Factors of Production vs. Factor Services

Traditionally economists have divided the resources used in production into land, labor, capital, and—sometimes—entrepreneurship, calling these the *factors of production* or *productive factors.* This somewhat arbitrary classification reflects the fact that there are inherent differences in productive factors such that one cannot be a perfect substitute for another. Land, labor, and capital differ in physical attributes, in the units in which they are measured, and in the roles that they play in production. Only within limits can more capital compensate for less land or more labor for less capital.

Distinct from the factors of production themselves are the *services yielded by these factors* or *factor services,* the contribution made by factors of production to the productive process. This distinction between productive factors and factor services reflects not only the difference in the units in which productive factors are measured and in the units in which they contribute to production but also the fact that these units exist at different levels of abstraction. The distinction between *productive factors* and *factor services* is of great importance to the theory of production.

Consider land. It may be measured and purchased in such units as acres or square feet. But of land used in the production of refrigerators it is nonsensical to ask what particular part went into the production of a specific refrigerator. Not the land itself but something more abstract—the *services* of land—go into the production of refrigerators. Moreover, while we have no readily available unit in which to measure the services of land, it is clear that any such unit would have a temporal dimension, for the services of land are yielded *through time*. Finally, it is apparent that at least some of the services of land are yielded *automatically* through time. The land upon which the refrigerator factory sits may contribute its services to the productive process for any portion of the 24 hours of the day or seven days of the week. Many of its services are yielded continuously. Operation of the factory for only part of the day or week means that many of the services of land do not enter into production and are simply lost. Thus possession of a unit of land may be conceived of as possession of a stock of the services of land, these services being yielded through time, and all of which may or may not enter into the productive process.[1]

The case of capital is similar but more complex. Capital is customarily measured and purchased in units appropriate to the form in which it exists. Thus a farmer may purchase four hoes or four tractors, and a textile manufacturer may purchase fifty looms or a building that he thinks of in terms of square feet of floor space and cubic feet of storage. But again, while hoes, tractors, looms, and buildings are tangible, we find no physical trace of hoes and tractors in carrots, or of looms and buildings in sport shirts. Quite evidently something that we may call the *services* of capital enters into production—not capital itself.[2]

Further, the services of capital, like those of land, are yielded through time. Like the services of land also, but to a lesser extent, some of the services of capital are yielded *automatically* through time. The forces of nature, which work with land to permit its services to be productive in agriculture, may have an opposite effect upon hoes, tractors, looms, or buildings. If not utilized in production, the services of capital become prey, in time, to nature.

To a considerable extent *intertemporal substitution* of capital services is possible. Thus in a given period machinery may be operated at a faster or slower rate, altering to some extent the distribution of its services through time, and buildings and/or machinery may be designed to last

---

[1]Since land includes all natural resources, the distinction between a factor and its services is not clear in some production processes in which land enters as a raw material. In most such cases, however, the input is obviously divisible in use and poses no difficulties for the analysis other than determination of whether the raw material constitutes land or capital. For the importance of the distinction between divisibility in acquisition and divisibility in use see the next section.

[2]Some forms of capital raise the same problem as that discussed in footnote 1. Again the difficulty is only that of classification of the raw material as either capital or land.

different periods of time. But in a going concern this type of substitution is limited, and future capital services may be at least as imperfect a substitute for present ones as are the services of other factors of production. Operating a machine at less than its normal rate in this time period does not insure an equivalent surplus of its services in future periods, and generally it means that some services have been permanently precluded from entering production. Operating the machine at greater than its normal rate may well have the same result. And there may well be no way to alter the rate at which many of the services of the building are yielded through time.

It is readily apparent that capital in the form of buildings is like the land upon which it rests in that many of its services are yielded *automatically* through time. The building will continue to yield many of its services whether any output is produced or not. Neither the building nor all of the services it yields come to an abrupt halt at the sound of the five-o'clock whistle, to resume only at the sound of the eight-o'clock whistle next day. What may not be so apparent is that some of the services of other forms of capital are also yielded automatically through time.

To see this point in terms of the services of machinery, consider a situation in which, instead of altering the rate of operation, we alter the *hours* during which a machine is operated at its normal rate. Suppose, for example, that the machinery is operated for two shifts a day rather than one. In such a case, the total services contributed to production (as measured by total hours of operation of the machine over its useful life span) may even be increased by the decrease in its idle time. Machinery that rusts is perhaps a good example: some of its services are lost if not utilized in production. More obvious examples would include the services yielded by furniture, furnishings of one kind and another, and so on.

Thus, as in the case of land, possession of a unit of capital may be conceived of as possession of a stock of factor services of a particular kind, these services being yielded through time, and all of them perhaps entering into production and perhaps not.

The nature of the concept of labor as a factor of production depends to some extent upon whether or not the classification of factors includes a fourth factor, entrepreneurship. The entrepreneur is, conceptually, the human agency that oversees and supervises the combining of factor services, so that all other human activity in the firm is, by default, that of labor—by implication requiring little intellect other than an ability to be supervised. In reality the most unskilled laborer must often use his intellect if his services are to be combined with those of land and capital, and thoughtless routine exertion may characterize some of the activities even of the manager of the firm. The distinction between labor and entrepreneurship is not very important in the theory of production, though it may be of considerable merit in other contexts. We may thus define labor as the source of the human activity, physical or mental, that is used in the process of production. It should be noted that this definition of labor includes, in terms of a factory, the management, clerical, and staff personnel, as well as production workers.

The definition of labor as an entity separate from its services is consistent with our earlier treatment of land and capital as different from their respective services. It is immediately apparent, however, that the firm cannot purchase labor, so defined (so long as slavery is not legal), and can only purchase labor services. The units in which we sometimes speak of these services (labor hours, man days, and so on) reflect a realization that the services of labor are yielded through time. Nonetheless, labor services, like other factor services, are intangible. We cannot put our finger on a unit of labor service or stack up a pile of them in a corner. Moreover, labor services are like capital services in that, while some temporal substitution is possible, some labor services are yielded automatically through time. If a worker is hired by the week, more or less of the labor services yielded may actually enter into production.

In this view factors of production are analogous to blocks of ice, which, while they may be purchased in various sizes, melt through time yielding so many gallons of water per hour. The ice may sometimes be made to melt slower or faster, but it will melt at a certain rate, anyhow, regardless of whether or not the water is put to use. Purchase of a specific quantity of a factor constitutes the purchase of a specific quantity of factor services.

An alternative conceptualization is that factor services are yielded only as they are used in production. This view preserves the distinction between factors and factor services, regarding the latter as often being capable of being yielded (and used) at various rates. Its major shortcoming is that a given quantity of a factor is not necessarily coincident with a specific quantity of factor services. This deficiency may be remedied by the assumption that for any given quantity of the factor there is a maximum rate at which it may be made to yield its services and that there are thus available during any given period a maximum quantity of factor services coincident with the given quantity of the factor. If the rate at which the factor services are utilized in production is less than this maximum rate, this is equivalent (in the first view) to not using in production some of the services yielded during the period.

Divisibility in Acquisition vs. Divisibility in Use

An important related distinction is that between divisibility *in acquisition* and divisibility *in use*. Since *factors* of production are purchased or hired and factor *services* used in production, the distinction is thus basically between the divisibility of factors and the divisibility of factor services. *Factors* of production must often be purchased or hired in "lumps," and so, typically, they are far from completely divisible in *acquisition.* The firm purchases land, machinery, and buildings in certain discrete sizes. Labor is hired in units and often for discrete time periods, such as days, weeks, months, or even years.

Further, factors of production must often be acquired in units that are not completely *compatible.* As noted above, such factors as buildings and land may yield many of their services throughout the twenty-four hours of the day. Yet the firm may be combining with these services those of labor purchased for only eight hours of the day.

Finally, the nature of the process of acquisition of factors is typically such that the firm must commit itself prior to the actual utilization of factor services in production. In essence the firm in purchasing factors of production purchases stocks of factor services that will only be used in production as they are yielded in time, after their purchase.

Thus indivisibility characterizes the *acquisition* of factors of production. They can often be acquired only in discrete "lumps," which often are not completely compatible, and factors of production usually cannot be purchased at a rate simultaneous with the rate at which they yield factor services.

The *services* of factors of production are, however, far more divisible than the factors themselves, primarily because they are yielded through time. The indivisibility that characterizes the acquisition of factors imposes, in effect, an upper limit or constraint upon the quantity of services yielded during any period in which the quantity of factors is not changed, but it does not prevent the use of *less* than this quantity of services in production. Thus, so long as the size of a building is not changed we cannot use in production a *greater* quantity of its services than the total services yielded during any period. Millions of factories, stores, shops, and so on are closed during many hours of the day, providing ample evidence that we can use in production less than all of the services yielded by a building. And the fact that hours of operation differ widely, and have differed greatly through time, supports the contention that the *services* yielded by buildings are highly divisible up to the constraint imposed by the indivisibility of the units in which they are acquired. The same would, of course, be true of the services yielded by the land upon which the building stands.

Similarly, machinery—even if capable of operation at only one rate and consisting of only a single machine—may typically be operated for a variable proportion of the twenty-four hours of a day, so that the services it yields to production may be varied up to the constraint of the total quantity of services that it can yield to production. And given that the firm has acquired a specific quantity of labor, there is an upper limit to the quantity of labor services that may be utilized in production during any period equal to or less than the period during which the quantity of labor is not changed, but lesser quantities of labor service than this maximum may well enter into production.

Typically, then, factor services are highly divisible up to the constraint imposed by the indivisibility of the units in which factors of production are acquired. Quite obviously, indivisibility in the *acquisition* of *factors* of production is not coincident with indivisibility in the *use* of the *services* of factors of production.

THE PRODUCTION FUNCTION

If a firm is to reach meaningful decisions concerning factor acquisition it must have some idea of the result, in terms of output, of combining various quantities of factor services. It must know, in other words, the technical relationship between inputs of factor services and output. This relationship, termed by economists "the production function," may be expressed mathematically as

$$x = f(a, b, c),$$

where x is output and a, b, and c are inputs of different kinds of factor services. The expression can, of course, be expanded so as to relate output of the good or service produced to any number of factor-service inputs.

Conceptually the production function is a general term for a partial description of the situation confronted by the firm in carrying out the activity of production. It does not specify the respective quantities of factor services of various kinds at the command of the firm, nor does it pass judgment upon the wisdom—or lack of wisdom—of various factor-service combinations. It merely states mechanistically the (maximum) outputs that will result if different quantities of factor services are combined in a particular process.

The production function is thus analogous to the utility function discussed in Chapter 2. Just as the utility function relates utility to quantities of goods irrespective of whether or not the consumer actually possesses, or would choose to possess, any particular quantities of goods, the production function relates output to the various quantities of factor services that might be combined, irrespective of whether or not the firm actually possesses these quantities of factor services or would choose to combine them if it did possess them.

Returns to Proportion vs. Returns to Scale

The general expression for the production function given above merely states that the quantity of output produced depends upon the quantities of the respective factor services combined. Economists, however, typically assume more specific characteristics for the production function, and these more specific characteristics can perhaps be best explained in terms of "returns to proportion" and "returns to scale."

"Returns to proportion" refers to the results, in terms of output, of performing a specific operation with the production function. "What will be the result," the economist asks, "if we vary the quantity of the services of one factor only, while combining with the services of this factor a constant quantity of the services of all other factors?" If, for example, there are only two factors of production, land and labor, what will happen—in terms of output—if a constant quantity of the services of land is combined with different quantities of the services of labor?

It should be noted that the question is not one of the *advisability* of combining various quantities of labor services with a given quantity of the services of land. The question concerns only the nature of the results if the firm *were* to do so.

For ease of discussion let us refer to labor as the *variable* factor, since the quantity of its services that enter into production can be varied, and let us refer to land as the *fixed* factor, since in this hypothetical case all the services of land enter into production. In terms of our earlier distinction, labor services are variable in use and those of land are fixed in use.

That factors of production are distinguished from one another by such terms as "land" and "labor" implies that their services are imperfect substitutes in production. This in turn implies that a relative scarcity of the services of one factor cannot be completely compensated for by the relative surplus of the other. We would also expect, on casual empirical grounds, that if a constant quantity of the services of land is combined with various quantities of the services of labor, some quantities of the latter could conceivably be "too much" in the sense that lesser quantities would result in greater output—that some ratios of labor services to the given quantity of land services would produce less output than a smaller ratio.

From considerations such as these has come the economist's famous "law of diminishing returns," which states that *if successively greater quantities of the services of one factor are combined with a given quantity of another, output will increase, but beyond some point output will increase less than proportionately.* The "law of diminishing returns" or "law of

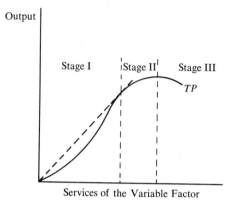

FIGURE 5.1

variable proportions," as it is also sometimes termed, is illustrated in Figure 5.1.

In stage III of Figure 5.1 (the state of "absolute decreasing returns to proportion") the total output or *total product* declines for successively larger inputs of the services of the variable factor. The ratio, or proportion, of the services of the variable factor to those of the fixed factor is so great that smaller quantities of the services of the variable factor, when combined with the same quantity of the services of the fixed factor, would yield greater outputs. There exists in stage III an excess of the variable factor's services relative to those of the fixed.

Though it is by no means so obvious, stage I (the stage of "increasing returns to proportion") is the logical converse of stage III, in that stage I is characterized by too large a proportion of the services of the fixed factor relative to those of the variable. Consequently, output increases very rapidly as the quantity of the variable's services is increased. In stage III the services of the variable factor are redundant and cannot compensate for a *relatively* lesser amount of the services of the fixed factor. In stage I the services of the fixed factor are redundant and cannot compensate for a lesser amount of the variable factor's services. Stage II (the stage of "decreasing returns to proportion") is thus the range of output in which neither factor's services are redundant.

The nature of returns to proportion may be more readily grasped in terms of the relationships of *marginal product* and *average product* to total product. Marginal product is the rate of change of total product relative to variation in the quantity of the variable factor's services, or—somewhat less accurately—the change in total product resulting from a unit change in the quantity of the variable factor's services. Average product is simply total product per unit of the services of the variable factor. The relationships between marginal product, average product, and total product are

TABLE 5.1

Services of the Variable Factor A	Total Product	Marginal Product of the Services of Factor A	Average Product of the Services of Factor A
1	10	10	10
2	22	12	11
3	37	15	12.33
4	50	13	12.50
5	62	12	12.40
6	71	9	11.83
7	76	5	10.86
8	78	2	9.75
9	76	−2	8.44
10	72	−4	7.20

illustrated in Figure 5.2 and Table 5.1. Stages I, II, and III coincide with those of Figure 5.1.

Marginal product is highest in stage I because of the relative redundancy of the fixed factor. The services of the variable factor are so scarce, relatively, that even small changes in their quantity cause large changes in output. At some point within stage I, as the input of the services of the variable factor is increased, the overabundance of the services of the fixed factor becomes somewhat less severe and the marginal product declines, its intersection with average product marking the end of stage I and also the end of the relative surplus of the services of the fixed factor. In stage II, as the services of the variable factor are increased, the marginal

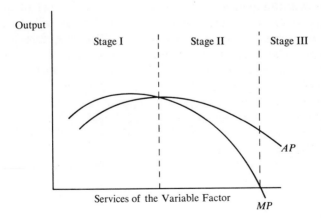

FIGURE 5.2

product continues to decline, marking by its intersection with the axis the end of stage II and the end of the two ranges in which it contributes positively to output. In stage III marginal product is negative, and increasing the services of the variable factor causes total product to fall.

Average product rises throughout stage I because marginal product is greater than average product. So long as equal increases in the services of the variable factor cause total product to rise by amounts greater than the average product, the average product must rise. Since, by the same token, average product must fall when marginal product is less than average product, the two are equal at the point of maximum average product, and average product must decline in stages II and III. Put in other terms, average product rises in stage I both because the excess services of the fixed factor are spread over a larger quantity of the services of the variable factor as the latter increases, and also because the extent of the excess decreases with every increase in the services of the variable factor. In stage II average product declines because the services of both factors are, in this productive process, scarce, and as the scarcity of one is alleviated, that of the other increases. In stage III not only is there a scarcity of the services of the fixed factor, but increases in the quantity of the variable factor make this relative scarcity so much worse that average product declines and total product also declines. Or, the excess services of the variable factor cause total and average product to decline.

"Returns to scale," like "returns to proportion," refers to the results, in terms of output, of performing an operation with the production function, although the operation is different from that implied by returns to proportion. Again it is true, however, that the question does not concern the *advisability* or *feasibility* of performing the operation but merely the nature of the results if the operation were performed.

The operation involved in "returns to scale" is that of multiplying all factor-service inputs by a given constant. "What will be the result, in terms of output," the economist asks, "if all factor services are changed by a given percentage?" If, for example, the services of land, labor, and capital were increased by 10 per cent, would output increase by 10 per cent, more than 10 per cent, or less than 10 per cent?

Unfortunately, while economists appear to agree on the question, they are far from agreement on the answer. Logically it would appear that a 10 per cent increase in *all* factor services would necessarily mean an increase of 10 per cent in output, and some economists agree that this would occur ("constant returns to scale"). Others, however, would maintain that the increase in output could be either less than 10 per cent ("decreasing returns to scale") or more than 10 per cent ("increasing returns to scale").

The area of disagreement can be reduced by careful consideration of the nature of the question. First, as indicated earlier, the question is not an empirical one. It may well be that the firm *in reality* cannot change the quantity of all factor services by the same proportion. An inability to do so would automatically mean a change in the *proportions* in which factor services are combined, violating the conditions of the question. It would also automatically mean that any type of result, in terms of output, is acceptable, but irrelevant—for under these circumstances there is no dispute that there can be any type of returns *to proportion*. The question requires that the proportions between the various types of factor services remain unchanged throughout the (conceptual) operation. Thus the fact that machinery may be acquired only in certain discrete sizes is irrelevant— not only because a given degree of indivisibility *in acquisition* does not necessarily imply the same degree of indivisibility in the *services* yielded by the machinery, but also because the question of whether or not the firm can, *in reality*, change capital services (and all others) by 10 per cent is irrelevant. "Returns to scale" refers to the nature of the result if the firm (conceptually) *does so*, not to the question of whether or not the firm *can* (in reality) do so.

Similarly, we must be aware (though it hardly seems necessary to point it out) that the operation specified by "returns to scale" requires the same proportionate change in *all* factor *services* (again without regard to the feasibility of such a change). Thus the fact that a given size of management may be able to supervise a larger enterprise as easily as a smaller one is again irrelevant. If, at both the larger and smaller outputs, *all* the *services* of management enter into production, then, quite obviously, the *proportion* of these factor services to all others has altered—violating the conditions of the question. If, at the larger output, a greater quantity of management *services* enters into production, the operation requires that the percentage increase in these services be neither more nor less than that of the other types of factor services. Unfortunately, factor services are intangible and we have no independent quantitative measure of them. In its absence we cannot specify, in reality, that the quantity of management services entering into production has, or has not, increased by a specified percentage. Thus if output *were* to increase by a percentage other than the percentage increase in all other types of factor services, and if we were attempting to attribute this result to the services of management, we would either have to conclude that the quantity of management services entering into production had changed by other than the specified percentage or we would be faced with the quite impossible task of establishing that this was not indeed the case. Since a ready explanation exists for any type of result other than constant returns, if the *proportion* of mangement services to all other services has changed, any case of what might appear to be increasing or decreasing returns to scale attributable to the services of management can be justifiably suspected to follow from the law of variable proportions.

Note also that the productive process is assumed to remain unchanged during the conceptual operation posed by "returns to scale." The meaning of this assumption, however, is far from clear. All economists would agree that "the state of the arts" or technology is given. But is it not undeniably true that some techniques can be used at some scales of production and not at others—that specialization of workers, for example, can occur at some scales of output and not at others? And does this not yield increasing returns to scale? Those who dispute this can contend that in such instances either the production function has been altered or else a 10 per cent increase in the factor is not, and cannot be shown to be, a 10 per cent increase in the quantity of that factor's *services* entering into production. Thus a result other than proportionate change in output indicates an alteration in the proportion in which factor *services* are combined.

Finally, questions arise in instances in which the units in which output is measured are not homogeneous. In making barrels, for example, twice as much wood can be used to make a barrel that will hold more than twice as much. Similarly, in fencing land, twice as many feet of fence can enclose more than twice as many acres. Critics can reply that the units in which output is measured must be homogeneous and that the conditions of the question require, by analogy, that barrels of the same size be produced and plots of equal size be enclosed. Alternatively they can argue in terms of factor *services*, as before.

In the heat of the argument it is easy to overlook that in reality no one would expect returns to scale not to be commingled with returns to proportions. Since the latter can, it is agreed, result in increasing or decreasing returns, it is probably best to regard what appear to be returns to scale other than constant as attributable to changes in the proportions in which factor services are combined.

Mathematically, it is very convenient to do so. If the production function is what is termed "linearly homogeneous" the result of a proportional change in the quantities of all factor services is a proportional change in output. Thus, if $x = f(a, b)$, where a and b are the services of factors A and B,

$$\lambda x = f(\lambda a, \lambda b), \qquad \text{where } \lambda \text{ is any positive constant,}$$

and

$$x = a\frac{\partial x}{\partial a} + b\frac{\partial x}{\partial b}, \qquad \text{by Euler's theorem.}[3]$$

---

[3] For a proof of Euler's theorem see W. T. Baumol, *Economic Theory and Operations Analysis*, 2nd ed. (Englewood Cliffs, N.J.: Prentice-Hall, Inc., 1965), pp. 404–405fn. The result shown applies to a *linear homogeneous production function*, a term which we shall use as synonymous with constant returns to scale.

Since $\partial x/\partial a$ = marginal product of a, and x/a = average product of a,

$$\frac{x}{a} = \frac{\partial x}{\partial a} \quad \text{when } \frac{\partial x}{\partial b} \text{ (the marginal product of } b\text{)} = 0.$$

Also, when $\partial x/\partial a = 0$,

$$\frac{x}{b} = \frac{\partial x}{\partial b}.$$

Thus in stage I of Figures 5.1 and 5.2 the average product of a is less than the marginal product of a and the marginal product of b is negative.

$$\frac{x}{a} < \frac{\partial x}{\partial a} \quad \text{so} \quad \frac{\partial x}{\partial b} < 0.$$

At the end of stage I (and beginning of stage II) the marginal and average products of a are equal and the marginal product of b is zero. At the end of stage II the marginal product of a is zero and the marginal and average products of b are equal. Thus, whenever production is occurring in stage I, in terms of the services of one factor, it is occurring in stage III, in terms of the services of the other. Stage II is the only stage that can occur for both simultaneously, and it is the only stage in which the marginal product of the services of neither factor is negative.

The Production Surface

The production function can be portrayed geometrically as a surface in space, the points comprising the surface representing the outputs that would result if the quantities of factor services represented by the coordinates of the point (other than output) were combined in production. Figure 5.3 represents sections through such a surface. It will be noted that each of these sections is a replica of Figure 5.1. Thus the operation involved in "returns to proportion" consists (in terms of a production surface) of taking a vertical section or "slice" through the production surface perpendicular to the axis showing the quantity of the services of one of the factors, and parallel to the other. In Figure 5.3 the section on which lie the points Y, P, and M indicates the results of combining various quantities of the services of labor with OY of the services of capital. The section on which lie the points S, R, and P indicates the results of combining various quantities of *capital* services with OS of *labor* services.

The relationship *between* sections should be carefully noted. Point P

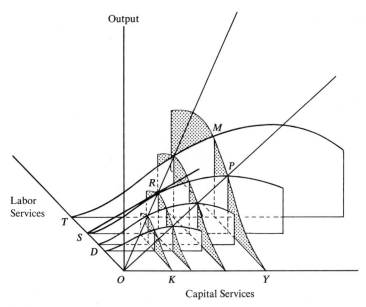

FIGURE 5.3

on section *YPM* marks the end of stage I and the beginning of stage II on this section. On the section *SRP* the same point marks the end of stage II and the beginning of stage III. Thus at *P* the marginal product of labor services equals the average product of labor services, while the marginal product of capital services equals zero. At *R* the marginal product of labor services is zero, and the marginal and average products of capital services are equal.

Figure 5.3 represents the case of constant returns to scale. The surface is thus ruled by straight lines through the origin, indicating that if the ratio between factor services is not altered, proportional changes in the services of both factors yield proportional changes in output. A section through *O* and any point on the surface consists of a straight line, and rays from the origin connect points of equal slope on sections such as *YPM* (or *SRP*) and other sections parallel to them. Thus, for example, the maximum points on sections such as *YPM* (or *SRP*) and sections parallel to them would form straight lines through the origin.

Figure 5.4 presents the production surface in terms of *isoquants*. In a manner analogous to an indifference curve, an isoquant shows all the various combinations of the two *inputs* that can yield the same *output*. As in the case of indifference curves, isoquants may not intersect (by definition) and their convexity (to the origin) reflects the fact that the two inputs are imperfect substitutes in production. The straight lines of which *OR* and *ON* are

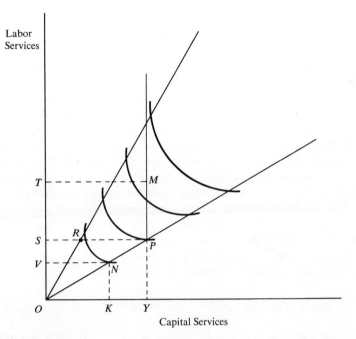

FIGURE 5.4

portions connect points of vertical and zero slopes, respectively, and are termed the *ridge lines* of the surface—since they indicate the highest points one could reach by movement perpendicular to each of the axes (at particular values on that axis). Thus along *SRP* the highest point on the surface is *P*, whereas *R* is the highest point on the surface that can be reached for any combination of labor services and *SR* capital services. Unlike indifference curves, however, specific numerical values may be assigned to isoquants. The letters in Figure 5.4 correspond to those of Figure 5.3.

THE MARKET-PERIOD OUTPUT-EXPANSION PATH

The Market Period

An essential characteristic of the productive process is that it occurs through time. Factor services are yielded through time, output occurs through time, and commitments and other decisions made by the firm possess a temporal dimension. The concept of a "period" reflects a realization of this characteristic.

In the market period it is assumed that all stocks of factor services have already been acquired by the firm and cannot be altered during the period. The firm has acquired certain quantities of land, labor, and capital and can secure no more during this period, nor can it act as a seller of factors of production. There is thus a maximum quantity of factor *services* of each type available to the firm, or a maximum rate at which each type of factor yields its services. Further, it is assumed that the factor services at the command of the firm can only be utilized in the particular productive process to which the production function refers, and that the use in production of more rather than less (or less rather than more) of the available quantities of factor services occasions no additional cost to the firm. As this implies, factor *services* are assumed to be divisible *in use*, in the sense that factor services may be excluded from production if rationality so dictates. Finally, it is assumed that no intertemporal substitution of factor services is possible—that is, the factor services at the command of the firm during this period can be utilized only in this period. Thus the situation posed is analogous to that of a firm which has leased specific quantities of land, labor, and capital for a given period of time.

The Output-Expansion Path

Given the situation just described, what are the best factor-service combinations to use in producing the various outputs that the firm *can* produce? In other words, what is the *output-expansion* path on the production surface?

Assume, in terms of Figures 5.3 and 5.4, that the firm has at its disposal OY of capital services and OT of labor services and that labor and capital are the only factors of production. In this situation point M represents the maximum output that can be produced, and only by combining OY of capital services and OT of labor services can this maximum output be produced. The range of possible combinations is bounded by the rectangle $OTMY$, however, so that there is no unique output-expansion path connecting O and M. Any output other than that represented by M could be produced by any of the factor-service combinations within the rectangle $OTMY$ that yield that output (as shown by the relevant isoquant). The rectangle $OTMY$, in other words, indicates the segments of each isoquant that are relevant for this situation, and no combination comprising a part of a relevant segment is unique. Any combination on the relevant segment of the isoquant could be chosen to achieve the output which that isoquant represents.

In this situation the proportion OT/OY could be maintained for all outputs, yielding a straight-line expansion path from O to M, and alterations in output would occur only by changes in scale. The market period in this case would be characterized entirely by returns to scale. Alternatively, the output-expansion path could be YM or TM. In either of the latter two cases there would be only returns to proportion in the market period. All other output-expansion paths connecting O and M would reflect a mixture of returns to proportion and returns to scale. Thus in the market period there can be returns to scale, returns to proportion, or a mixture of the two.

It might seem, initially, that rational expansion paths would have to lie within the rays of which OR and OP constitute segments and the rectangle $OTMY$. On the isoquant on which R occurs, for example, using more than OS of labor services requires additional capital services to maintain this output. The marginal product of labor services is negative, along this isoquant, for inputs of labor services greater than OS. But, under our assumptions, using more labor services and more capital services occasions no additional cost to the firm (so long as no more than OT of labor services and OY of capital services are used). The firm may therefore rationally select, in producing a given output, any of the combinations shown by the relevant isoquant so long as those combinations occur on a part of the isoquant that lies within the rectangle $OTMY$.

Thus the decision-making process of the firm is a relatively simple one during the market period. There is one, and only one, combination of factor services that will yield the maximum output, but there is a wide range of combinations of factor services that will yield any smaller output that the firm might choose to produce. A decision to use less than the total available stocks of either or both types of factor services is simultaneously, however, a decision to preclude from entry into production some of the available factor services. Machines, for example, may be operated at a rate less than their normal rate (or some of them left idle) and/or restrictions on visits to the water cooler relaxed. But, guided by the production function, the firm would also have to determine *which* lower-than-normal rate of machine operation (or what number of machines to leave idle) and/or *what degree* of laxity in restrictions on its labor force would mean entrance into production of a specific factor-service combination. Thus, while there is no unique output-expansion path in the market period, the choice of any specific output-expansion path implies that—for any output other than the one that the use of all factor services would yield—specific quantities of the available factor services are being excluded from production.

THE OUTPUT-EXPANSION PATH OF THE FIRM
IN THE SHORT RUN

The Short Run

In the preceding section complete indivisibility in acquisition was assumed. It was assumed that the firm had already acquired given quantities of the factors of production and thus possessed given stocks of factor services. In the situation termed the "short run" this assumption is relaxed, and it is assumed instead that at least one factor of production is divisible in acquisition and at least one factor is not. All other assumptions remain unchanged.

Thus the short run is a situation in which the firm has already acquired a certain quantity of one or more of the factors of production but can purchase greater or lesser quantities of at least one other. The services of at least one factor are divisible in acquisition as well as in use, while those of at least one other factor are divisible only in use. There is thus a maximum quantity of factor services of one or more types available (or maximum rates at which one or more factors yield their services) but no such constraint with respect to the services of at least one of the other factors of production. It is again assumed that stocks of factor services that have already been acquired can be utilized only in the productive process to which the production function refers and that the use in production of more rather than less (or less rather than more) of such services occasions the firm no additional cost. No intertemporal substitution of factor services is possible, and factor services may be excluded from production if rationality so dictates. The situation is thus analogous to that of a firm that has leased a specific quantity of capital for a given period of time but can vary at will the quantity of labor services it purchases and uses.

The Short-Run Output-Expansion Path

Given the situation posed, what are the best factor-service combinations to use in producing the various outputs that the firm can produce? Or, what is the output-expansion path of the firm on the production surface?

Assume again (in terms of Figures 5.3 and 5.4) that the firm has at its disposal OY of capital services and that capital is referred to as the "fixed" factor. Assume that labor is the only other factor of production and that the firm can purchase and use various quantities of labor services— so that labor may be referred to as the "variable" factor.

In this situation the output-expansion path proceeds from O along the ray of which OP is a segment until the output corresponding to P is attained, after which the output-expansion path proceeds across the surface along the line on which M is a point. Thus the range of output from O to P is characterized by returns to scale, greater outputs than that corresponding to P being the result of varying the proportion of labor services to the maximum available quantity of capital services. The short-run output-expansion path is characterized by returns to scale and returns to proportion, the latter following the former in terms of output. The output-expansion path does not represent a chronological ordering of output, nor does it, per se, indicate the *optimum output* that the firm *should* produce. It does indicate, however, the optimum *factor-service combinations* to utilize in producing the various outputs that the firm *can* produce. The maximum output that the firm *can* produce would be indicated by the intersection of the line of which *PM* is a segment with the ray of which *OR* is a segment, for at this point the marginal product of labor services would be zero.

The decision-making process of the firm is considerably more complex in the short run than in the market period, for there exists in the short run an optimum factor-service combination for every output that the firm is capable of producing. In other words, there exists a minimum-cost factor-service combination for every possible output, and a rational firm could select only these combinations.

In Figure 5.4 the relevant segments of the isoquants are bounded by the rays of which *OR* and *OP* constitute segments and the line of which *PM* is a segment. But if the firm were to produce an output such as that to which *N* refers, it should rationally purchase and use *OV* of labor services and combine with them the quantity *OK* of capital services—precluding from entry into production *KY* of the available capital services. For, with *OV* of labor services, *capital* services should not be added beyond the point at which their marginal product is zero (the quantity *OK* of capital services). And it would not be rational to use any quantity of capital services less than *OK* in producing *N*, for the quantity to which *N* refers could then be produced only by the use of additional labor services and the incurring of additional cost. Similarly, to produce the output to which *P* refers, the firm should purchase and use *OS* of labor services and use all of its available capital services (*OY*). Rational production of outputs greater than that to which *P* refers requires the combining of more than *OS* of labor services with *OY* of capital services, again excluding none of the available capital services from entry into production.

Thus in the short run there is a unique output-expansion path, a portion of which (*OP* in Figure 5.4) implies a specific type of cost-minimizing behavior on the part of the firm. For, at each input of labor services over this portion of the path, the firm must determine the correct amount of the available capital services *not* to use. Again, for example, machines may be operated at less than their normal rate (or some of them left idle) or used for only a portion of the day—in operating in the range of the output-expansion path characterized by returns to scale. Nonetheless, for any input of the services of the variable factor(s) the firm would have to determine the proper quantity, or quantities, of the services of the fixed factor(s) that are not to be utilized in production. That part of the output-expansion path characterized by returns to proportion does not, of course, require this type of decision.

Mathematically, if the production function is $x = f(a, b)$, where a represents the services of the variable factor and b represents the services of the fixed factor, then the "returns to scale" portion of the output-expansion path can be represented by

$$dx = \frac{\partial x}{\partial a} da + \frac{\partial x}{\partial b} db.$$

Given constant returns to scale it is also true that

$$x = a \frac{\partial x}{\partial a} + b \frac{\partial x}{\partial b}.$$

From the second equation it is possible to define the *marginal gross product* of a (the change in output attributable to changes in the input of a with "appropriate" adjustment of the quantity of b) as

$$\frac{dx}{da} = \frac{\partial x}{\partial a} + \frac{\partial x}{\partial b} \frac{db}{da}.$$

Since in this case the "appropriate" adjustment in the quantity of b causes its marginal product to equal zero, the line OP in Figure 5.4 constitutes a locus of partial maximum values (subject to the condition that $\partial^2 x/\partial b^2 < 0$). As noted earlier, the condition that $\partial x/\partial b = 0$ means (from the third equation, above) that

$$\frac{x}{a} = \frac{\partial x}{\partial a},$$

or the marginal and average products of a are equal and x/a is also a maximum.

Thus, along OP the marginal product of capital services is zero and the marginal and average products of labor services equal and constant. Reasonably enough, the firm is maximizing the output per unit from the services of the factor for which it must pay as it uses, by combining with them other factor services (for which it has already paid) only so long as the latter contribute positively to production.

On the output-expansion path beyond P, returns to proportion supersede returns to scale. There can be no "appropriate" adjustment of the quantity of b because all available b is entering into production. Since there can be no change in b, $db = 0$ and

$$dx = \frac{\partial x}{\partial a} da.$$

The marginal product of b, equal to zero at P, rises for greater outputs along the "returns to proportion" portion of the output-expansion path, while the marginal and average product of a decline. At the point at which the marginal product of a equals zero, the marginal product of b (which has already begun to decline) equals the average product of b.

THE OUTPUT-EXPANSION PATH OF THE FIRM
IN THE LONG RUN

The Long Run

In the market period it is assumed that all factor services are indivisible in acquisition but divisible in use. In the short run it is assumed that the services of at least one factor of production are divisible in acquisition and in use and that the services of at least one factor are indivisible in acquisition but divisible in use. In the situation known as the "long-run" it is assumed that the services of *all* factors of production are divisible in acquisition and in use. Thus the long run is the logically limiting case of a progression of cases that can be conceived of in terms of the number of factors whose services are divisible in acquisition, as well as in use.

Put in a somewhat different way, the long run is a situation in which the firm has *a choice* of short runs. The firm has a choice of the size of stocks of factor services of all types that it wishes to acquire. As soon as it exercises this choice, it is in a short run defined in terms of the factor or factors the size of whose stocks of factor services it has selected. Until this decision is reached, however, the firm can consider the acquisition of any quantity of the services of any factor of production. Moreover, the choice of any short run is not binding upon the firm. If the firm wishes to alter output by changing the quantities of all factor-service inputs, there is no physical constraint upon its doing so. Thus, while there is a short-run position coincident with any long-run position, the long-run position means that the firm can shift to other short-run positions at will. This requires not only freedom for the firm to acquire any quantity of factor services but also the further freedom to resell factor services at will. As the foregoing implies, no problem arises of excluding factor services from entry into production or of user cost (the cost of using more rather than less, or less rather than more, of the services of a fixed factor). Similarly there is no problem of intertemporal substitution of factor services, since factor services are either only acquired as used or resold if in excess.

The long run is analogous to a situation in which the firm has an arrangement with suppliers to provide any quantity of factor services upon demand. The firm can thus vary the quantity of all the factor services that it purchases, and uses, at will.

The Long-Run Output-Expansion Path

In the market period there is no unique output-expansion path because, in effect, the services of all factors of production are free up to the constraints of the quantities previously acquired. In the short run there is a unique output-expansion path because, in essence, the services of at least one factor are *not* free. Since this need be true of the services of only one factor, the long-run output-expansion path is also unique. Since a minimum of one constraint is needed to determine a maximum physical output, there exists a terminal point on the market-period and short-run expansion paths but none on the long-run expansion path (so long as the assumption of constant returns to scale is maintained).

Figure 5.5 depicts the long-run output-expansion path of the firm. The line *DE* and the lines parallel to it are termed *isocost* curves and are analogous to the budget lines employed in indifference-curve analysis. The slope of the isocost curve (*OD/OE*) equals the ratio of the price of capital services to that of labor services, and the isocost curve thus indicates the various combinations of labor services and capital services that can be purchased, and used, for a given cost outlay. Tangency of the isocost curve with the isoquant indicates the least costly combination of factor services that can be used to produce any output on the output-expansion path.

The curvature of the isoquant reflects the degree of substitutability in

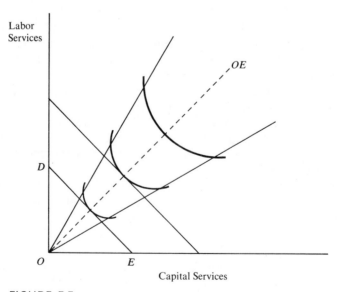

FIGURE 5.5

production of the services of the two factors of production. Posing a unit withdrawal of labor services at various points along a given isoquant in Figure 5.5, it is clear that the quantity of capital services needed to compensate for the withdrawal increases as one moves down the isoquant, reflecting the fact that it becomes increasingly difficult to maintain output by substituting capital services for labor services as the quantity of the latter decreases and that of the former increases. Since the magnitude of a change in output resulting from a change in input depends upon the marginal productivity of the input, the slope of the isoquants in Figure 5.5 equals the ratio of the marginal product of capital services to the marginal product of labor services (ignoring the fact that the slope is negative in the relevant range).

The slope of the isoquant thus indicates the substitutions that, *if made*, will leave output unchanged. The isocost curve indicates, in contrast, the substitutions that *can be made* for a given cost outlay. The decision-making process of the firm is that of reconciling these two types of substitutions so as to equate the slope of the isocost curve and the slope of the isoquant, or of equating the ratio of marginal products to the ratio of prices.

Mathematically, if the production function is $x = f(a, b)$, the firm acts so as to cause

$$\frac{\dfrac{\partial x}{\partial a}}{\dfrac{\partial x}{\partial b}} = \frac{P_a}{P_b},$$

where P_a and P_b are the respective factor-service prices. This can also be expressed as

$$\frac{\dfrac{\partial x}{\partial a}}{P_a} = \frac{\dfrac{\partial x}{\partial b}}{P_b},$$

yielding a result analogous to the principle of rational consumer expenditure derived in demand theory. The equation of the isoquant is

$$f(a, b) = \text{constant.}$$

Differentiating, we secure

$$\frac{\partial x}{\partial a} da + \frac{\partial x}{\partial b} db = 0.$$

Hence the slope of the isoquant through any point becomes

$$\frac{db}{da} = -\frac{\dfrac{\partial x}{\partial a}}{\dfrac{\partial x}{\partial b}}.$$

The numerical value of this slope is termed the *marginal rate of substitution* of the services of factor B for those of factor A and reflects the relative ease of substituting the services of factor B for those of factor A. The relative change in the marginal rate of substitution is called the elasticity of substitution.[4]

---

[4]The elasticity of substitution may be expressed as

$$\sigma = \frac{\dfrac{d\left(\dfrac{b}{a}\right)}{\dfrac{b}{a}}}{\dfrac{d\left(\dfrac{db}{da}\right)}{\dfrac{db}{da}}}.$$

Alternatively

$$\sigma = \frac{\dfrac{d\left(\dfrac{b}{a}\right)}{\dfrac{b}{a}}}{\dfrac{d\left(\dfrac{\dfrac{\partial x}{\partial a}}{\dfrac{\partial x}{\partial b}}\right)}{\dfrac{\dfrac{\partial x}{\partial a}}{\dfrac{\partial x}{\partial b}}}}.$$

Finally, assuming the ratio of factor-service prices to equal the ratio of marginal products,

$$\sigma = \frac{\dfrac{d\left(\dfrac{b}{a}\right)}{\dfrac{b}{a}}}{\dfrac{d\left(\dfrac{P_a}{P_b}\right)}{\dfrac{P_a}{P_b}}}.$$

Thus the elasticity of substitution is a measure of the relative change in the relative quantities of factor services divided by the relative change in relative factor prices.

SUMMARY AND CONCLUSIONS

In the present chapter the theory of production has been developed in terms of three conceptually possible cases or situations—the market period, the short run, and the long run. Like the demand situations posed in the preceding chapter, these situations are not exhaustive; they merely indicate three of a large number of possibilities. Similarly, actual situations can be expected to incorporate some of the features of two or more of these situations and often will be more complex than any of them.

The market-period analysis was characterized by the absence of a unique output-expansion path and the fact that returns could be returns to proportion, returns to scale, or both. If user cost were assumed for the services of one factor, however, there would be a unique output-expansion path, and the analysis of this period would be similar to that of the short run. If user cost is assumed for both factors, the analysis becomes similar to that of the long run. Similarly, if user cost is assumed for the services of the fixed factor in short-run analysis, a different output-expansion path is generated and the analysis becomes closer to long-run analysis. Finally, any purportedly long-run situation in which factor proportions must be altered becomes short-run in terms of the limiting factor. If, for example, the services of management cannot be increased beyond some point, the analysis becomes a short-run analysis in terms of these services, returns to proportion succeeding returns to scale (in terms of output) at the point at which the constraint on management services takes effect.

SELECTED REFERENCES

(The following do *not* distinguish divisibility in acquisition from divisibility in use.)

ALLEN, R. G. D., *Mathematical Analysis for Economists* (London: Collier-Macmillan, Ltd., 1938), chap. 11 (sec. 11.8) and chap. 12 (secs. 12.6–12.9).

DUE, JOHN F., and ROBERT W. CLOWER, *Intermediate Economic Analysis*, 4th ed. (Homewood, Ill.: Richard D. Irwin, Inc., 1961), chap. 7.

HENDERSON, JAMES M., and RICHARD E. QUANDT, *Microeconomic Theory: A Mathematical Approach* (New York: McGraw-Hill Book Company, 1958), chap. 3 (secs. 3.1–3.4).

LEFTWICH, RICHARD H., *The Price System and Resource Allocation*, 3rd ed. (New York: Holt, Rinehart and Winston, Inc., 1966), chap. 7 (including appendices).

from production theory to cost curves

INTRODUCTION

In the present chapter we shall continue to develop the line of thought connecting resources to the market for final goods and services. Previous chapters have provided an explanation of how some wants come to be expressed in the market. We continue in this chapter the explanation of how resources are converted into forms suitable to the satisfaction of those wants and offered in the market. From production theory we shall go to the cost curves of the firm, for the costs of the firm play a major role in determining the conditions under which goods are offered for sale in the market.

This is only one of several directions in which we could proceed, for the subject matter of the previous chapter is basic to a number of areas of thought in price and distribution theory and its applications. Subsequently we shall return to this point of departure for development of some of the other topics for which we have provided a common base. For the present, however, we continue the task of providing an explanation of the process by which the services of land, labor, and capital are converted into the goods and services that consumers have expressed a willingness to purchase and the conditions under which this desire to purchase will be gratified.

Thus the specific task in this chapter is to depict the nature of the cost curves generated by different types of output-expansion paths. We retain the assumption of rationality and its attribution to the producer as a dominant characteristic. We also assume (unless stated otherwise) that the prices of factor services, while they may vary, are not affected by changes in the quantity of factor services purchased by the individual firm. The firm is purely competitive, in other words, in purchasing factor services. Subsequently we shall alter this assumption, but it is made for the present chapter because doing so permits us to understand more readily the relationship of the production function to the firm's cost functions.

As before, we shall employ the three heuristic devices (or logical situations) of the market period, the short run, and the long run. Again these three sets of subsidiary assumptions by no means include all possible situations that we might assume, and it is recognized that the decisions of the producer would not be so neatly compartmentalized as this classification suggests. The classification indicates, however, the range of situations that could be assumed.

Finally, the method of analysis is unchanged. Given the fundamental assumption of rationality and its attribution to the producer, and given the subsidiary set of assumptions that comprise the situation posed, what conclusions can be deduced from the conjoining of these assumptions?

THE COST CURVES OF THE FIRM IN THE MARKET PERIOD

In the market period, it will be recalled, it is assumed that all stocks of factor services have been acquired and cannot be altered. Alternatively, the market period is that class of producers' decisions which relates to the *utilization* of stocks of factor services of various types and not to their acquisition. Factor services are assumed divisible in use, in the sense that in combination with a given quantity of any one type of factor service others may be excluded from production if rationality so dictates, but no greater stock of any kind of factor service may be acquired. Thus the firm has a maximum number of machine hours, man hours, building services, and so on at its disposal, and the problem is to determine the nature of its cost functions under these assumptions.

Economists have traditionally divided the costs of the firm into those that vary with output (variable costs) and those that remain unchanged in total as output changes (fixed costs). This division of costs is roughly comparable to the businessman's distinction between operating expenses and overhead. Thus

$$total\ costs\ =\ variable\ costs\ +\ fixed\ costs.$$

Dividing both sides of the equality by output to express the relationship on a per-unit or average basis, we get

average total costs = average variable costs + average fixed costs.

So long as we maintain the assumption, for the market period, that there are no user costs, all the costs of the firm are fixed costs. In this case there is no relationship between the production function and the firm's cost functions. The firm's total and fixed costs coincide, as do its average total costs and average fixed costs. Graphically, total and fixed costs constitute a horizontal line, and average total and average fixed costs constitute a rectangular hyperbola (since the product of the coordinates is a constant). Thus for outputs up to and including the maximum output that can be produced (*M* in Figure 6.1) the cost curves of the firm are unaffected by the output-expansion path selected. As previously shown, there is no unique output-expansion path on the production surface.

If we assume positive user cost, a unique output-expansion path on the production surface is dictated thereby and the firm's cost curves are no longer independent of the production function.[1] Figure 6.2 is a duplicate of Figure 5.4 of the previous chapter. The firm has at its disposal OY of capital services and OT of labor services; these constitute the only factors of production, and M represents the maximum output that can be produced, given the two constraints.

In Figure 6.2 the ratio OF/ON is the ratio of the user cost (per unit) of *capital* services to those of labor. If we assume user cost to be a linear function of the quantity of services utilized, the output-expansion path

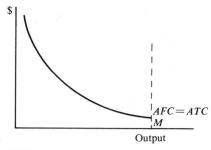

FIGURE 6.1

---

[1] The assumption of a positive (or negative) user cost forces a slight breach in the set of assumptions comprising the market period. If it were true of *all* factor services that no intertemporal substitution is possible and *all* opportunity costs are zero, there could be no meaningful concept of user costs. Thus it must be true for the particular factor services giving rise to user costs that some intertemporal substitution is possible, or other form of (nonzero) opportunity costs exists.

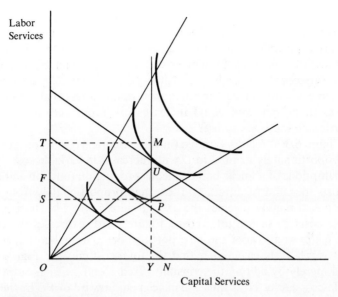

FIGURE 6.2

would be linear from O to U (assuming, as in Chapter 5, a linear homogeneous production function), and returns to scale would characterize this portion of the path. From U to M the output-expansion path would not be linear, and returns to proportion would succeed (in terms of output) returns to scale. If the ratio of the user cost of capital services to that of labor services did *not* remain constant as output increased, the output-expansion path would *not* be linear over the range of output characterized by returns to scale, despite the assumption of a linear homogeneous production function. In this event the slope of lines such as FN (isocost curves) would not remain the same for all inputs less than OT and OY, and the points of tangency of these isocost curves and isoquants would not lie on a ray from the origin.

Since user costs are assumed to vary (in total) with output, we now have a variable-cost component of total cost. Total costs are no longer identical with fixed costs, and the average-total-cost function is no longer the same as that of average fixed cost. One component of total cost is thus independent of output and one is not: one component of *average* total cost is necessarily a rectangular hyperbola and one is not. If the user cost per unit of capital services and that per unit of labor services remain constant over the range of output characterized by returns to scale, *marginal cost* (the rate of change of variable cost relative to variation in output, or—more loosely—the increase in variable cost attributable to a unit change in output) is also constant over this range of output, as is the *average* variable cost.

Over the range of output characterized by returns to *proportion* (*UM* in Figure 6.2) no more capital services are available. Increased user costs are incurred (in total) if additional labor services are combined with *OY* of capital services (in order to achieve outputs larger than *U*), but increases in labor services alone result in less-than-proportionate increases in output. Thus, increases in user cost in this range result in less than proportionate increases in output, and equal increases in output occasion more-than-proportionate increases in user cost.

Figure 6.3(a) relates variable (in this case user) cost to output. Output rises proportionately from *O* to *U* with increases in variable cost, reflecting the assumptions of a linear homogeneous production function and constant user costs (per unit of input), and less than proportionately from *U* to *M*. Figure 6.3(b) merely reverses the axes. Figure 6.3(c) adds fixed costs and variable costs to secure total costs. Figure 6.3(d) expresses the curves of Figure 6.3(c) as averages and also portrays the marginal-cost curve.

It is relatively easy to see that the total-cost curve in Figure 6.3(c) is derived merely by adding the constant (fixed costs), at each output, to the variable-cost curve. *TC* is thus a displacement upward of *VC* by the amount of the fixed costs. What may not be so apparent is the procedure by which the cost curves of Figure 6.3(d) are derived from those of Figure 6.3(c). Figures 6.4(a) and 6.4(b) attempt to portray these relationships more clearly

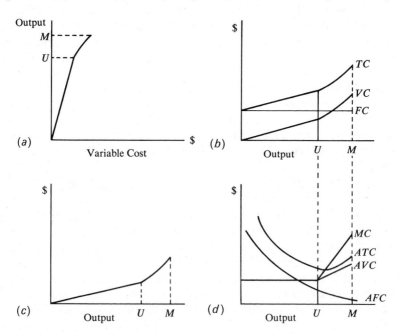

FIGURE 6.3

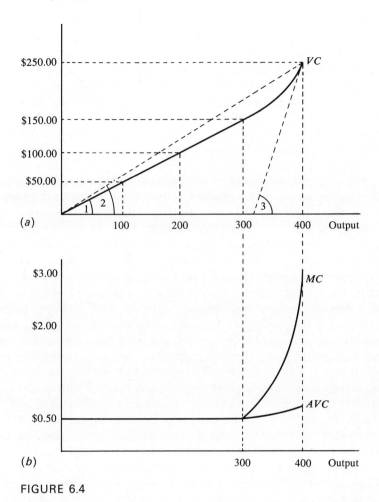

FIGURE 6.4

by assigning numerical values to some of the points on an illustrative variable-cost curve and computing the corresponding values of average variable cost and marginal cost.

In Figure 6.4(a), for outputs of 300 or less, average variable cost is $0.50($50/100, $100/200, $150/300) and is the tangent of angle 1. For outputs greater than 300, however, average variable cost is greater than $0.50. At an output of 400, for example, average variable cost is $250/400 or $0.625 and is the tangent of angle 2. Marginal cost, the rate of change of variable cost (or of total cost, since variable cost is the only part of total cost that varies with output) is the slope of the tangent to the curve at any point. Since the curve is linear for outputs of 300 or less and passes through the origin, marginal cost and average variable cost coincide in this range of output. For outputs greater than 300, however, marginal cost is greater than $0.50 and also greater than average variable cost. Thus at an output of 400 marginal cost is the tangent of angle 3 and has a value of approximately $3\frac{1}{3}$ ($250 divided by approximately 75). Average total cost may be derived from total cost, and average fixed cost from fixed cost by the same method as that by which the average variable cost at an output of 400 was determined (that is, by constructing a line from the origin to the point and determining the tangent of the angle formed by the construction line and the horizontal axis).

The important point in this discussion is that the assumptions made concerning the nature of the production function and concerning variable cost determine the shape and configuration of the firm's cost curves. If, in the market period, user costs are assumed zero, the firm's cost curves become as shown in Figure 6.1, irrespective of assumptions made about the production function. In this case marginal cost and variable cost are zero. But if positive user costs are assumed, the resulting cost curves reflect the assumptions made concerning the production function and user costs (that is, all curves reflect these assumptions except the fixed- and average-fixed-cost curves). If the production function, though linear and homogeneous, reflects decreasing returns to *proportion*, and if user cost (per unit of input) is constant throughout, the cost curves of the firm are as shown in Figure 6.3(d). If user cost (per unit of input) increases with the quantity of input, marginal cost and average variable cost increase with output (marginal cost being greater than average variable cost at all outputs) and over no range of output are they constant. Further, in the range *UM* of Figure 6.3(d) marginal cost and average variable cost would rise more rapidly, and over the range *OM* average total cost would fall less rapidly and rise more rapidly. Altering the assumption of constant returns to scale would result in corresponding alterations in the shape and configuration of the firm's cost curves.[2] The relevance of our concern with the nature of the firm's cost functions will become more apparent in subsequent chapters.

THE COST CURVES OF THE FIRM IN THE SHORT RUN

The short run has been defined as a situation in which the firm has previously acquired (or contracted for) a given stock of the services of at least one factor of production, while there is at least one other factor the services of which

---

[2] To represent increasing returns to scale on an isoquant diagram, isoquants representing equal increases in output can be crowded closer together as one moves out from the origin. Similarly, decreasing returns to scale may be represented by increasing the space between isoquants representing equal increases in output. And equally spaced isoquants representing equal increases in output would portray, in this method, constant returns to scale.

may be purchased at will. The services of at least one factor are indivisible in acquisition but divisible in use (up to the limit of the total stock purchased), while the services of at least one other factor are divisible in acquisition as well as in use. Thus the services of one factor may be used as needed (up to a constraint), while those of at least one other factor may be purchased (and used) as needed.

This definition of the short run differs from that customarily adopted. It is traditional to assume that the services of at least one factor are indivisible in *use*, as well as in acquisition. As we have seen, this is not a very plausible assumption but it has great intellectual appeal, for on this definition the dichotomy of returns to proportion versus returns to scale coincides with the short-run, long-run dichotomy. Consequently the short-run production function becomes merely the result of taking a section through the production surface at the given quantity of the services of the fixed factor, and (assuming constant factor prices) the variable-cost curve becomes the direct converse of the upper edge of the section.

Thus, on the traditional definition, the short-run output-expansion path becomes, in terms of Figure 6.2, movement along the section on which lie the points Y, P, U, and M, yielding total-product and variable-cost curves such as those shown in Figures 6.5(a) and 6.5(b). Since there is no constraint on the quantity of the services of the variable factor purchased (and used),

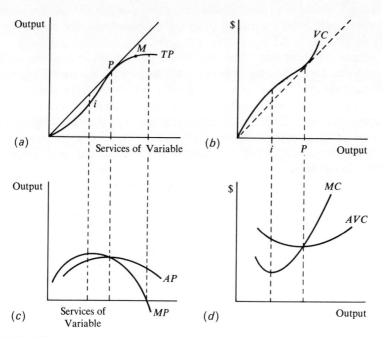

FIGURE 6.5

M no longer indicates the maximum output that can be produced. The traditional short run yields cost curves such as those depicted in Figure 6.5(d),
in which (for the one-variable case) the marginal-cost curve and the average-
variable-cost curve are obviously inverse functions of (respectively) the
marginal-product and average-product curves of Figure 6.5(c) [derived from
the total-product curve of Figure 6.5(a)].

But, as argued in the previous chapter, complete indivisibility in *use*
does not generally characterize the services of a fixed factor in the short run.
Indivisibility in *acquisition* does not imply an equal degree of indivisibility
in the *use* of factor services. Less than all of the available services of a fixed
factor may be combined with a given quantity of the services of a variable
factor, if not using some of the services of the fixed factor would result in
greater output. Consequently, unless we wish to impute irrationality to the
producer or to choose the less realistic of two alternative assumptions concerning the nature of factor services, we must abandon the traditional
derivation of short-run cost curves outlined in Figure 6.5.

Assuming no user costs and returning to the preferred definition of
the short run, the output-expansion path becomes, in terms of Figure 6.2,
the path on which lie the points O, P, U, and M. In essence the services of
capital are free up to the constraint OY (assuming no intertemporal substitution or resale of factor services is possible), and the isocost curves are
horizontal. Returns to scale characterize the portion OP of the output-
expansion path, and returns to proportion characterize the remainder of
the path.

Thus the short-run output-expansion path yields cost curves similar
to those that depict the market period when user cost is assumed (Figure 6.6).
Assuming the cost of the services of the variable factor to be constant (per
unit), marginal cost and average variable cost are constant and equal over
the range of output OP, rising thereafter. Since there is no constraint on the
quantity of the services of the variable factor that may be purchased (and
used), the cost curves do not end abruptly at a specified output as in the case
of the market period.

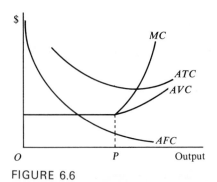

FIGURE 6.6

If positive user costs are assumed for the services of the variable input, this does not alter the output-expansion path or the nature of the firm's cost curves, assuming user cost to be constant per unit of input. The firm's cost curves would merely be shifted upward by this assumption (except for *AFC*). If positive user costs are assumed for the services of the fixed factor, however, a new output-expansion path is generated and the derivation of the firm's cost curves becomes even more similar to that of the market period when positive user costs are assumed. Thus, as in the market period, the nature of the firm's short-run cost curves is dependent upon the assumptions made about the production function and costs of the services of the factors of production.

THE COST CURVES OF THE FIRM IN THE LONG RUN

The long run, it will be recalled, is a situation in which all factor services are variable in acquisition as well as in use. Assuming constant factor-service prices and a linear homogeneous production function, the output-expansion path is linear. Thus in Figure 6.2, if *FN* and the isocost curves parallel to it reflect the ratio of factor prices, *OU* constitutes a segment of the output-expansion path. The path would continue (with the same slope) indefinitely beyond *U*, since in the long run there are no constraints on the quantity of factor services purchased (and used).

As one would suspect (since there is no change in direction of the path at *U*), long-run marginal cost and long-run average cost are equal and constant throughout. Since there are no constraints, there is no reason for marginal cost or average cost to rise. Since there are no fixed factors, there is only one type of average cost and only returns to scale.

Figure 6.7 depicts the long-run cost curves of the firm. Since the long

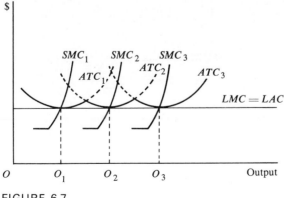

FIGURE 6.7

run is a situation in which there exists a choice of short runs, various sets of
short-run marginal-cost and average-total-cost curves are also shown.

An understanding of the relationship of the long-run cost curves of
Figure 6.7 to the short-run cost curves requires a closer examination of certain relationships on the production surface. Figure 6.8 depicts the long-run
output-expansion path on a linear homogeneous production surface, the
path being the ray on which lie the points D_1 and D_2. Since factor-service
prices are assumed constant, the ratios of factor-service inputs at every point
along the output-expansion path are constant $(Ob_1/Oa_1 = Ob_2/Oa_2$, and
so on). At any input of a the rate of change of output, for variation in b
alone, is the same—that is, the slope of the tangent to D_1 is the same as the
slope of the tangent to D_2. Similarly, if tangents were taken at D_1 and D_2
for variation in a *alone*, their slopes would be the same. Put otherwise, the
returns-to-proportion or (traditional short-run) marginal product of a is the
same at every point on the output-expansion path, as is that of b. Likewise, the returns-to-proportion average product of b $(D_1C_1/a_1C_1, D_2C_2/
a_2C_2, \ldots)$ is constant as is that of a $(D_1C_1/b_1C_1 = D_2C_2/b_2C_2, \ldots)$.

The important thing, however, is that the marginal *gross* product (the
rate of change along the long-run output-expansion path, for variation in
both inputs, taken together) is constant, and equal to the average *gross*
product $(D_1C_1/OC_1 = D_2C_2/OC_2, \ldots)$. Each increment in output occasions the same increment in cost, even though the cost increment is comprised of two separate components—that due to the increase in a, and that
due to the increase in b. Since this is true throughout, long-run marginal
cost and long-run average cost are equal and constant.

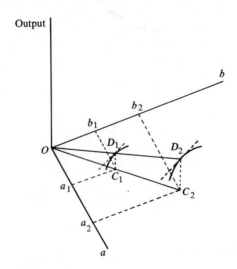

FIGURE 6.8

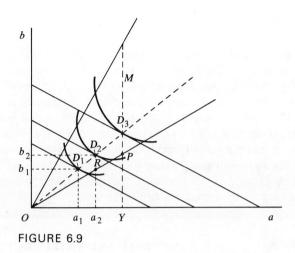

FIGURE 6.9

Now consider Figure 6.9. Outputs D_1 and D_2 again lie on the long-run output-expansion path, as does D_3. If there is a short run defined in terms of OY of factor services a, however, D_3 also lies on the *short-run* output-expansion path on which lie the points O, P, D_3, and M (assuming zero user cost). Similarly, O, R, *and* D_2 lie on a short-run output-expansion path defined in terms of the quantity Oa_2 of the services of factor a. Every point on a long-run output-expansion path coincides with a point on a short-run output-expansion path. For every long-run position there is a corresponding short-run position, and every value of long-run marginal cost is also the value of the short-run marginal cost of the corresponding short run, at the same output. An incremental change in output from D_3 secured by varying b *only* will occasion an increment in cost equal to that accompanying the same increment in output if it results, instead, from variations of b *and* a. The change in the quantity of b will, of course, be greater if a cannot change. Thus in Figure 6.7 the long-run and short-run marginal costs of the output D_1 are the same, SMC_2 equals LMC at D_2, SMC_3 equals LMC at D_3, and so on.

Similarly, since at any point along the long-run output-expansion path the same quantities of the two inputs are used as in the corresponding short run, total cost is the same. Thus in Figure 6.9 Ob_2 of b and Oa_2 of a are combined to produce an output of D_2 irrespective of which of the two output-expansion paths was taken to arrive at D_2 (O, D_1, D_2 or O, R, D_2). If factor-service prices have not changed, the cost of Oa_2 of a has not changed, so that the fixed cost of short-run analysis becomes merely the variable cost of one of the two factor services in long-run analysis. Since in each instance the cost of Oa_2 of a is added to that of Ob_2 of b, short-run and long-run total costs are the same for output D_2. Consequently, average total cost and long-run average cost are equal for outputs $D_1, D_2, D_3, \ldots$ in Figure 6.7.

The short-run cost curves of Figure 6.7 are often taken to represent alternative plant sizes. Given divisibility in acquisition, there are an infinity of plant sizes, so that LMC becomes the locus of the values of SMC where $ATC = LAC$, and LAC becomes the locus of the values of ATC where $SMC = LMC$. An output greater than D_1 would occasion increased marginal cost if produced in the plant size represented by SMC_1 and ATC_1, but the increase in marginal cost could be avoided by choice of a slightly larger plant size, the short-run marginal cost of which would equal LMC at the larger output. Since LMC is constant, the size of plant selected would be determined entirely by demand considerations.

INTERNAL AND EXTERNAL ECONOMIES AND DISECONOMIES

As noted earlier, one would expect returns to proportion and returns to scale to occur simultaneously in reality. Returns to scale, it will be recalled, does not refer to *feasibility*. It merely asks what would happen to output if the quantities of all factor services *were* increased proportionally. Often, however, it is not possible to increase or decrease the quantities of all factor services proportionally, so that output changes partly as a result of changes in the inputs of several types of factor services and partly because the proportions between quantities of factor services of different types are altered. At larger outputs, for example, the firm may be able to utilize larger and more complex machines rather than more machines of the same type, and a given quantity of labor may yield a greater quantity of labor services because of the increased specialization of function that is possible at greater outputs. Similarly, over some range of output there may be increasing returns to proportion in combining the services of management with larger quantities of the services of all the other factors of production, or a larger proportion of the available stock of management services may be utilized in production. Thus over some range of output there may be *internal economies of size* (sometimes misleadingly termed "internal economies of scale"). These economies are referred to as internal (to the firm) because the reductions in cost per unit are attributable to the firm rather than to the actions of all firms in the industry.

Internal economies of size result from the inability of the firm to maintain at all outputs the optimal ratios of factor-service inputs. Internal *diseconomies* of size result from this same inability. Thus, beyond some point *decreasing* returns to proportion may result from combining a given stock of the services of management with greater quantities of all other types of

factor services, or proportional increases in management *personnel* may not
result in proportionate increases in the quantity of the *services* of management entering into production—since a part of their time must be spent in
coordination of their own efforts. Thus, while benefits may accrue over
some ranges of output from specialization of management and/or other
forms of labor, it may also be true that, over other ranges of output,
coordination is so difficult that proportional increases in personnel constitute less-than-proportional increases in the quantity of labor services
entering into production, with a resulting increase in cost per unit of output.

This pattern of cost behavior (of which economists are rather fond)
is illustrated in Figure 6.10. Again the different sets of "short-run" cost
curves may be viewed as representing different plant sizes, and the relationship of "long-run" marginal cost to "short-run" marginal cost and of "long-
run" average cost to average total cost is the same—that is, LMC is the locus
of the values of SMC at the outputs at which ATC and LAC are equal and
LAC is the locus of the values of ATC where $SMC = LMC$. Because portrayal of all conceptually possible plant sizes would obviate the necessity of
drawing LAC separately, the "long-run" average-cost curve of Figure 6.10
is often referred to as the "envelope curve."

For outputs smaller than OK, internal economies of size outweigh
internal diseconomies of size, whereas the latter outweigh the former for
outputs greater than OK. As implied by our previous discussion, a pattern
of cost behavior such as that depicted by Figure 6.10 does not necessarily
mean that the firm cannot have a linear homogeneous production function.
The entire analysis, for example, may refer to a given stock of management
services, and may result from alterations in the proportions of these services
to all others, in which case LAC and LMC refer to a *short run* defined in
terms of a given quantity of management services. Or, the cost per unit of

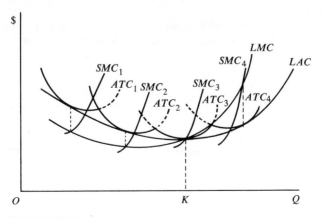

FIGURE 6.10

factor services may vary at different outputs because proportional changes in the units in which factors are *acquired* does not result in proportional changes in the quantity of services entering into production, yielding in effect an alteration in factor-service prices and causing the output-expansion path to be nonlinear. Finally, the firm may not maintain the same ratio of factor-service inputs at all outputs, because, for example, the same type of machine is built only in certain discrete sizes, and/or proportional changes in the outlay upon machines yield other than proportional changes in the quantity of services that can enter production—also an alteration, in effect, of factor-service prices.

Whatever their origin, internal economies and diseconomies are always within the cognizance of the firm. If Figure 6.10 is viewed as a *planning curve*, the firm is aware of, and can plan for, the increases or decreases of cost due to internal economies and diseconomies of size. *External* economies and diseconomies, on the other hand, are changes in cost arising from the actions of all firms in the industry, which the individual firm may be unaware of or unable to plan for. Thus the growth of one localized industry may lower the costs of an adjacent industry that utilizes by-products of the first industry or depends upon labor with similar skills. Or, as an industry grows, the prices of its factor-service inputs may rise as a result of the increased demand of all firms in the industry for specialized resources. Such external economies and diseconomies may be represented, respectively, as downward and upward shifts in the entire pattern of cost curves depicted in Figure 6.10.

SIMPLE MATHEMATICS OF COST FUNCTIONS

Market Period

Let $x = f(a, b)$ be a linear homogeneous production function, where x represents output and a and b represent the services of two factors of production. Then, by Euler's theorem,

$$(1) \qquad x = a\frac{\partial x}{\partial a} + b\frac{\partial x}{\partial b}.$$

Let C represent total cost, F represent fixed cost, and U_1 and U_2 be, respectively, the user cost per unit of factor services a and b. The total cost can be represented as

$$(2) \qquad C = F + U_1a + U_2b.$$

Average total cost becomes

(3)
$$\frac{C}{x} = \frac{F}{x} + \frac{U_1 a + U_2 b}{x},$$

or the sum of average fixed cost and average variable (user) cost, respectively.

Let x_0 be a certain value of output. Then the equation of the isoquant becomes

(4)
$$x_0 = f(a, b),$$

and the problem becomes that of minimizing C for each x_0. Using the method of the Lagrangian multiplier, we define the function

(5)
$$S = F + U_1 a + U_2 b - \lambda[f(a, b) - x_0].$$

$$\frac{\partial S}{\partial a} = U_1 - \lambda \frac{\partial x}{\partial a} = 0,$$

or
$$\frac{U_1}{\dfrac{\partial x}{\partial a}} = \lambda$$

$$\frac{\partial S}{\partial b} = U_2 - \lambda \frac{\partial x}{\partial b} = 0,$$

or
$$\frac{U_2}{\dfrac{\partial x}{\partial b}} = \lambda$$

$$\frac{\partial S}{\partial \lambda} = f(a, b) - x_0 = 0.$$

$$\frac{U_1}{\dfrac{\partial x}{\partial a}} = \frac{U_2}{\dfrac{\partial x}{\partial b}}, \qquad \frac{U_1}{U_2} = \frac{\dfrac{\partial x}{\partial a}}{\dfrac{\partial x}{\partial b}},$$

yielding the conclusion that for any output in the range in which both

a and b are variable in use, the ratio of the user cost (per unit of input) of a to that of b must equal the ratio of their respective marginal products. Let the total user cost be represented by T. Then

(6) $$T = U_1 a + U_2 b.$$

For each output it will be true[3] that

$$\text{marginal cost} = \frac{dT}{dx} = \frac{U_1}{\dfrac{\partial x}{\partial a}} = \frac{U_2}{\dfrac{\partial x}{\partial b}},$$

and

$$\frac{\partial x}{\partial a} = \frac{U_1}{\dfrac{dT}{dx}}, \qquad \frac{\partial x}{\partial b} = \frac{U_2}{\dfrac{dT}{dx}}.$$

Substituting in equation (1), we have

(7) $$x = \frac{U_1}{\dfrac{dT}{dx}} a + \frac{U_2}{\dfrac{dT}{dx}} b$$

---

[3] Since

$$dT = U_1\, da + U_2\, db,$$

and [from (5)]

$$\lambda = \frac{U_1}{\dfrac{\partial x}{\partial a}} = \frac{U_2}{\dfrac{\partial x}{\partial b}},$$

$$dT = \lambda \frac{\partial x}{\partial a}\, da + \lambda \frac{\partial x}{\partial b}\, db.$$

Since

$$dx = \frac{\partial x}{\partial a}\, da + \frac{\partial x}{\partial b}\, db,$$

$$\frac{dT}{dx} = \frac{\lambda \left(\dfrac{\partial x}{\partial a}\, da + \dfrac{\partial x}{\partial b}\, db \right)}{\dfrac{\partial x}{\partial a}\, da + \dfrac{\partial x}{\partial b}\, db} = \lambda,$$

$$\therefore \quad \frac{dT}{dx} = \frac{U_1}{\dfrac{\partial x}{\partial a}} = \frac{U_2}{\dfrac{\partial x}{\partial b}}.$$

$$= \frac{1}{\frac{dT}{dx}} (U_1 a + U_2 b),$$

$$\frac{dT}{dx} = \frac{U_1 a + U_2 b}{x}.$$

Thus average variable (user) cost and marginal cost are equal so long as both a and b are variable (in use). Since

(8)
$$\frac{dT}{dx} = \frac{T}{x},$$

then
$$\frac{d^2 T}{dx^2} = \frac{x \frac{dT}{dx} - T}{x^2} = \frac{x \frac{T}{x} - T}{x^2} = 0,$$

or equality of marginal cost and average variable (user) cost necessarily implies that they are also constant.

When all of the services of one factor are employed,

(9)
$$T = k + U_2 b,$$

where $k = a U_1$ and is constant. Since output now increases only as a result of increases in b, then (for increases in output) marginal cost becomes [by the same reasoning as in (6)]

$$\frac{dT}{dx} = \frac{U_2}{\frac{dx}{db}}.$$

Since $d^2 x / db^2 < 0$,

$$\frac{dT}{dx} \text{ is increasing as } x \text{ increases.}$$

Average variable cost is also increasing and is less than marginal cost.

(10)
$$\frac{d\left(\frac{T}{x}\right)}{dx} = \frac{x \frac{dT}{dx} - T}{x^2} > 0,$$

$$\frac{x \dfrac{dT}{dx}}{x^2} > \frac{T}{x^2},$$

$$\frac{dT}{dx} > \frac{T}{x}.$$

Short Run

The short run is very similar to the market period, except that the price of one of the factor services is, in effect, zero (so long as some of the previously acquired stock of services is not employed in production). Thus if factor services a are fixed in acquisition but variable in use (up to the constraint of the available stock), then in the returns-to-scale portion of the output-expansion path the equivalent of equation (1) becomes

(11) $\quad x = b \dfrac{\partial x}{\partial b} \quad$ (since $\dfrac{\partial x}{\partial a}$ is equated to zero at each value of b),

$$\frac{x}{b} = \frac{\partial x}{\partial b}.$$

Similarly, the equivalent of equation (6) becomes

(12) $$T = V_2 b$$

(where V_2 is the price of b, assuming no user cost). Thus

(13) $$\frac{dT}{dx} = \frac{V_2}{\dfrac{\partial x}{\partial b}}.$$

Equation (11) implies constant marginal and average productivity of the services of factor b. Hence marginal cost, dT/dx, is constant in this part of the output-expansion path. The same is true of average variable cost, since [from (11) and (13)]

(14) $$\frac{dT}{dx} = \frac{V_2}{\dfrac{x}{b}} = \frac{V_2 b}{x}.$$

For outputs greater than that at which all the stock of factor services *a* is being employed in production, returns to proportion succeed returns to scale, and by argument equivalent to equations (9) and (10) marginal cost and average variable cost rise, the former being greater than the latter at each output.

Long Run

In the long run the services of all factors are variable in acquisition as well as in use, so that the equivalent of equation (3) (average cost) becomes

(15)
$$\frac{C}{x} = \frac{V_1 a + V_2 b}{x}.$$

Similarly, by argument analogous to equation (7), marginal cost equals average cost:

(16)
$$\frac{dC}{dx} = \frac{V_1 a + V_2 b}{x}$$

—implying, as in equation (8), that the two are also constant.

SUMMARY AND CONCLUSIONS

This chapter has been devoted primarily to the implications, in terms of the firm's cost functions, of the production situations posed in Chapter 5. In the market period, if there are no user costs, there is no unique output-expansion path and there exists only an average-fixed-cost curve (identical with an average-total-cost curve) up to the maximum output that the firm can produce. If positive user costs are assumed, there exists a unique output-expansion path characterized by returns to scale over the range of output in which only a part of each stock of factor services is entering into production, and marginal and average variable (user) cost are equal and constant (assuming a linear homogeneous production function and constant user costs). Output beyond this range is characterized by returns to proportion, marginal cost exceeding average variable cost, and both increasing with output until the maximum possible output is attained.

In the short run the output-expansion path is unique and (assuming no user costs) is one of the ridge lines of the production surface (over the range of output in which only a part of the stock of the services of the fixed factor is being utilized in production). At each input of the services of the variable (in acquisition and in use) factor, that quantity of the services of the fixed (in acquisition) factor is utilized at which the marginal product of the services of the fixed factor is zero. Assuming again a linear homogeneous production function and constant prices for the services of the variable (in acquisition and in use) factors, marginal cost equals average variable cost and is constant. For larger outputs, returns to proportion succeed returns to scale, marginal and average variable cost rise (the former exceeding the latter at any given output), and there is no discrete maximum output.

The long-run output-expansion path is characterized only by returns to scale, and (assuming a linear homogeneous production function and constant factor prices) marginal cost equals average cost and is constant throughout. Each long-run position is, however, coincident with a short-run position, so that long-run marginal cost is the locus of the values of short-run marginal cost at the outputs at which long-run average cost and average total cost are equal. Conversely, long-run average cost is the locus of the values of average total cost at the outputs at which long-run and short-run marginal costs are equal.

The envelope cost curve is a geometrical portrayal of a set of assumptions in which long-run and short-run considerations are mingled, yielding a pattern of cost behavior that economists think to be frequently applicable. As a firm increases in size, internal economies of size predominate over some range of output succeeded by another range in which internal diseconomies of size predominate. In between the two may be a single output or a range of output over which long-run average cost is constant. Finally, *external* economies or diseconomies of size may cause downward or upward shifts in the level of the firm's cost curves.

Thus the assumptions made in the theory of production determine the nature of the firm's cost functions. Obviously, only a few of all possible situations have been posed, and it is apparent that the firm's decisions would not be so neatly compartmentalized as these situations suggest. Period analysis, despite its usefulness, can be misleading. Some of the difficulties involved will become more apparent in subsequent chapters.

SELECTED REFERENCES

CHAMBERLIN, EDWARD H., "Proportionality, Divisibility, and Economies of Scale," *Quarterly Journal of Economics* (Feb. 1948), reprinted in Richard V. Clemence, *Readings in Economic Analysis*, vol. 2 (Cambridge, Mass.: Addison-Wesley Publishing Company, Inc., 1950), pp. 70–103.

DUE, JOHN F., and ROBERT W. CLOWER, *Intermediate Economic Analysis*, 4th ed. (Homewood, Ill.: Richard D. Irwin, Inc., 1961), chap. 8.

ELLIS, HOWARD S., and WILLIAM FELLNER, "External Economies and Diseconomies," *American Economic Review*, vol. 33 (Sept. 1943), reprinted in American Economics Association, *Readings in Price Theory* (Homewood, Ill.: Richard D. Irwin, Inc., 1952), pp. 242–63.

ROBINSON, JOAN, *Economics of Imperfect Competition* (London: Collier-Macmillan, Ltd., 1933), appendix, pp. 337–43.

STIGLER, GEORGE, "Production and Distribution in the Short Run," *Journal of Political Economy*, vol. 47 (June 1939), reprinted in American Economics Association, *Readings in the Theory of Income Distribution* (New York:

McGraw-Hill Book Company, Blakiston Division, 1949), pp. 119–42.

VINER, JACOB, "Cost Curves and Supply Curves," *Zeitschrift für National-okonomie*, vol. 3 (1932), reprinted in Richard V. Clemence, *Readings in Economic Analysis*, vol. 2 (Cambridge, Mass.: Addison-Wesley Publishing Company, Inc., 1950), pp. 8–35.

7
equilibrium of the firm and industry

In Chapter 4 some of the implications of six different sets of assumptions relating to the demand for the output of the firm were explored—yielding the market situations of pure competition, monopoly, monopolistic competition, oligopoly, price discrimination, and joint production. In Chapters 5 and 6 various sets of assumptions relating to the firm's production function and the cost of its factor services were posed and the implications for the cost curves of the firm deduced. In the present chapter we continue this construction of the theory of the firm by adding to assumptions concerning the demand situation in which the firm finds itself other assumptions depicting the nature of its costs. Given rationality, and given the subset of assumptions relating to both demand and cost conditions, the optimum output(s) and/or price(s) are deducible for each situation. This explanation of the equilibrium of the firm is not only a further step in building the theory of the firm but also permits—in some instances—the derivation of the industry, or market, supply curve.

Thus, in the present chapter we shall revisit the situations posed in Chapter 4, adding additional information concerning these situations and deducing certain conclusions that can now be reached given the initial assumptions and the additional assumptions posed. The cost situations developed in Chapters 5 and 6 are, as previously indicated, far from comprising the set of all such situations, and the same limitation applies to the demand situations depicted in Chapter 4. Nonetheless, all combinations of these two limited sets would yield too many situations to be treated in worthwhile detail. Consequently, no attempt will be made to depict for each demand situation all of the cost situations previously discussed. The reader, however, by this point should be able to construct and analyze situations other than those treated in this chapter, including (but not confined to) situations in which the cost conditions assumed are among those described in the previous chapter but not utilized in conjunction with a given market situation.

THE EQUILIBRIUM OF THE PURELY COMPETITIVE FIRM AND INDUSTRY

Typically it is assumed, in the case of pure competition, that there are a large number of sellers. This is not an independent or necessary assumption, strictly speaking, but making it lends credence to other assumptions that *are* necessary. It must be assumed that buyers are indifferent in their choice of sellers—that, so far as buyers are concerned, the product or service sold is homogeneous. It must also be true that there is no collusion among sellers, that no seller is aware of any effect that changes in the quantity he sells may have upon market price, and that (in the long run) there be freedom of entry into and exit out of the industry.

The above assumptions imply, as we have seen, that the firm views the demand for its output as a horizontal line. As we have also seen, however, the cost conditions of the firm depend upon the set of entrepreneurial decisions to be analyzed, or the period chosen, the conditions of supply and use of the services of the factors of production, and the nature of the production function.

The Market Period

In its simplest form the market period refers to a situation in which the firm can sell a specific maximum quantity of output, or lesser quantities, its total costs being unaffected by the quantity sold. The essential assumption, therefore, is that marginal cost is zero for all outputs that the firm can sell.

The traditional example (conceived in the days before refrigeration) is that of the fisherman returning to the dock with his day's catch. All costs have already been incurred, there is no feasible alternative to immediate sale at the market price, and no cost savings result from a decision to sell only a part of his catch. Analytically, however, the analysis is unchanged if we regard it as dealing with all decisions made *after* the decision to embark upon the venture—provided that the services of such inputs as bait, nets, and so on yielded during the period must be utilized during the same period or not at all. Thus, in its simplest form the market period may refer either to a situation in which the firm possesses an inventory of its finished product that it must sell at existing market conditions, or to a situation in which the firm possesses inventories of factor services that it has already acquired and the use (or nonuse) of which occasions the firm no additional cost. The essential condition, therefore, is that marginal cost is zero for all outputs that the firm can produce.

Figures 7.1(a) and (b) refer to a purely competitive firm and industry, respectively, and the simplest type of market-period situation. Since selling any quantity less than the maximum that the firm can sell [OM in Figure 7.1(a)] would mean foregoing some revenue while leaving total costs unchanged, each of the n firms sells its maximum output regardless of the price established in the market, and the market supply curve is vertical.

If the market period is defined in terms of inventories of factor services that have already been acquired, *and* if it is also assumed that there are positive user costs (constant per unit of input), then the equilibrium of the competitive firm and industry in this period may be represented geometrically as in Figures 7.2(a) and (b). Since, at outputs smaller than OW, increases in output would occasion smaller increases in total cost than in total revenue, such outputs could not be optimal. Similarly, a rational firm would not choose outputs larger than OW, because at such outputs decreases in output would occasion larger decreases in total cost than in total revenue. Hence OW is the optimum output for the firm. If, however, AR should lie below AVC, the firm would not operate, since average revenue

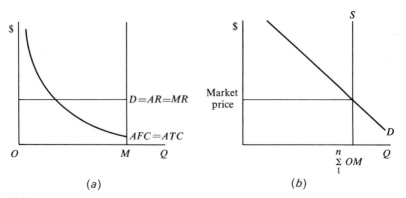

(a)   (b)

FIGURE 7.1

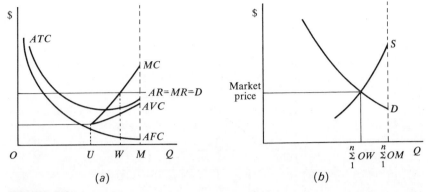

FIGURE 7.2

then would be insufficient to cover even the user costs (per unit of output). Thus the supply curve of the competitive firm is that portion of its marginal cost curve *above* the lowest value of its average-variable-cost curve. Horizontal summation of the supply curves of the firms in the industry yields the industry supply curve shown in Figure 7.2(b).

Essentially the same analysis holds for a market period defined in terms of a product inventory consisting of goods for which there is an alternative to immediate sale in the particular market considered. If, for example, our fisherman has access to refrigeration facilities or if the product is not so highly perishable, the seller himself may well have a *reservation* demand for his own product. Or if the product may be diverted, in part or in toto, to alternative markets, sellers in this market will have a reservation demand for their own product.

Figure 7.3 depicts a market situation in which sellers have a reservation demand (D_r). The reservation demand is actually implicit in the supply curve and may be derived simply by subtracting the supply curve from the given product inventory. Thus at the price OK sellers would be willing to sell all of the product inventory OM and would demand none of it for themselves. At prices below OH sellers would be willing to sell none of the product inventory OM and would demand all of it for themselves. At the market price OL sellers are willing to sell OW of their inventory, retaining for themselves WM (equal to LS).[1]

Just as a firm may have a reservation demand for its product, it may also have a reservation demand for its inventories of factor services. Some intertemporal substitution of factor services may be possible, or inventories of factor services may be adequate to produce other products or services. Thus the "user cost," which yielded a determinate output-expansion path

---

[1] Since at prices below OH sellers would wish to keep all of the product inventory for themselves, D_r could logically be extended rightward along the line of which HD_r constitutes a segment to the point on this line above M, and then vertically down to M.

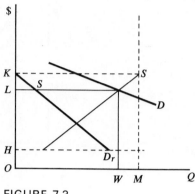

FIGURE 7.3

for the market period in the previous chapter (and the accompanying cost curves), could equally as well have been the cost of using factor services now rather than later or in the production of this particular good rather than some other. Costs are no less real because they involve subjective estimates by the firm of opportunities foregone.

Finally, the market period may well be characterized by inventories of factor services *and* of product, with the result that the cost of some outputs is merely the cost of selling now rather than later from an already-produced stock, while the costs of larger outputs include user costs for factor services. In turn these user costs may consist, in whole or in part, of the cost of producing now rather than later.

Thus, in its simplest form the market period is characterized by the fact that marginal costs are zero, so that profit maximization (or minimization of loss) is equivalent to maximization of total revenue. More complicated cases may involve consideration of alternative markets, alternative uses of factor services, and user costs—causing the process of profit maximization to be that of maximizing the *difference* between the total revenue and total cost, the latter varying with output. All forms of the market period are characterized by a specific maximum output.

Mathematically, the equilibrium of the firm in the more complex forms of the market period may be expressed as follows (assuming the second-order conditions to be met):

(1) Let $R = f(q)$ be total revenue, and $\pi = F(q)$ be total cost.

(2) Maximize $R - \pi$:

$$\frac{d(R - \pi)}{dq} = \frac{dr}{dq} - \frac{d\pi}{dq} = 0,$$

$$\frac{dR}{dq} = \frac{d\pi}{dq},$$

or the optimal output is such that

marginal revenue = marginal cost.

The Short Run

That the firm is purely competitive again dictates that, for the firm, marginal revenue equals average revenue and that the demand for the output of the firm can be represented as a horizontal line at the market price. Figures 7.4(a) and (b) depict the equilibrium of the firm and industry, respectively—the optimal output of the firm again being that at which marginal cost and marginal revenue are equal. Similarly, since no output would be forthcoming if price were to fall below the lowest value of AVC, the industry supply curve is the horizontal summation of marginal cost curves above this point.

In the situation represented by Figure 7.4(a) the firm is making a profit of $EDCB$, or BC per unit. So long as price exceeds minimum average total costs, profits will exist. As implied earlier, however, "costs" to an economist means something other than the overt expenditures made by the firm for the services of the factors of production. In accordance with the concept of "opportunity costs," the cost curves of Figure 7.4(a) include the costs of using factor services in this particular productive process at this time rather than in others or in this one at some future time. Thus if the manager of an enterprise is also its owner, or if the firm happens to own the land that it utilizes, the costs of the firm include not only the *explicit* or overt expenditures for the services of factors of production but also the *implicit* costs of managerial wages or rent that the firm would have had to pay if it had purchased these factor services in a market transaction.

The purely competitive firm enjoys a profit only if price is greater than

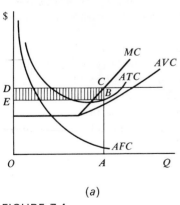

(a)

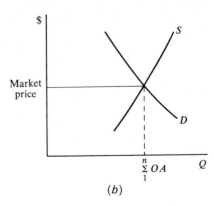

(b)

FIGURE 7.4

minimum average *total* cost, yet it will continue to operate in the short run so long as price exceeds minimum average variable cost. The difference between total cost and variable cost, it will be recalled, is fixed cost. Fixed costs, while playing no part in determination of the optimum output, are expenditures that the firm must make (or has already made) irrespective of output. Thus, so long as price exceeds minimum average variable costs it is sufficient to cover these costs and make some contribution toward fixed costs. Consequently, the firm reduces its loss by operating, rather than not operating, when price is greater than average variable costs but less than average total costs. In the long run, however, the firm must meet all of its costs if it is to remain in the industry.

The horizontal portion of the marginal-cost and average-variable-cost curves reflects, it will be recalled, a specific type of cost-minimization behavior by the firm. At each input of the services of the variable factor (variable in acquisition as well as in use) the services of the fixed factor are added until their marginal productivity is no longer positive. Thus the firm must determine, at each input of the services of the variable, the optimal quantity of the services of the fixed factor that should be excluded from production. Given constant factor-service prices and a linear homogeneous production function, marginal and average variable costs are constant and equal over this range of output. Beyond this range, returns to proportion succeed returns to scale, it is no longer necessary to exclude factor services from production, and marginal and average variable costs increase with output. While again there is a maximum output, this maximum is determined by the production function itself rather than by the imposition of two constraints upon the function (as in the market period), and this maximum output would never be produced. This maximum will not be reached so long as any cost is associated with the acquisition or use of the services of the variable factor, since this maximum is characterized by the fact that the marginal product of the services of the variable factor is zero at this point. The firm can hardly be expected to pay for services that occasion no increase in output.

The short-run equilibrium of the firm can be portrayed in terms of its total-cost and total-revenue functions. Since marginal revenue is constant, the total-revenue curve shown in Figure 7.5 is a straight line. Over the range in which marginal cost is constant the total-cost curve is also a straight line. The intercept of the total-cost curve is the value of the firm's fixed costs. Since profit is the difference between total revenue and total costs, the firm's optimum output occurs where this difference is the greatest. At this output the rate of change of total cost (marginal cost) is equal to that of total revenue (marginal revenue)—as shown by the fact that the tangent to the total-cost curve is parallel to the total-revenue curve at the output OA.

Mathematically, the equilibrium of the purely competitive firm in the

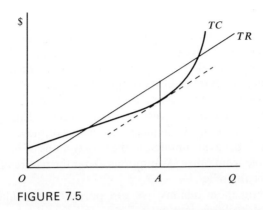

FIGURE 7.5

short run can be expressed in the same manner as in the market period, the equilibrium condition being that

$$\frac{d(R - \pi)}{dq} = \frac{dR}{dq} - \frac{d\pi}{dq} = 0 \quad \text{or} \quad \frac{dR}{dq} = \frac{d\pi}{dq}.$$

The second-order condition is that

$$\frac{d^2 R}{dq^2} < \frac{d^2 \pi}{dq^2}$$

or the rate of change of marginal revenue be less than the rate of change of marginal cost. Since the rate of change of marginal revenue is zero (marginal revenue is constant), the second-order condition is that marginal cost have a positive slope.

The Long Run

It will be recalled that in the long run, strictly speaking, the services of all factors of production are variable in acquisition as well as in use. *Given constant factor-service prices* and a linear homogeneous production function, the output-expansion path is linear. Long-run marginal cost and long-run average cost are equal and constant.

Again strictly speaking, the assumptions of the previous paragraph can be added to the assumptions of pure competition (in particular, the assumption that no seller is aware of any influence that changes in the quantity he sells may have upon market price), and—granted rationality—certain conclusions can be deduced. Many economists find doing so less than completely satisfactory, however, because one of the conclusions deduced is that there is no unique output for the firm. Any scale of operation is equally as profitable as any other. Others object because only the assumptions of pure competition preclude a given firm from selecting a scale of operation at which its share of the market would be so large that it would have to recognize the influence of changes in its output upon price. If it *did* occur, we would no longer have pure competition. Thus, if we have *assumed* pure competition, the situation in question cannot occur. This answer, while logically correct, may not fully assuage the qualms of those who prefer that the type of seller's behavior implicit in the assumptions of pure competition be itself deducible from other assumptions about the nature of the situation that is posed for the seller.

Disregarding these qualms, we can portray the equilibrium of the industry geometrically as in Figure 7.6(a) and (b). While any firm may choose any scale of operation, each will be producing at *some* scale at any given time. Consequently there will be at any time a short-run supply curve, such as SRS_1, derived by horizontal summation of marginal-cost curves (above minimum average variable cost), even though the short-run marginal-cost curves do not reflect the same scale of operation by all of the individual firms. SRS_1 will be, in other words, a horizontal summation of short-run marginal-cost curves, but there is no reason to assume it to be a summation of all SMC_1 curves. Finally, since any long-run equilibrium is coincident with a short-run equilibrium, the intersection of the industry demand curve and the long-run supply curve occurs at the point of intersection of industry demand with SRS_1.

The long-run supply curve answers the question of the conditions under which the industry would be willing to supply a greater (or smaller) output in the long run. But to pose the question requires us to posit some reason for expecting industry output to change. Thus the necessary procedure is for us to pose hypothetical changes in demand (shifts in the demand

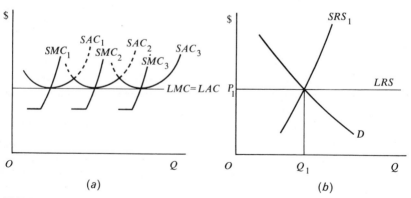

FIGURE 7.6

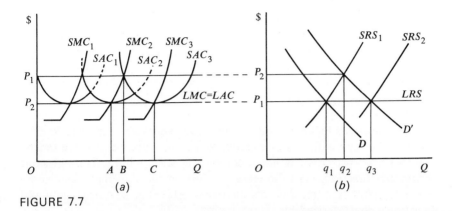

FIGURE 7.7

curve) and then ascertain the nature of the industry's response to these changes in demand—given the nature of the firm's cost curves and given also the assumption that firms can in the long run change their scale of operation and/or enter or leave the industry.

In Figure 7.7(b) an increase in demand is posited. The short-run response of the industry is an increase in output from Oq_1 to Oq_2 and an increase in price from OP_1 to OP_2. If we assume the firm whose cost curves are depicted in Figure 7.7(a) to be operating at the scale indicated by SMC_2 and SAC_2, that portion of the industry's response attributable to this particular firm is an increase in output from OA to OB. The industry's short-run response thus consists of movement up SRS_1, which consists simultaneously of movement by firms up the short-run marginal-cost curve in terms of which the particular scale at which they are operating is defined. For the firm the output-expansion path proceeds *across* the production surface, and given expenditures upon the services of variable factors yield less-than-proportionate increases in output, causing short-run marginal and average total costs to rise.

Despite the rise in average total costs, positive profits now exist. Furthermore, it appears to the individual firm that its profits could be increased by increasing the scale of its operations, and new firms would be attracted to the industry by the same prospect. Thus in the long run existing firms will increase their scale of operations and new firms will enter the industry—resulting in rightward shifts in the short-run supply curve and decreases in price. This process will continue until market price is reestablished at P_1, but at the same price the industry is now producing a larger quantity. Thus, since this industry would produce any quantity desired, in the long run, at the same price, the long-run supply curve is horizontal. Once the new long-run equilibrium is attained, there is no incentive for further entry and no incentive for alteration of the scale of operations by the firms in the industry. The firm whose cost curves are depicted in Figure 7.7(a) may well now be producing an output of OC rather than OA, but it has no reason to change further its scale of operations.

The "Envelope" Cost Curve

As noted in the previous chapter, economists are rather fond of a particular set of conditions that can yield an "envelope" cost curve for the firm. Such a cost curve is not incompatible with a linear homogeneous production function, even though a production function that was characterized by increasing returns to scale over some range of output, followed by a range characterized by decreasing returns to scale, could yield such a result. Equal increases in the quantity of a *factor* of production do not always mean equal increases in the quantity of factor *services* that enter into production. Thus, increased specialization may result in decreasing average costs, over some range of output, not because of increasing returns to scale but because a given increase in the quantity of *factors* results in a more-than-proportionate increase in the quantity of factor *services* entering into production. Such a result is, in effect, a decrease in factor-service prices. Similarly, there may be increasing and then decreasing returns to proportion in combining a given quantity of management services with varying quantities of all other factor services. Further, difficulties in coordinating the efforts of management or labor may become greater than the advantages of further specialization, so that factor-service prices, in effect, rise at larger outputs as less additional services are delivered into the productive process from equal increments in the acquisition of the factors themselves.

Whatever its origin, and despite the fact that it typically reflects a mixture of returns to proportion and returns to scale, the "envelope" curve has the significant advantage that the output of the individual firm is unique in "long-run" equilibrium. Figures 7.8(a) and (b) may be used to illustrate such an equilibrium for a purely competitive firm and industry.

Initially the firm may be presumed to produce an output of OA at a size of operation indicated by ATC_3 and SMC_3 at the initial price OP_1. If it did not, the firm could not be in the industry in the "long run" at this price. Given an increase in demand to D', the price in the market rises to OP_2, and the short-run adjustment of the firm is to increase output to OB. Since profit now exists, the individual firm would tend to increase the size of its operations, and there would also tend to be entrance of new firms into the industry. As a result of these effects the short-run supply curve would shift to the right, price would fall, and a new equilibrium would be established in which there would be a larger number of firms producing at the original size. The increased quantity supplied by the industry would thus be due

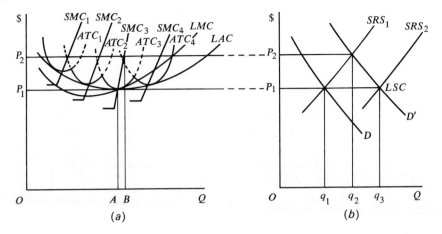

FIGURE 7.8

entirely to the entry of new firms. Since this increased quantity is supplied at the original market price, the "long-run" supply curve of the industry is again horizontal. (If the assumption of constant *factor-service* prices were altered, this conclusion, of course, would not necessarily hold.)

External Economies and Diseconomies

In the long-run case treated above and in the case of the envelope cost curve, the long-run supply curve of the purely competitive industry is horizontal (assuming constant factor-service prices). The effect of external economies would be to impart a downward slope to the long-run supply curve. External diseconomies would have the opposite effect. Industries characterized by an upward-sloping long-run supply curve (for whatever reason) are termed *increasing-cost* industries. Industries having a downward-sloping long-run supply curve (for whatever reason) are known as *decreasing-cost* industries.

MONOPOLY EQUILIBRIUM

Figure 7.9 depicts a short-run equilibrium for the monopolist. The profit-maximizing (or loss-minimizing) output is that at which marginal cost and marginal revenue are equal, as in the case of any other type of firm. The monopolist's optimum output, in the situation posed by Figure 7.9, is OA and its optimum price is OP_1.

It is a common fallacy to assume that because a firm is a monopolist it must receive a profit. In Figure 7.9 the monopolist, however, has a loss

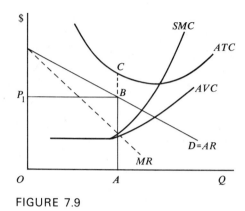

FIGURE 7.9

of *BC* per unit of output. Only if its average revenue is greater than its average total cost will any firm make a profit. True enough, the situation described by Figure 7.9 cannot continue in the long run. In the long run either demand must increase or the monopolist must be able to reduce his costs (perhaps by reducing the size of his plant or by winning price concessions from his suppliers). Nonetheless, the monopolist minimizes his losses, in the situation posed, by choosing an output of *OA* and a price of *OP₁*. If these losses cannot be eliminated in the long run, the monopolist will be out of business, transferring the resources over which he has control into an industry in which they will receive at least a normal return.

It is also sometimes thought that a monopolist will charge the highest price at which he can make any sales. The monopolist is restrained in his price policy, however, by the fact that at higher prices lesser quantities can be sold. Thus in Figure 7.9 a higher price than *OP₁* would increase the firm's losses.

While it may be safely concluded that any short-run losses the monopolist incurs must disappear in the long run (if the monopolist is to continue operations in this industry), a similar fate cannot be presumed for any short-run *profits* that the monopolist may enjoy. By changing the size of his plant or by other means the monopolist may even be able to increase his profits in the long run. He can continue to enjoy monopoly profits, however, only so long as there exist barriers to the entry of other firms (that is, only so long as he can remain a monopolist).

As a moment's reflection will indicate, we cannot derive the supply curve of a monopolistic industry. By definition a supply curve indicates the quantities that will be supplied at various *prices*. Since the monopolist's output is determined by equating marginal *revenue* with marginal cost, and since a given value of marginal revenue can coincide with any number of different prices, we are unable to say what quantity a monopolist will sell at a given *price*.

EQUILIBRIUM OF THE MONOPOLISTIC COMPETITOR

It will be recalled that in monopolistic competition we make the following assumptions:

(a) Each firm is so small relative to the market that it need fear no retaliation from other firms to changes in its output or price.

(b) The product or service sold is differentiated—so that at least some of the customers of the firm do not regard the products or services of other firms as perfect substitutes.

(c) There are no significant barriers to entry. Firms may easily enter the industry and produce products or services that are very similar, but not identical (in the eyes of consumers), to those produced by the existing firms.

Figure 7.10 portrays the short-run equilibrium of the monopolistic competitor. The optimum output is OA and the optimum price is OP_1. This output and price could not be maintained in the long run, however, since the pure profit that exists would cause entry of new firms into the industry. The entry of new firms producing similar products or services would cause the demand for the output of the individual firm to fall and, in general, to become more elastic.

Confronted with a situation in which its demand is falling and becoming more elastic, the original firm might well react by increasing its advertising or by other measures that might be expected to raise its demand curve (or prevent a decline) and decrease its price elasticity (or prevent an increase in price elasticity). Since such measures can be presumed to increase the firm's costs, the long-run equilibrium depicted by Figure 7.11 may come about partly as a result of downward shifts in demand and partly as a result of upward shifts in the firm's cost curves. Whatever the combination of these forces bringing it about, the long-run equilibrium would be characterized

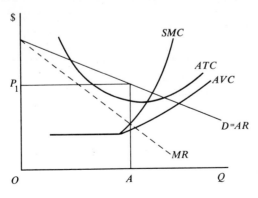

FIGURE 7.10

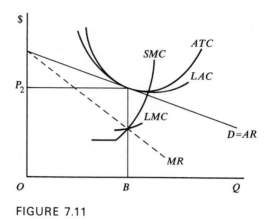

FIGURE 7.11

by tangency of the demand curve to the short-run (and long-run) average-cost curves.

It may not be immediately apparent that marginal cost must equal marginal revenue, in Figure 7.11, at the same output at which the tangency occurs. Since, at the output at which this tangency occurs, the rates of change of average cost and average revenue are equal, it will also be true at this output that the rates of change of total cost (marginal cost) and total revenue (marginal revenue) will be equal. Average cost and average revenue having been multiplied by the same magnitude (OB) to get total cost and total revenue, the latter two will possess equal rates of change, since this was true of the former two. Mathematically, at the point of tangency, $R = \pi$ (where R is total revenue and π is total cost), and

$$\frac{d\left(\dfrac{R}{q}\right)}{dq} = \frac{d\left(\dfrac{\pi}{q}\right)}{dq},$$

$$\frac{q\dfrac{dR}{dq} - R}{q^2} = \frac{q\dfrac{d\pi}{dq} - \pi}{q^2}.$$

Since $R = \pi$,

$$\frac{dR}{dq} = \frac{d\pi}{dq}.$$

OLIGOPOLY EQUILIBRIUM

Oligopoly, it will be recalled, is a situation in which there are only a few sellers in the industry, the output of each seller constituting so large a proportion of industry output that any change in the output or price of one seller is very likely to provoke retaliation from the other sellers in the industry. This reaction can take any of a large number of forms; consequently, there are many oligopoly situations that can be analyzed.

The oligopoly situation discussed in Chapter 4 was that of the "kinked" demand curve. In this situation the individual oligopolist expects that if he were to increase his price above the customary price, his rivals would not do likewise, whereas if he were to lower his price below the customary price, his rivals would quickly match the price cut. Consequently there is a "kink" in the individual firm's demand curve at the customary price.[2]

Figure 7.12 portrays geometrically the short-run equilibrium of this type of oligopolist. Because of the discontinuity in the marginal-revenue curve, price could remain at its customary value (OP_1) despite large variations in the firm's cost. Understandably, this analysis has been widely used as an explanation of "sticky" prices in particular industries (prices that remain the same despite significant changes in cost).

For the particular oligopoly situation presented, no unique pattern of events is to be expected in the long run. Nonetheless, since the time of

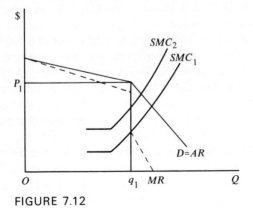

FIGURE 7.12

[2]It should be noted that the analysis, itself, provides no explanation of how the customary price is selected.

Adam Smith economists have noted the tendency of businessmen to collude —or, as the latter might prefer to put it, to "stabilize" an industry or to "rationalize" production. Tacitly or overtly, the oligopoly situation we have discussed may well change over time into a price-leadership cartel, in which one firm—in effect—determines industry price.

EQUILIBRIUM OF THE PRICE DISCRIMINATOR

In the case of price discrimination discussed in Chapter 4, the firm sells the same product or service in separate markets at different prices, its cost being unaffected by the allocation of output between markets. In the present chapter we shall again defer treatment of more complicated (and perhaps more meaningful) cases of price discrimination in order to concentrate upon the basic nature of the equilibrium of the price discriminator.

In order to be *able* to engage in price discrimination, the firm must be able to separate its total market into a number of submarkets. It must be able to distinguish, in other words, separate groups of customers whom it can treat differently in terms of price. This means that if different prices are to be charged in the various submarkets there must be no significant *leakage* between markets—that is, customers charged higher prices must not be able to enter submarkets in which lower prices obtain, and customers in lower-priced submarkets must not act as sellers in higher-priced submarkets.

Assuming that the firm can separate its total market into submarkets, it will be *profitable* for the firm to do so *only* if the demand elasticities in the several submarkets are different (assuming marginal cost to be unaffected by the allocation of output between markets). As we have seen, the price discriminator will so allocate any output between markets as to cause the marginal revenue to be equal in each. Only if the price elasticities of demand are different in the several submarkets will the condition of equality of marginal revenue require that different prices be charged. Necessary for an equilibrium to exist, however, is the further condition that marginal revenue, equal in each submarket, must also be equal to marginal cost. Thus equilibrium is fully defined, in this case, by the conditions that marginal revenue is equal in each submarket and also equals marginal cost.

Figure 7.13 illustrates the equilibrium of the price discriminator in the case that we have posed. D_T is the horizontal summation of the two separate demand curves comprising it. The equilibrium output Oq_t is divided between the two submarkets in such a way as to equalize the marginal revenues in each (as shown by the horizontal line). The price q_1P_1 is charged in the first submarket, q_2P_2 is charged in the second submarket, and the price q_tP_t is the price that the firm *would have* charged if it were not engaging in price discrimination. As shown in Chapter 4, the price charged in the submarket

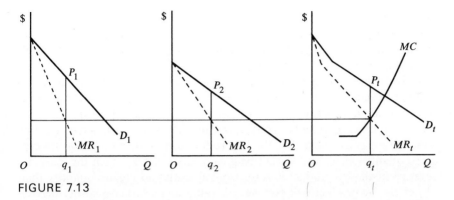

FIGURE 7.13

possessing the smaller price elasticity of demand will be higher than that charged in the submarket having the greater price elasticity of demand, and the higher price will be higher and the lower price lower than the single price q_tP_t that would be charged if the firm were not engaging in price discrimination.[3]

The price discriminator may have any of the short-run and long-run cost conditions that we have previously described. And, as in all cases in which some degree of monopoly exists, we cannot derive an industry supply curve. Since the differential price elasticities of demand to which the price discriminator responds often reflect differential degrees of competition faced by the firm in various submarkets, price discrimination is sometimes the path toward a more competitive organization of the industry. A firm initially possessing a large degree of monopoly power yields ground reluctantly in those submarkets in which the entry of new firms has caused the demand curve to be characterized by greater elasticity, while it maintains higher prices in those submarkets in which other firms have not yet made inroads. Or the initiative may lie with the price-discriminating firm itself. Knowing that it possesses certain relatively "safe" or "home" markets, the firm may venture forth into other markets characterized by higher demand elasticities, its entrance into those markets increasing the demand elasticity (to the firm) and the degree of competition.

THE EQUILIBRIUM OF THE PRODUCER
OF JOINT PRODUCTS

It will be recalled that the case of joint products refers to a situation in which the firm produces more than one product, there being a fixed ratio

---

[3]There are conditions under which price discrimination can result in a lowering of price in *both* submarkets (relative to the single price that a nondiscriminatory monopolist would charge). This case will be considered in a later chapter.

between the quantities of the products produced. The example used in the previous discussion of this case was that of the steer and his hide. Production of any quantity of carcasses for sale in the meat market results in simultaneous production of an equal number of hides for the hide market.

In Figure 7.14 the demand for the major product is represented by D_2 and the demand for the by-product by D_1. The horizontal axis is expressed in composite units so that one unit represents, for example, one steer (with hide), two units represents two steers (with their two hides), and so on. For simplicity it is assumed that the by-product can be disposed of at no cost if the quantity produced should be greater than that at which the marginal revenue of the by-product is zero. Consequently, no greater quantity than OS of the by-product will ever be *sold* (although a larger quantity may be produced), and the price of the by-product will never be lower than SP_3. Since no greater quantity than OS of the by-product would ever be *sold*, the total marginal revenue and the marginal revenue received from the major product (MR_2) coincide for outputs greater than OS. Since the *total revenue* received from sale of the by-product remains constant for outputs greater than OS, the *average* revenue (D_T) does not remain the sum of D_1 and D_2 beyond OS but is, instead, D_2 plus the result of dividing the constant sum received from the sale of the by-product by the quantity of both products produced.

Even conceptually one cannot separate the marginal cost of one of the products from the other. MC_1 thus refers to the marginal cost of producing

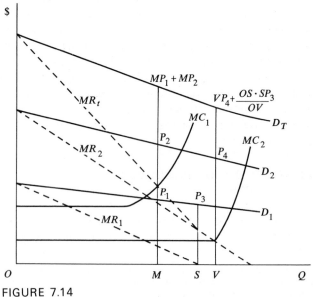

FIGURE 7.14

the major product and the by-product. If the marginal-cost curve intersects the total-marginal-revenue curve above its intersection with the marginal-revenue curve of the major product (as MC_1 does), the prices charged for the two products can be immediately determined from their respective demand curves (MP_1 and MP_2 in Figure 7.14).

If the firm's marginal-cost curve is as shown by MC_1, however, an output larger than OS will be *produced*, but only OS of the by-product will be *sold*. The prices of the by-product and the major product in this case will be SP_3 and VP_4, respectively.

Again we cannot derive a supply curve in the case of joint production (unless the producer is purely competitive with respect to both products), nor is there any specific set of long-run cost conditions to be expected.

SIMPLE MATHEMATICS OF FIRM EQUILIBRIUM

The equilibrium of the firm occurs simultaneously on the input and output sides—that is, a firm in maximizing its profit by choosing an output at which marginal cost equals marginal revenue is simultaneously minimizing the cost of producing that output, or maximizing the output that can be produced for the given cost outlay. Below, we offer a limited proof that minimizing the cost of the prescribed level of output requires satisfaction of the same condition as does maximization of the output that can be produced for the given cost outlay, and that this condition is also a condition for profit maximization.

Minimizing the Cost of the Prescribed Level of Output

Let

$$(1) \qquad\qquad X = f(a, b)$$

be the production function, where X is output and a and b are the quantities of two types of factor services. Let

$$(2) \qquad\qquad X_0 = f(a, b)$$

be the prescribed output, and

$$(3) \qquad\qquad \pi = V_1 a + V_2 b,$$

where π is total cost and V_1 and V_2 are the factor-service prices of a and b, respectively.

Then, in order to minimize (3) subject to (2), form the function

(4) $$S = V_1 a + V_2 b + \lambda[X_0 - f(a, b)],$$

$$\frac{\partial S}{\partial a} = V_1 - \lambda \frac{\partial X}{\partial a} = 0,$$

$$\frac{\partial S}{\partial b} = V_2 - \lambda \frac{\partial X}{\partial b} = 0,$$

$$\frac{\partial S}{\partial \lambda} = f(a, b) - X_0 = 0,$$

yielding as a condition of equilibrium

(5) $$\frac{\dfrac{\partial X}{\partial a}}{\dfrac{\partial X}{\partial b}} = \frac{V_1}{V_2}.$$

The second-order conditions (not shown) require that the isoquants be convex from below.

Maximizing the Output of the Prescribed Level of Costs

Given equations (1) and (3) above, let the prescribed cost outlay be

(6) $$\pi_0 = V_1 a + V_2 b.$$

Then, in order to maximize (1) subject to (6), form the equation

(7) $$L = f(a, b) + k(\pi_0 - V_1 a - V_2 b),$$

$$\frac{\partial L}{\partial a} = \frac{\partial X}{\partial a} - k V_1 = 0,$$

$$\frac{\partial L}{\partial b} = \frac{\partial X}{\partial b} - k V_2 = 0,$$

$$\frac{\partial L}{\partial k} = \pi_0 - V_1 a - V_2 b = 0,$$

yielding as a condition of equilibrium

$$\frac{\dfrac{\partial X}{\partial a}}{\dfrac{\partial X}{\partial b}} = \frac{V_1}{V_2},$$

the second-order conditions remaining the same.

Maximizing Profit

In the case of pure competition, let the price of the good be represented by p and profit by M. Then, from (1) and (3),

(8) $$M = pX - \pi.$$

Substituting from (1) and (3) for X and π, respectively,

(9) $$M = pf(a, b) - V_1 a - V_2 b.$$

Maximizing M,

$$\frac{\partial M}{\partial a} = p \frac{\partial X}{\partial a} - V_1 = 0 \qquad \text{or} \qquad p \frac{\partial X}{\partial a} = V_1$$

(the value of the marginal product equals the factor-service price),

$$\frac{\partial M}{\partial a} = p \frac{\partial X}{\partial a} - V_2 = 0 \qquad \text{or} \qquad p \frac{\partial X}{\partial b} = V_2,$$

$$\frac{\dfrac{\partial X}{\partial a}}{\dfrac{\partial X}{\partial b}} = \frac{V_1}{V_2},$$

or a condition for profit maximization is that

$$\frac{\dfrac{\partial X}{\partial a}}{\dfrac{\partial X}{\partial b}} = \frac{V_1}{V_2},$$

assuming the second-order conditions to be met.

SUMMARY AND CONCLUSIONS

This chapter has been designed to explain, in some of the cases in which it is possible to do so, the nature of the firm and industry's equilibrium and the derivation of industry supply curves. The output of the individual firm was found to be determinate in all the cases considered except that of a purely competitive firm operating under conditions of constant long-run average cost. Even in this case the output of the industry is determinate and we know that, at whatever scale the firm is operating, marginal cost must equal marginal revenue. Determination of the optimum price occasioned little difficulty.

Our efforts to derive industry supply curves necessarily met with much more limited success. Since the supply curve is by definition a geometrical representation of a schedule of the quantities that will be supplied at a corresponding schedule of prices, we could only derive supply curves in those cases in which price must equal (for the firm) marginal revenue. We can fairly safely assume in most instances, however, (at least in the short run) that the industry will supply a larger quantity only at a higher price, all other things being equal.

Two tasks remain in this brief treatment of price theory. The first is to provide an explanation of the determination of factor-service prices. Having accomplished this, we can then direct our attention to a summary exposition of the interrelatedness of all parts of the economic system. The next chapter undertakes these tasks.

SELECTED REFERENCES

BAUMOL, WILLIAM J., *Economic Theory and Operations Analysis*, 2nd ed. (Englewood Cliffs, N.J.: Prentice-Hall, Inc., 1965), chap. 14.

HENDERSON, JAMES M., and RICHARD E. QUANDT, *Microeconomic Theory: A Mathematical Approach* (New York: McGraw-Hill Book Company, 1958), chap. 4.

LEFTWICH, RICHARD H., *The Price System and Resource Allocation*, 3rd ed. (New York: Holt, Rinehart and Winston, Inc., 1966), chaps. 9–12.

LIEBHAFSKY, H. H., *The Nature of Price Theory* (Homewood, Ill.: The Dorsey Press, 1963), chaps. 9–11.

MACHLUP, FRITZ, *The Economics of Sellers' Competition* (Baltimore: The Johns Hopkins Press, 1952).

ROBINSON, JOAN, *The Economics of Imperfect Competition* (London: Collier-Macmillan, Ltd., 1934).

factor service pricing and
economic interdependence

Previous chapters have provided an explanation of how some of man's wants come to be expressed in the market, yielding simultaneously an explanation of consumer behavior. Previous chapters also have offered an explanation of the process by which factor services are combined so as to yield products and services in a form suitable to the satisfaction of man's wants, and of the conditions under which goods will be offered in the market, providing simultaneously an explanation of the behavior of the firm and of the industry of which the firm is a part.

The behavior of consumers, on the one hand, and the behavior of firms and industries, on the other, are not independent. In varying degrees (depending upon such factors as the form of market organization) firms and industries respond to changes in consumer preferences by reallocating resources in accordance with those altered preferences. If the desirability of a particular good, to consumers, increases, this is manifested by an increased demand. As a result, the price will rise and, generally, a greater quantity of the good will be produced and a greater proportion of society's resources devoted to its production. Thus the allocation of resources is determined in large part by the relative strength of consumer preferences for particular goods. In a purely competitive economy there would be "consumer sovereignty"—the allocation of resources would be dictated by the relative strength of consumer preferences, and economic profits would be transitory.

Interdependence is a much more pervasive characteristic of the economic system, however, than the foregoing might suggest. The ability of a consumer to express his desires in the marketplace is constrained by his income, and his income in turn is primarily determined by the economy's evaluation of the services he contributes to production (and/or of the services of factors of production that he owns). Since the primary goal of this book (as noted in Chapter 1) is to provide an understanding of the economic system, and since the economic system is characterized by interdependence, we shall as a major task of the present chapter consider a major source of that interdependence—the determination of factor-service prices. As usual, the explanation of this particular phenomenon yields an explanation of another aspect of economic behavior.

The ultimate statement of the interrelatedness of all economic activity is the concept of *general equilibrium*. Conceptually, every price is related to every other price and any change in one alters the forces affecting every other. Having treated factor-service pricing, we shall be in a position to develop, in a simple way, the concept of general equilibrium.

THE DEMAND FOR FACTOR SERVICES

Initially it would seem that since factor-service prices, like final-product prices, are determined by the forces of supply and demand, their explanation should proceed in the same manner. Since it is firms that demand factor services, it would appear that we need only isolate the factors affecting the firm's demand for factor services and then horizontally sum individual firms' demands to secure the market demand for input. This procedure is more complex in the case of the demand for input, however, because one of the parameters of what would otherwise be the firm's demand for factor services is in most cases altered by changes in the factor-service price. Similarly, on the supply side the determination of input prices is more complex. Even under conditions of pure competition not all types of factor services are related to the cost of producing them in the manner true of final products. We therefore require a separate discussion of factor-service pricing.

The method employed in arriving at the demand for factor services is the same as that used throughout the book. The assumption of a rational producer will be conjoined with various subsets of assumptions (various heuristic devices or various logical situations) to arrive at deductions concerning the firm's behavior. As usual, only a few of the situations that could be constructed will be posed. Having derived the demand for factor services, we shall consider the factors affecting the price elasticity of demand for input, or the *elasticity of derived demand*.

The Purely Competitive Firm's Short-Run Demand for Factor Services

Assume a firm that is purely competitive in selling its product and in purchasing its input, so that the quantity it sells cannot affect the product price, and the quantity of input purchased cannot affect its price. Assume further that the firm is operating in the short run and that there are no user costs. In such a situation the firm's output-expansion path (assuming a linear homogeneous production function) is that on which lie the points O, P, and L in Figure 8.1(a). It is assumed that factor service a is variable in acquisition and in use and that the firm possesses a divisible stock, OK, of factor service b. Returns to scale characterize the output-expansion path from O to P, and the path is linear over this range. From P to L the output-expansion path is nonlinear and characterized by returns to proportion. Figure 8.1(b) depicts the marginal and average product of factor service a, OS of a being the input of a at which returns to proportion succeed returns to scale in terms of output. Assuming a constant price for input a, Figure 8.1(c) indicates the type of marginal-cost and average-variable-cost curves yielded, P in this figure corresponding to P in Figure 8.1(a).

The first step in the derivation of the firm's demand for input, in this situation, is to evaluate MP_a, or—more specifically—the downward-sloping portion of MP_a. As previously established, a purely competitive firm would not produce an output less than P in Figure 8.1(c) (that is, it would not produce if price fell below minimum AVC) and thus would not purchase

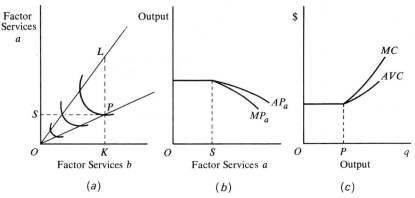

FIGURE 8.1

an input less than OS [Figure 8.1(a) or (b)]. Further, since the firm (in deciding how many units of input to acquire) is interested in the contribution to output of each unit of input rather than their average contribution, it is interested in the marginal product rather than the average product of a. Since the price of the output is constant (for a purely competitive firm), multiplying the marginal product of any unit of input by product price will indicate the increase in total revenue attributable to that unit of input. This result can then be compared with the price of the input, since this is the addition to total cost attributable to that unit of input.

The result of multiplying the marginal product by the price of the product is called the *value of the marginal product*. This linear transformation of the marginal product is labeled *VMP* in Figure 8.2. Since the individual firm cannot affect the price of the input, the *average factor cost* (cost per unit of input) equals the *marginal factor cost* (rate of change of total or variable cost relative to variation in input), and both are equal to the input price. At this input price the firm purchases OQ units of input, since larger quantities of input would include units whose contribution to total revenue was not as great as the amount by which their acquisition caused total cost to rise. Purchasing a quantity of input less than OQ would mean that some units of input were *not* purchased that would have added more to total revenue than to total cost. Thus at the factor-service price indicated in Figure 8.2 the firm purchases that quantity of input at which the value of the marginal product equals marginal factor cost, or $VMP = MFC$.

It may well appear at this point that VMP constitutes the firm's demand for input. To treat it as such, however, is to ignore the interdependence we wish to stress. The VMP curve of Figure 8.2 exists only so long as the price of a, or OP_1, is not changed. A fall in the price of a factor service, for example, means a downward shift in the firm's marginal-cost curve. Since the fall in input price could not occur for *only one* of the firms

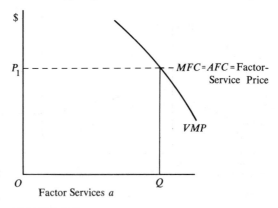

FIGURE 8.2

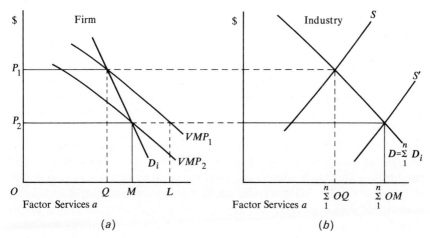

FIGURE 8.3

in an industry that is purely competitive in buying, the marginal-cost curves of all firms in the industry would shift downward, the short-run supply of output would increase, product price would fall, and—consequently—there would be a downward shift in the VMP curve. Thus in Figure 8.3(a) the firm would not purchase OL of input at input price OP_2 but OM instead.[1]

Put otherwise, the individual firm might *think* that it would purchase OL of input at factor-service price OP_2, but it would not do so, and aggregation over all firms of the VMP curves would *not* yield the purely competitive industry's demand for input. Thus the firm's demand for input, in this situation, is constructed in the manner indicated in Figure 8.3(a)—utilizing a different VMP curve for each input price. Horizontal summation of all D_i curves over all firms *would* yield the competitive industry's short-run demand for input a, as indicated in Figure 8.3(b).

The Purely Competitive Firm's Long-Run Demand for Input

When the services of more than one factor are variable in use and in acquisition, the derivation of the firm's demand for input becomes more

---

[1] Because one of the major topics of this chapter is economic interdependence, an analysis of factor-service pricing was selected that takes into account certain aspects of this interdependence. Quite obviously, there is no attempt to be all-inclusive. The making explicit of the interrelationship between factor-service price and product price in this analysis is not a denial of other economic interrelationships. The aim is to introduce the student to economic interdependence, despite the lack of parallelism with the analysis of earlier chapters. It seems more important to build a bridge to the concept of general equilibrium, and to construct a more realistic analysis of factor-service pricing, than to maintain the traditional partial-equilibrium analysis up to the point at which the student is suddenly confronted with the concept of general equilibrium.

complex. The reason basically is that a change in any one input price may lead to an alteration in the quantity not only of that input but others as well. Initially no change in *product price* will be assumed in order to take account of this further complicating factor. In other words, what may be termed the "external" effect upon product price arising from the change in output by firms will initially be disregarded. Having derived what would otherwise be the firm's demand for input, we shall then take the external effects into account.

Assume that Figure 8.4 represents a linear homogeneous production function and that the firm is at the initial equilibrium indicated by A. At this equilibrium the firm is purchasing (and using) a_1 of factor service a and b_1 of factor service b. With no change in input prices the output-expansion path would be the straight line through the origin on which lie the points A and A', and these points would, of course, be on isoquants having at these points the same slope. Given a fall in the price of a, the firm moves to a second equilibrium indicated by B, at which it purchases (and uses) a_2 of a and b_2 of b.

Given the fall in the price of input a, more a is purchased (and used)—for two reasons: the *substitution effect* of the price change and the *output effect* of the price change. If the two effects are separated, as in consumer demand theory, $a_3 - a_1$ reflects the substitution effect of the price change, $a_2 - a_3$ the output effect, and $a_2 - a_1$ the total effect of the price change. While the services of some factors of production may be complementary in production, the relationship of any one to all others as a whole must be that of substitution. Consequently, one effect of the price reduction is to cause a substitution of the factor services that are now relatively less expensive for those that remain at the same prices. Note that this would occur even if no change in output occurred. The second reason for purchasing (and using) more a when its price falls (and, generally, more b as well) is to

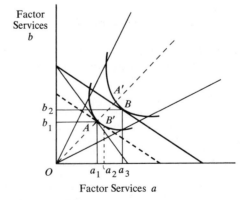

FIGURE 8.4

make possible the increase in output that the firm's now lower marginal-cost curve makes necessary. A larger output is now required, in other words, to equate marginal cost with product price (assumed, at this point in the analysis, not to have changed).

If we use F_a to represent the initial price of a, F_b to represent the price of b, and F_a' to represent the lowered price of a, then at A

$$\frac{MP_a}{MP_b} = \frac{F_a}{F_b}$$

and at B

$$\frac{MP_a}{MP_b} = \frac{F_a'}{F_b}.$$

At B, relative to A, MP_b is greater because the ratio of b to a has declined: $b_2/a_2 < b_1/a_1$. For the same reason MP_a is less. Thus both the ratio of factor-service prices and the ratio of marginal products have altered in the same direction so as to maintain the equality.

Since product price is assumed constant, so far in the analysis, then at A

$$\frac{VMP_a}{VMP_b} = \frac{F_a}{F_b}$$

and at B

$$\frac{VMP_a}{VMP_b} = \frac{F_a'}{F_b}.$$

Thus at B, relative to A, the value of the marginal product of b is greater and the value of the marginal product of a is less.[2]

What is involved in the argument up to this point is illustrated in Figure 8.5. The inputs of a are the same as those shown in Figure 8.4. VMP_a is the value of the marginal product of a if various quantities of a are combined with the initial quantity (b_1 in Figure 8.4) of b. If these same quantities of a were combined with the larger quantity of b (b_2 in Figure 8.4), this would yield the higher curve, VMP_a'. At the initial input price F_a the

---

[2] Note that while the *magnitude* of the value of the marginal product of a is less at B than at A, the VMP_a *function* is higher (see Figure 8.5), since the original quantities of a are combined with a greater quantity of input b.

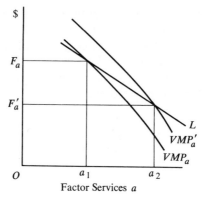

FIGURE 8.5

firm purchases (and uses) a_1 of a, equating F_a and VMP_a. At the lower input price F_a' the firm purchases (and uses) a_2 of a, equating F_a' and VMP_a'. The equating of input prices with the relevant value of the marginal product yields a necessarily downward-sloping curve, such as L in Figure 8.5.

At this point we are ready to take into account the "external" effect of the input-price change. In an industry that is purely competitive in buying, the fall in the price of input a can be presumed to have occurred for all firms. Consequently, the output of all firms would increase, product price would also fall, the value of the marginal-product curve would not shift as far as shown in Figure 8.5, L would be an overstatement of the firm's long-run demand for input, and such curves as L could not be summed to secure the industry's long-run demand for input.

The firm's long-run demand for input is thus as shown (D_i) in Figure 8.6. Ignoring the product price change, the firm would purchase

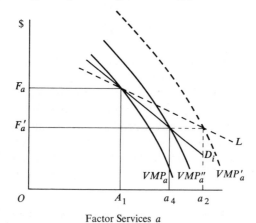

FIGURE 8.6

(and use) a_2 of a at the input price F'_a, but, taking the product price change into account, the firm at the input price F'_a would purchase only a_4 of input. Some increase in a would have to result from the fall in its price, not only because of the substitution effect but also because the product price falls only as a result of greater output, and this increase in output necessitates some increase in the quantity of a.

Some Degree of Monopoly in Selling

Any firm that is not purely competitive, in considering the desirability of a larger output, must take into account the fact that the larger output can be sold only at a lower price. Such a firm evaluates the marginal product not by product price but by *marginal revenue*. Multiplying the marginal product by marginal revenue yields the *marginal-value product* or *marginal-revenue product*. Since, in the short run, it is quite possible that an other than purely competitive firm may operate in the range of output characterized by returns to scale, all of the marginal-product curve must be evaluated (and not the downward-sloping portion only). Since marginal revenue may be assumed to decline, in most instances, as output increases, the curve depicting the marginal-value product is, however, downward sloping throughout.

Thus, retaining the assumptions made earlier concerning the production function in the short run, the nature of factor services, the absence of user cost, and the inability of this firm to affect input prices—in short, changing only the assumption concerning the conditions under which the product is sold—we may illustrate the relationship between the value of *marginal product* of the variable input and its *marginal-value product* as in Figure 8.7.

No problem arises from the "external" effects of input price changes if the less than purely competitive firm (in selling) is a monopolist. In this case the effects of industry output change upon marginal revenue have been

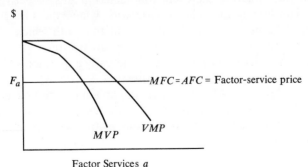

FIGURE 8.7

taken into account in computing the *MVP* of various outputs. The *MVP* curve of the monopolist (in selling) would be this firm's demand curve for the factor service. In all other instances in which there was some degree of monopoly in selling, a change in input price would cause changes in the outputs of all firms in the industry, thus shifting the product demand curve confronting any given firm. As a result there would be shifts in the firm's *MVP* curve at various input prices, and the firm's demand for input would have to be derived like that of the purely competitive firm (with the substitution of *MVP* for *VMP*).

The absence of "external" effects of input-price changes also simplifies the derivation of the monopolist's long-run demand for input. Substituting *MVP* for *VMP* in Figure 8.5, *L* could represent the monopolist's demand for input. Derivation of the long-run demand curves of other types of firms possessing some degree of monopoly power (in selling) would have to take "external" or industry effects into account and would more closely resemble the process depicted in Figure 8.6 (substituting *MVP* for *VMP*).

Derived-Demand Elasticity

The producer desires factor services not as consumption items for himself but as a means by which he hopes to make a profit. With them he can produce something that consumers are willing to buy. Since it is the consumer's wish to buy products that causes producers to buy factor services, the producer's demand for input is said to be a *derived* demand (derived from the consumer's demand for the product). The input-price elasticity of the producer's demand for factor services is therefore referred to as the elasticity of *derived* demand.

Assume initially that factor services in the productive process are combined in fixed proportions. Marshall's classic example is that of knife blades and knife handles, which are combined in a ratio of one to one to make knives.[3] In this situation there are four determinants of derived-demand elasticity. The first is the relative ease with which the factor service in question may be used in other processes, or that with which other factor services (not presently being used in the productive process) may be substituted for the input in question. This is actually a question of the relative difficulty of changing the production function.

The example that Marshall used in explaining the first determinant was that of the services of plasterers.[4] If the wages of plasterers were to increase, one of the factors determining the relative decrease in the quantity demanded of their services would be the feasibility of altering the productive

---

[3] Alfred Marshall, *Principles of Economics*, 8th ed. (London: Collier-Macmillan, Ltd., 1952), p. 318.

[4] Marshall, *Principles of Economics*, p. 317.

process so as to use the services of bricklayers, instead. The more feasible the change, the more elastic the demand for the services of plasterers.

The second determinant of derived-demand elasticity is the *product* (price) demand elasticity. A change in input price will change product price and output. The greater the change in output, the greater the change in the quantity demanded of the input. The elasticity of derived demand therefore tends to be greater if *product*-demand elasticity is greater, and less if product (price) elasticity of demand is less.

The third determinant of derived-demand elasticity is sometimes called "the importance of being unimportant." The greater the proportion of the cost of the product attributable to the price of the factor service in question, the greater will be the elasticity of derived demand for it. Thus if the price of an input that is a major cost component should increase, there is apt to be a relatively large decrease in the quantity demanded of this input. If the cost of the particular factor service is a small element in the cost of producing the product, there is apt to be a relatively small decrease in the quantity demanded of this input when its price increases. Hence "the importance of being unimportant."

Finally, the fourth determinant of the derived-demand elasticity of a given factor service is the price elasticity of supply of *other* factor services (currently being used in the productive process). If purchase of less of these services causes a decrease in their prices, the "savings" accruing to the firm from purchasing less of them can be used to offset the reduction in the quantity demanded of a given factor service, the price of which has increased. Thus if the price of one input increases, the quantity demanded of this input will decrease less if decreases in output cause other factor-service prices to fall than if these prices are not affected. The derived-demand elasticity for a given input will thus be greater, the larger is the elasticity of supply of other inputs.

Dropping the assumption that inputs must be combined in fixed proportions does not require any important qualifications to the preceding argument, so long as the *elasticity of substitution* (the relative change in the marginal rate of substitution—see Chapter 5) is less than *product-demand elasticity*. A fall in the price of an input will now cause an increase in quantity demanded because of the output effect of the price change *and* its substitution effect. The relative ease with which this input is substituted for others will depend upon the elasticity of substitution. So long as the elasticity of substitution is less than product-demand elasticity, the elasticity of derived demand is simply increased by the fact that this input can be substituted for others and others for it. Given the inequality, the greater the elasticity of substitution, the larger the derived-demand elasticity.[5]

---

[5] If the elasticity of substitution is *greater* than the product-demand elasticity, the third determinant ("the importance of being unimportant") operates perversely. If the

THE SUPPLY OF FACTOR SERVICES FROM THE
VIEWPOINT OF THE FIRM

It was noted in Chapter 4 that the demand for the output of the individual firm is, in all cases except that of monopoly, a distortion of the market demand curve—the degree of distortion depending upon the form of market organization characterizing the industry. Thus, under pure competition the demand for the output of the individual firm may be represented as a horizontal line, despite the fact that the market demand curve is downward sloping.

An analogous situation exists in the relationship of the supply of factor services to the individual firm relative to the supply curve in the market for factor services. If a group of firms are purely competitive in purchasing, the supply of factor services appears to the firm as a horizontal line, since the firm cannot affect input prices by its purchases—even though the market supply of the input may be upward (or downward) sloping. If there is only one buyer, no such distortion exists. In between lies a range of factor-service market positions, corresponding to that between monopoly and pure competition in selling, and characterized by lesser or greater differences between the elasticity of supply of input to the firm and the elasticity of supply in the input market (at a given input price).

Monopsony

One factor-service market situation is that of monopsony—defined as the case in which there is only one buyer in the market for factor services. As in the case of its counterpart, monopoly, this situation serves mainly to mark the end of a logical continuum but is approximated in certain local markets for factor services (for example, in the local labor market in a village in which there is only one employer).

In the case of monopsony the market supply of factor services is the firm's supply of factor services and no distortion need exist. If the market supply is upward sloping, the supply of factor services to the firm will also, of course, be upward sloping. This gives rise to a distinction between *marginal factor cost* and *average factor cost* corresponding to the distinction, for a monopolist, between average revenue and marginal revenue. The monopsonist, being the only buyer, will offer a price no higher than that necessary to secure the quantity of input he desires. If he wishes to secure a

---

elasticity of substitution and the elasticity of product demand are equal, the fourth determinant is irrelevant. See Joan Robinson, *The Economics of Imperfect Competition* (London: Collier-Macmillan, Ltd., 1933), pp. 258–62.

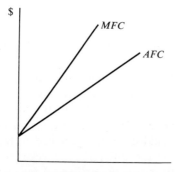

FIGURE 8.8

larger quantity of input, rather than this quantity, he must offer a higher price rather than the original input price. For this reason, the monopsonist's marginal factor cost will exceed the average factor cost or supply curve. This relationship is illustrated in Figure 8.8, *MFC* being marginal to *AFC*.

Assuming the monopsonist to be purely competitive in *selling*, his equilibrium in terms of input can be portrayed by Figure 8.9. The firm in this situation would operate at the input of *a* at which marginal factor cost equals the value of the marginal product, and it would pay the *average* factor cost *OL* for an input of *OQ*. If the monopsonist were *not* purely competitive in selling his product, *VMP* in Figure 8.9 would be replaced by *MVP*, after which the analysis would proceed as before.

The concept of rent, although originally applied to the return of the services of land, may be applicable to the return to the services of any factor of production. Rent may be defined as the difference between what is *paid* to owners of factor services and what the owners would have to

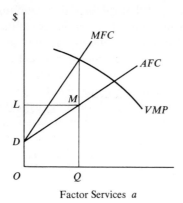

FIGURE 8.9

receive in order for those services to be committed to the particular use under consideration. Oddly enough, it is necessary to pay rent (so long as one price is paid for all the factor services purchased) but not necessary to receive it.

Thus the monopsonist in Figure 8.9 must pay a price of OL if he wishes to secure OQ of input. The *marginal* unit of input (the OQth unit) receives no rent. But all units other than the marginal unit receive rent, since there are differences between the price paid for them (OL) and the prices at which they would have been devoted to this particular use. Rent is sometimes defined as the difference between *price* and *transfer* price. "Price," in this context, means the price paid for factor services. "Transfer price" is the price at which a given unit of input would have transferred into this particular use. The AFC curve of Figure 8.9 shows for any particular input the transfer price, or the price this particular unit of input must receive if it is to be devoted to this particular use. Thus the rent received by any particular unit of input is the difference between AFC and OL.

Consequently, the rent paid by the monopsonist, in toto, is the triangle DLM in Figure 8.9. Just as consumer's surplus may be represented as the area underneath the demand curve, above the price, rent may be represented as the area underneath the input price above the supply curve of the factor services to the firm.

Oligopsony

Oligopsony is a situation in which the firm knows that changes in the price it pays for input will result in changes in the input prices paid by other firms, and vice versa. As in all input-market situations other than monopsony, the price elasticity of input supply to the firm can be expected, in general, to be greater than that of the market supply of factor services. Typically it can be expected that the high degree of input-price interdependence is due to there being only a few purchasers of the input in the market.

As in the case of oligopoly, oligopsony may take many forms. And, just as in oligopoly, there is a strong incentive to cartelize so that oligopsony becomes, for most purposes, monopsony. Tacit or overt collusion is likely to occur. If it does not, it is quite possible that the AFC curve for a particular oligopsonist will have in it a "kink" (analogous to the "kinked" demand case in oligopoly), reflecting a conviction or belief that other firms would match any increase in input price made by a given oligopsonist but would not match any decrease in input price. The MFC curve for a particular oligopsonist would be characterized in this case by a "gap" or discontinuity (corresponding to the marginal-revenue "gap" in the "kinked" oligopoly demand case).

Assuming the oligopsonist to be purely competitive in selling, the

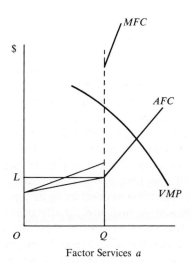

Factor Services *a*

FIGURE 8.10

"kinked" oligopsony case may be illustrated as shown in Figure 8.10. This analysis may be applied to local market situations in which, for example, employers attempt to pay no more than the "prevailing local wage rate," believing that any increase in the wage rate that one firm might offer would be quickly matched by the other firms but that a decrease would not. *VMP* in this case could be anywhere within the "gap" without affecting the quantity of input purchased, and the "prevailing local wage rate" would tend to be quite "sticky." Shifts of the *VMP* curve within the "gap" (resulting, for example, from changes in product price) would not occasion changes in input price or in the quantity of input purchased.

As in the case of monopsony, rent may accrue to the owners of factor services. From the standpoint of the individual *firm*, however, rent is the difference between the price *paid by this firm* and the input price necessary to cause the factor services to be devoted to *this* firm rather than others. Rent from the standpoint of the group of firms as a whole (which in this analysis may be called the industry) will be larger than rent from the standpoint of the individual firm. For any given quantity of input, transfer price to the industry can be expected to be less than transfer price to the individual firm. Transfer price to the industry reflects alternative opportunities outside this industry. Transfer price to the individual firm reflects alternative opportunities outside this firm. Thus rent will differ in magnitude from the standpoint of the firm and the standpoint of the industry of which the firm is a part. Rent from the standpoint of the *economy* as a whole would be of yet a different magnitude. The differing elasticities of supply to the economy, to the industry, and to the firm reflect these differences in rent.

Price Discrimination in Buying

The firm cannot be expected always to view with equanimity the fact that it is paying rent—for this means paying to the owners of some factor services a higher price than that at which the owners would be willing to devote these services to this particular firm. Given that the firm can separate its suppliers into different groups having different elasticities of supply to the firm (and keep them separate), and given that the marginal-value product for any quantity of input is not affected by the allocation of purchases from the different groups of suppliers, the firm can reduce the rent it pays by engaging in price discrimination in purchasing its input. If, for example, the labor services of men and women are equally productive in a particular process but the elasticities of supply of these services to the firm are not the same, the firm may reduce the rent it pays by paying different prices for the services purchased from the two groups of suppliers.

In Figure 8.11, AFC_t represents the total supply of factor services to the firm and is the horizontal summation of AFC_1 and AFC_2. Similarly, MFC_t is the horizontal summation of MFC_1 and MFC_2. The purchase of *any* quantity of input would be so distributed between the two groups of suppliers that the marginal factor cost would be the same in each of the input markets (input markets 1 and 2 in Figure 8.11). Assuming pure competition in *selling the product*, the equilibrium input OQ_t would be so distributed (OQ_1 in market 1 and OQ_2 in market 2) that $MFC_1 = MFC_2 = MFC_t = VMP$.

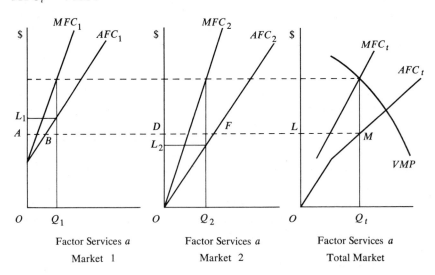

FIGURE 8.11

If the firm were *not* engaging in price discrimination in purchasing its input, it would pay OL—purchasing AB of input from market 1 and DF of input from market 2. This would mean that the marginal factor cost of some of the units purchased from market 2 is greater than their value of the marginal product, and that there remain units *not* purchased in market 1 of which it is true that marginal factor cost is less than the value of the marginal product. By curtailing the quantity of input purchased from the market with the less elastic supply (market 2) and increasing the quantity of input purchased from the market with the more elastic supply (market 1), the firm can increase its profitability. This increase in profitability must be equivalent to some decrease in the average input price paid for OQ_t. Since rent is the area below input price above AFC_t, a decrease in the average price paid for OQ_t would decrease rent.

As a matter of fact (or logic), if the firm were able to engage in *perfect* price discrimination it would pay *no* rent. Under perfect price discrimination the firm would pay a different price for *each unit* of input and would pay in total only the area underneath the AFC_t or supply curve for the quantity of input purchased.

THE MARKET SUPPLY OF FACTOR SERVICES

For cases in which the input of one industry consists of the output of another, the explanation previously given of the industry or market supply curve is fairly adequate. Thus, for example, in a competitive industry the short-run market supply curve is derived by horizontal summation of firms' marginal cost curves (above minimum average variable costs). If the output of this industry constitutes the input of a second industry, we have already indicated (in deriving the first industry's supply curve) the conditions under which input will be offered to the second industry. The problem is more complex than this may suggest, in the case of capital goods, for the services purchased may be yielded to the firms over a considerable period of time. Nonetheless, the previously derived rationale for the supply curve is basically sound in this case, in which the input of one industry consists of the output of another.

If the input in question, however, is not itself the result of production (in the normal economic sense), we have provided no explanation thus far of the conditions under which it will be offered to the industry. The services of land and of labor fall into this category of what may be termed *primary* factor services, to distinguish them from secondary factor services (or factor services that are the result of previous production).

It is relatively easy to provide an explanation of the supply of primary factor services to a particular industry or market if this market is but one of

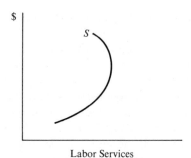

Labor Services

FIGURE 8.12

a number of related markets in which these factor services are sold. In this situation it would be necessary, in order to increase the quantity supplied to any particular market, to bid these inputs away from the alternative markets in which they would otherwise be sold (assuming full employment). Thus the quantity of the services of land or labor devoted to any particular industry could be expected to be greater at high input prices than at lower input prices, yielding an upward-sloping supply curve. As the quantity supplied to this particular industry increased (assuming full employment), the supply to other industries would decrease, increasing the input price paid in those industries and raising the opportunity cost of further transfers to the particular industry initiating the transfer.

In a market that is relatively isolated from others, or in a period of time too short for transfers between input markets to be effectuated, the supply of primary factor services may be vertical or even—in the case of labor services—backward bending. In a short period of time transfer of land from one use to another may not be feasible, so that the same quantity of land service is supplied at every input price. The *total* supply of land services *to the economy* is of this nature at any time. In a relatively isolated labor market there may well be some critical wage rate above which the owners of labor services would offer on the market a *smaller* quantity—preferring at the higher wage rate to work fewer hours and have more leisure. Such a backward-bending supply curve is depicted in Figure 8.12.

THE CONCEPT OF GENERAL EQUILIBRIUM

A change in the price of any consumer good changes the demand for other consumer goods, since the demand for any good is affected by changes in the prices of other goods. Further, a change in the price of any good may change the price paid for inputs used in producing that good, which in turn may affect the prices paid for inputs used in the production of other goods, cause a redistribution of incomes earned by owners of factor services, and occasion changes in the prices of other consumer goods—both because the cost of producing those goods has been altered by changes in input prices and because the redistribution of income has altered the demands for various consumer goods. Posing a change in an input price would lead to a similar chain of alterations in other input prices, in consumer goods prices, in supply and demand schedules, and in the distribution of income.

Thus the economy is characterized by many types of interdependence. Consumer goods prices are interdependent through the interrelatedness of consumer goods markets. Consumer goods prices are also interdependent with input prices because of the interrelatedness of the two types of prices in production. Input prices themselves are interdependent, owing to the interrelatedness of input markets. Thus, a change in any price can cause widespread ramifications throughout the economic system, because all input and consumer goods markets are conceptually interrelated, laterally (between markets of the same type) and vertically (between input markets and consumer goods markets). Because changes in quantity affect price, all quantities are interrelated.

The interdependence of magnitudes in the economic system raises the question of whether or not the many relationships between these magnitudes can be consistent. Is there conceptually a set of prices and quantities that could satisfy all the relationships involved? Can there be, in other words, a *general equilibrium* of the entire economy? The question is a difficult one, and we shall attempt only a conditional answer for a vastly simplified model of the economy.[6]

Let us assume a simple economy in which there are n individuals, each of whom can be represented by the subscript i, so that i takes the values $1, 2, \ldots, n$. Let there also be m goods, each of which can be represented by the subscript j, so that this subscript takes the values $1, 2, \ldots, m$. Let $\overline{X}_{ji}$ be the initial holding of good j possessed by individual i, so that the individual's total initial holdings may be represented as $\overline{X}_{1i}, \overline{X}_{2i}, \ldots, \overline{X}_{mi}$.

Typically the quantity of a particular good that the individual has ($\overline{X}_{ji}$) is not the quantity he would like to have, so that if we represent the latter by X_{ji}, our individual is going to have to trade with others if his consumption plan is to be realized. Only *relative* prices can be determined by our model, so let the prices of all other goods be expressed in terms of the mth good, so that $p_m = 1$. If we then regard the individual's holdings as being his real income for this period, we can express the monetary value of his income (before exchange takes place) as

$$M = p_1\overline{X}_{1i} + p_2\overline{X}_{2i} + \cdots + \overline{X}_{mi}$$

---

[6]The exposition that follows is patterned after that of Ferguson [C. E. Ferguson, *Microeconomic Theory* (Homewood, Ill.: Richard D. Irwin, Inc., 1966), pp. 354–62].

or

$$(1) \qquad M = \sum_{j=1}^{m} p_j \overline{X}_{ji}.$$

If our individual now, with knowledge of the relative prices, allocates all of his income so as to get the quantities he desires of each good, then

$$M = p_1 X_{1i} + p_2 X_{2i} + \cdots + X_{mi}$$

or

$$(2) \qquad M = \sum_{j=1}^{m} p_j X_{ji}.$$

Thus

$$(3) \qquad \sum_{j=1}^{m} p_j (X_{ji} - \overline{X}_{ji}) = 0.$$

Our individual must, of course, act in accordance with the principle of rational consumer's expenditure developed in Chapter 2. He must so allocate his income that the ratio of the marginal utility of any one good to its price equals the ratio of the marginal utility of any other good to that good's price. Since this must be true of all individuals in the economy, and since $p_m = 1$, we may describe the *exchange equilibrium* for the economy by the following set of equations (letting *marginal* utility be represented by U):

$$(4) \qquad \begin{aligned} \frac{U_{ji}}{p_j} &= U_{mi} && \begin{array}{l} (j = 1, 2, \ldots, m - 1), \\ (i = 1, 2, \ldots, n), \end{array} \\[2ex] \sum_{j=1}^{m} p_j (X_{ji} - \overline{X}_{ji}) &= 0 && (i = 1, 2, \ldots, n). \end{aligned}$$

Let there be q business firms in our economy, each of which is purely competitive and can be represented by the subscript s, so that s takes the values $1, 2, \ldots, q$. Each firm converts inputs of factor services into outputs of commodities and services. If we let the x symbols represent *both inputs and outputs* (inputs as negative quantities and outputs as positive quantities), we can then represent the *transformation function* for firm s as

$$(5) \qquad f_s(X_{1s}, X_{2s}, \ldots, X_{ms}) = 0.$$

Underlying the transformation function is the production function for each good, and each firm must attempt to maximize its profits. This requires, for the production side of the economy, satisfaction of the following conditions:

(6)
$$\frac{f'_{js}}{p_j} = f'_{ms} \qquad \begin{array}{l} (j = 1, 2, \ldots, m - 1), \\ (s = 1, 2, \ldots, q), \end{array}$$

$$f_s(X_{1s}, X_{2s}, \ldots, X_{ms}) = 0 \qquad (s = 1, 2, \ldots, q).$$

Since the symbols X represent inputs and outputs, the meaning of the first of the two conditions in (6) requires elaboration. If both j and m are inputs, f'_{js} represents the marginal product of j, and f'_{ms} represents the marginal product of m. Since $p_m = 1$, the condition then becomes the familiar one that the ratio of the marginal product of one input to the price of that input must equal the ratio of the marginal product of any other input to its price.

If both j and m are outputs, the condition is not so readily grasped. If the firm is producing more than one good, it must so allocate its inputs to the production of these various goods that producing more of one of them, and less of another, could not increase the firm's profits. The ratio f'_{js}/f'_{ms} is called the *marginal rate of transformation* and shows the amount by which the output of good m could be increased by using inputs made available by reducing the output of good j by one unit. Clearly, in equilibrium no further advantage is to be gained by such transfers of inputs within the firm. If reducing production of good j by one unit makes possible an increase of two units in the output of m, the marginal cost of j must be twice that of m (since the total costs of the firm are unaffected by the transfer of inputs). This ratio of marginal costs (2:1) is the same ratio as the marginal rate of transformation. If, therefore, the firm cannot gain by the transfer of inputs from production of good j to good m, the *price* of j must be twice that of m. Thus the first of the two conditions of (6) is that

(7)
$$\frac{f'_{js}}{f'_{ms}} = \frac{MC_{js}}{MC_{ms}} = \frac{p_j}{p_m} = p_j \qquad (\text{since } p_m = 1).$$

Finally, if j is an output and m is an input, rearrangement of the first condition of (6) yields (since $p_m = 1$)

(8)
$$p_m = p_j \frac{f'_{ms}}{f'_{js}}.$$

The ratio f'_{ms}/f'_{js} is the marginal product of input m in producing j alone. Thus in this form the condition becomes the familiar one that the price of the input must equal the value of the marginal product.

Equations (4) and (6) impose certain equilibrium conditions on, respectively, the individuals and the business firms that comprise our simple economy. For general equilibrium, however, it must also be true, for the prices established in all markets, that the quantities demanded and supplied are equal for each input and output. In other words, the net amount of j supplied (if positive) or demanded (if negative) by business firms must equal the net amount of j demanded (if positive) or supplied (if negative) by individuals. Thus

$$(9) \qquad \sum_{s=1}^{q} x_{js} = \sum_{i=1}^{n} (X_{ji} - \overline{X}_{ji}) \qquad (j = 1, 2, \ldots, m - 1).$$

If the conditions specified by (4), (6), and (9) are met, a general equilibrium *may* exist. Comparison of the number of variables and equations in the system would reveal that there are an equal number of each, but this doesn't guarantee the existence of a general equilibrium.[7]

Our purposes will have been served if the reader's wrestling with the system presented has reinforced his appreciation of the interrelatedness of economic activity. For fuller treatment of the specific topic of general equilibrium the reader is directed to the references at the end of the chapter.

A MATHEMATICAL NOTE ON DERIVED-DEMAND ELASTICITY

Following Marshall's mathematical note XV[8] in which factor services are combined in fixed proportions to produce a product (one knife handle and one blade to produce one knife), let

q = output of knives,
$F(q)$ = demand for knives,
$\phi_2(q)$ = supply of blades,
m = price elasticity of the demand for handles.

---

[7] The variables are: the mn quantities demanded of the m goods by the n individuals; the mq quantities supplied of the m goods by the q firms; and the $m - 1$ prices. The variables thus total $mn + mq + (m - 1)$. The set of equations (4) yields $n(m - 1) + n$ equations; the set of equations (6) yields $q(m - 1) + q$ equations; and (9) yields $m - 1$. The equations thus also total $mn + mq + (m - 1)$.

[8] Marshall, *Principles of Economics*, pp. 701–702.

    Then, since the price that the firm is willing to pay for handles equals
the price it receives for knives minus the price it must pay for blades,

(1) $f_1(q) = F(q) - \phi_2(q) =$ demand for handles.

The price elasticity of demand for handles is thus

$$m = -\frac{f_1(q)}{q}\frac{1}{f_1'(q)} = -\left[\frac{qf_1'(q)}{f_1(q)}\right]^{-1}.$$

Substituting from (1),

$$m = -\left[\frac{qF'(q) - q\phi_2'(q)}{f_1(q)}\right]^{-1}.$$

Multiplying the first expression by $F(q)/F(q)$,

$$m = -\left[\frac{qF'(q)}{F(q)}\cdot\frac{F(q)}{f_1(q)} - \frac{q\phi_2'(q)}{f_1(q)}\right]^{-1}.$$

Multiplying the second expression by ϕ_2/ϕ_2,

$$m = -\left[\frac{qF'(q)}{F(q)}\cdot\frac{F(q)}{f_1(q)} - \frac{q\phi_2'(q)}{\phi_2(q)}\cdot\frac{\phi_2(q)}{f_1(q)}\right]^{-1},$$

(2) $$m = \frac{1}{-\dfrac{qF'(q)}{F(q)}\cdot\dfrac{F(q)}{f_1(q)} + \dfrac{q\phi_2'(q)}{\phi_2(q)}\cdot\dfrac{\phi_2(q)}{f_1(q)}}.$$

Verbalizing some of the component expressions of (2),

$$-\frac{qF'(q)}{F(q)} = \begin{array}{l}\text{inverse of price elasticity of demand for knives}\\\text{(necessarily positive),}\end{array}$$

$$\frac{F(q)}{f_1(q)} = \text{ratio of price of knives to the price of handles,}$$

$$\frac{q\phi_2'(q)}{\phi_2(q)} = \text{inverse of price elasticity of supply of blades.}$$

Thus:

1. The larger the price elasticity of demand for knives, the greater the elasticity of derived demand for handles (m).

2. The larger the ratio of the price paid for handles to the price of knives, the greater the elasticity of derived demand for handles (m).

3. The larger the elasticity of supply of blades, the greater the elasticity of derived demand for handles (m).

SUMMARY AND CONCLUSIONS

This chapter concludes Part I of the book. Part I, if successful, has given the reader a basic understanding of the functioning of the economic system. To provide such an understanding is the book's primary goal.

Part II is devoted to applications of price theory in various areas of business administration—yet it would be a mistake to think of this book as being neatly divided into a "theoretical" component (Part I) and an "applications" component (Part II). In a sense, the most important application that will be made is largely complete at this point. If successful, Part I has provided the reader a mental framework or screen through which he views a large part of economic reality, and by means of which he detects—or thinks he detects— order. This benign form of "brainwashing" is the most important application of price theory. To provide a way of, and tools for, thinking about a large part of economic reality is also an application that must come before other, more narrow, applications.

Furthermore, the more specific applications of Part II will require some further development of certain portions of price theory. In Part I we considered only those parts of price theory deemed necessary to the goals of Part I, and the depth of treatment followed the same criterion. In the more specific applications of Part II we will need to consider in greater depth some aspects of price theory already considered in Part I, and to build new tools of greater specificity from those we have already developed. Thus, for example, for some applications in transportation we shall need a deeper understanding of the theory of price discrimination, and for some in production management we shall have to modify the production theory developed in Part I.

SELECTED REFERENCES

DUE, JOHN F., and ROBERT W. CLOWER, *Intermediate Economic Analysis*, 4th ed. (Homewood, Ill.: Richard D. Irwin, Inc., 1961), chaps 13–16, 20.

FERGUSON, C. E., *Microeconomic Theory* (Homewood, Ill.: Richard D. Irwin, Inc., 1966), chap. 15.

KUENNE, R. E., *The Theory of General Economic Equilibrium* (Princeton, N.J.: Princeton University Press, 1963).

LEFTWICH, RICHARD H., *The Price System and Resource Allocation*, 3rd ed. (New York: Holt, Rinehart and Winston, Inc., 1966), chaps. 13–14.

ROBINSON, JOAN, *The Economics of Imperfect Competition* (London: Collier-Macmillan, Ltd., 1933), chaps. 18, 21, 22.

WALRAS, L., *Elements of Pure Economics*, trans. W. Jaffe (Homewood, Ill.: Richard D. Irwin, Inc., 1954).

APPLICATIONS IN BUSINESS ADMINISTRATION

the pricing of
motor-carrier services

INTRODUCTION

Motor trucking is something of a paradox. Much of it is characterized by a form of pricing seemingly at variance with the industry's economic characteristics. We can use the tools and concepts of Part I to provide *an* explanation of this form of pricing. The "intellectual spectacles" of Part I can also yield us *a* resolution of the paradox and *a* frame of reference in which to view governmental policy. Thus, this aspect of transportation is particularly fertile ground for the application of economic theory.

The first section of the chapter discusses briefly the economic characteristics of motor trucking. The second section reviews the theory of price discrimination and develops it somewhat further than Part I did. One of the major purposes of this section is to emphasize the economic prerequisites that permit this form of pricing. Moreover, we shall investigate whether these economic prerequisites or conditions are compatible with the natural economic characteristics of motor trucking. If not, we shall examine other factors that might explain the existence of price discrimination in this industry. We shall look particularly, in the third and fourth sections of the chapter, at the role of governmental regulation of motor trucking—therein may lie the solution to our puzzle.

A caveat: In examining government policy from the vantage point of economic theory we shall discern order and a rationale for governmental action vis-à-vis motor carriers. We may well dislike what we see—especially given the normative connotations often attached to many of the economic terms used. But our analysis will not be sufficiently comprehensive for over-all evaluations of governmental policy in this area. Our basic task is the far less ambitious one of understanding how price discrimination can characterize the pricing practices of what would be (in the absence of governmental action) a highly competitive industry.

THE ECONOMIC CHARACTERISTICS OF MOTOR TRUCKING

No one actually knows how many firms are engaged in motor trucking, but it is certain that their number is very great. In 1963 the "motor carriers of property" (in contradistinction to passenger carriers) in interstate commerce who were subject to economic regulation by the Interstate Commerce Commission totaled 15,618 firms.[1] The number of interstate (for-hire) motor carriers of property who were not regulated by the I.C.C. was estimated in 1954 to be 27,000.[2] The number of private carriers (firms transporting their own products) was estimated for the same year to be 119,197.[3] The number of *intrastate* for-hire carriers is unknown, but in California alone, in 1964, there were 15,895 motor carriers of property subject to regulation by the Public Utilities Commission of California.[4]

The size of the typical firm in motor trucking is small. Of the 15,618 firms regulated by the I.C.C. in 1963 the *largest* carriers were the Class I and Class II carriers (yearly gross revenues in excess of $200,000).[5] Yet these carriers numbered only 3708.[6] The average carrier in this group of carriers in 1962 operated 59 trucks ("power units"), of which approximately 24 were leased.

In contrast to the size of the firm, the industry is a large one, the revenues of those carriers subject to the economic regulation of the I.C.C.

---

[1] American Trucking Associations, *American Trucking Trends, 1964* (Washington, D.C.: American Trucking Associations, 1964), p. 13.

[2] Charles A. Taff, *Commercial Motor Transportation*, rev. ed. (Homewood, Ill.: Richard D. Irwin, Inc., 1956), p. 199.

[3] *Ibid.*, p. 120.

[4] Public Utilities Commission of California, *Report on Operations of Property, Year 1964*, cited in D. Phillip Locklin, *Economics of Transportation*, 6th ed. (Homewood, Ill.: Richard D. Irwin, Inc., 1966), p. 643.

[5] American Trucking Associations, *loc. cit.*

[6] *Ibid.*, p. 16.

alone totaling \$8.6 billion in 1963.[7] The growth of the industry has been rapid. The revenues of regulated carriers in 1939 were less than a billion dollars and less than \$4 billion in 1950.[8] Intercity ton miles of all motor carriers increased from 53 billion in 1939 to almost 350 billion in 1963.[9]

Firms in the industry are possessed of great natural ability to follow profit opportunities. The entire investment of a small carrier can be in motor trucks, and even for the largest carriers by far the greatest share of investment is in motor trucks. The location of the relatively minor share of investment that takes the form of "fixed plant" does not seriously restrict the natural ability of the firm to sell its services in widely separated markets. Furthermore, not only can the major portion of the firm's investment be easily transferred from place to place, but also a transfer of the entire investment can be accomplished at relatively small cost.

Determining whether or not there are significant natural economies of size in motor trucking is made more difficult by the fact of government regulation: the growth of the firm is a function, to a large extent, of what the firm is permitted to do. Thus one firm may be larger than another simply because it is permitted to transport more commodities for further distances, over more direct routes, with greater return-haul authority, with less interference from competitors, and so on. Despite this difficulty, most studies agree that there are few, if any, natural economies of size in motor trucking.[10]

The economic characteristics discussed above make it clear that there are no significant natural barriers to entry in motor trucking. A new firm (in the absence of governmental restriction) could enter the industry by having a sufficient sum for the down payment on one truck, provided the firm could meet any requirements that might apply concerning safety or financial responsibility.

The small size of the typical firm, the large number of firms, the natural mobility, and the absence of natural barriers to entry indicate that in the absence of regulation the motor trucking industry would be about as good an example of a purely competitive industry as we could expect to find. Justifiably or not, the effect of governmental regulation is to contravene, in a large portion of the industry, the natural economic characteristics that

---

[7] *Ibid.*, p. 6. This exceeds by \$67 million the gross operating income of all railroads for this year, but it was estimated to constitute only one third of the total value of all motor-carrier services produced in 1963.

[8] *Ibid.*, p. 9.

[9] *Ibid.*, p. 7.

[10] See, for example, Merrill J. Roberts, "Some Aspects of Motor Carrier Costs: Firm Size, Efficiency, and Financial Health," *Land Economics*, vol. XXXII (Aug. 1956), pp. 236–37. See also U.S., Congress, Senate, Select Committee on Small Business, *Trucking Mergers and Concentration*, Hearings, 85th Cong., 1st Sess. (Washington, D.C.: U.S.G.P.O., 1957), pp. 305–15.

would shape the industry in this way. The large number of firms is offset by the grouping of many of them into price-fixing cartels, and the small size of the typical firm and the absence of significant economies of size are offset by artificial barriers that make entry difficult. Mobility is also restricted by geographical restrictions upon the firm's operations, and the range of commodities it may transport is usually limited.

The for-hire motor carriers that are not subject directly to the control of the I.C.C. (the exempt carriers) remain highly competitive, but they are confined primarily to the transportation of agricultural products. The activities of private carriers are also circumscribed to limit the degree to which they may be substituted for regulated carriers. The effect of regulation is thus to convert what would otherwise be a highly competitive industry into one in a major portion of which significant monopolistic elements exist.

A significant element of monopoly is one of the prerequisites for price discrimination in an industry.

THE THEORY OF PRODUCT RATE DISCRIMINATION

The number of forms price discrimination may take in the sale of transport services is limited only by the ingenuity of the seller in finding profitable means of separating his customers into different groups, and by governmental action to proscribe the use of such means. The most important method of separating customers, however, is on the basis of the product to be transported, and regulatory authorities generally encourage this method. Since the price of transport services is generally referred to as the "rate," the most important form of price discrimination in transportation may be termed "product rate discrimination."

Prerequisites of Product Rate Discrimination

Any form of price discrimination requires that it be both possible and profitable for the seller to separate his customers into different groups. The fact that different groups of customers wish different products transported provides an easily available method of separating the market for transport services. Even if one individual wishes more than one product transported, he can be treated as a participant in separate markets. Thus leakage between markets is minimal. The purchasers of transport services for one product cannot readily resell these services in a higher-priced market, nor can they readily acquire the service in a market where a different product is transported at a lower rate. Hence it is quite possible to separate the purchasers of transport services on the basis of the products they wish transported.

Assuming the seller's costs to be unaffected by the allocation of transport services among markets, he would find it profitable to charge different rates for transporting different products only if the elasticities of demand for his services were also different in these product-delineated markets. Since the seller will so allocate his output as to equalize the marginal revenue received from each market, and since $MR = AR\,(1 - 1/\eta)$, the prices or rates charged in the various markets will differ only if the elasticities of demand for his services also differ in those markets. Solving for η, it would only be profitable to engage in product rate discrimination if the ratio $AR/(AR - MR)$ were different in the different markets for transport services. Since in equilibrium marginal revenue is not only equal in each market but also equal to marginal costs, product rate discrimination can occur only if the ratio $(AR - MC)/AR$, or the *degree of monopoly*,[11] is different in the various markets.

This final way of formulating the condition permits us to drop the assumption that the seller's costs are unaffected by the allocation among markets of the services he sells. Rate differentials based entirely upon differences in the marginal costs of transporting different products would not constitute product rate discrimination. By the same token, rate uniformity where such differences in marginal costs exist *would* be an instance of product rate discrimination. Thus a necessary condition of product rate discrimination is that the firm possess different degrees of monopoly power in the various markets in which it sells its services. This is a prerequisite regardless of whether the marginal cost of serving those markets is the same.

A corollary of the possession of a significant degree of monopoly in any market is a limitation of the number of *competitive* sellers with which one shares that market. In general, an increase in the number of competitive sellers in a market will increase the elasticity of demand for the output of the individual seller, thus decreasing the degree of monopoly he possesses. And to the extent that the rate that can be received exceeds the marginal cost of serving that market, it will be tempting to prospective sellers. Thus entry must be restricted if product rate discrimination is to be a significant characteristic of the rate structure. Finally, collusion among sellers (which can only work if entry is restricted) has much the same effect as reduction in their numbers. *As a group* the sellers in any market possess a higher degree of monopoly than if they compete individually. The demand for the output of the firms, as a group, has a lower elasticity. Thus product rate discrimination is increased, in likelihood and extent, by collusion among sellers.

The necessary conditions for product rate discrimination are thus an ability to separate customers into different markets on the basis of the products they wish transported and the possession in those markets of

---

[11]Abba P. Lerner, "The Concept of Monopoly and the Measurement of Monopoly Power," *Review of Economic Studies*, vol. I (June 1934), pp. 157–75.

differential degrees of monopoly power.[12] Product rate discrimination can be expected to be a more important characteristic of the rate structure if entry is restricted and if there is collusion among sellers of transport services.

A Simple Model of Product Rate Discrimination

The theoretical explanation of product rate discrimination can perhaps be best developed through treatment of several different but related "situations." Elements from each of these logical situations can then be grouped together to form a heuristic device or simple model of product rate discrimination.

As the initial step, consider the case of a seller with a significant degree of monopoly power, the purpose of the analysis being to determine his reaction to changes in the price elasticity of the demand for his output. Let it also be assumed that this seller is unrestricted in his ability to choose a price and output consistent with his revenue and cost conditions and that he is not colluding with any other seller.

Figure 9.1 depicts the reaction of the seller to an increase in the elasticity of the demand for his output. Initially he chooses an output q_1 and a price of p_1. Since the price elasticity of demand is the multiple of the ratio of the coordinates of point x and the inverse of the slope, we can unambiguously represent an increase in demand elasticity at point x by decreasing the slope of the demand curve as it passes through this point. In general, the reaction of the seller to an increase in the elasticity of demand for his output will be, as shown in Figure 9.1, an increase in output and a reduction in price.

Similarly, in general the reaction of a seller to a decrease in the elasticity of the demand for his output will be, as shown in Figure 9.2, an increase in price and a reduction in output. Thus, in general, *a seller will react to an increase in the elasticity of the demand for his output by lowering price and increasing output, and he will react to a decrease in this elasticity by raising his price and decreasing his output.*

As the second situation, assume that there are two different and unrelated sellers of the type assumed in the first situation, and that these sellers experience opposite changes in the price elasticities of demand for their respective outputs. On the basis of the first situation we can conclude that the seller who has experienced an increase in the elasticity of the demand for his output will react by lowering price and increasing output. Similarly, the seller who has experienced a decrease in the elasticity of the demand for

---

[12]It should be emphasized that these are the necessary and sufficient conditions (assuming profit maximization). Frequently discussions in the literature erroneously attribute to fixed costs (or "burden") a causal role in product rate discrimination (for example, Locklin, *Economics of Transportation*, pp. 135–36).

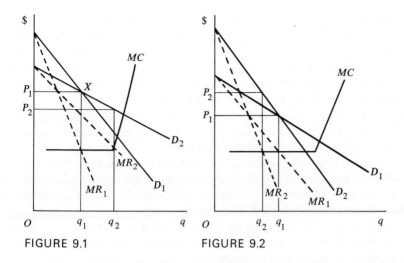

FIGURE 9.1   FIGURE 9.2

his output will react by raising price and decreasing output. Note that these profit-maximizing reactions are to be expected regardless of whether or not the two sellers sell the same product or service.

As the third situation, assume a single seller serving two markets, his costs being unaffected by the allocation of his output between markets. While he could be selling different products or services, it is perhaps easier at this point to envision him as selling a single product or service in two separate markets. The purpose of the analysis is to compare a policy of charging different prices in the two markets with a uniform price policy and the relationship of these prices to the uniform price. In Figure 9.3 the seller

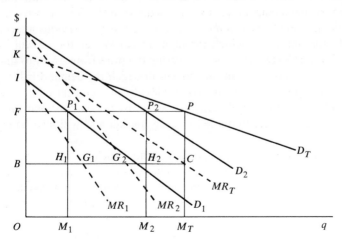

FIGURE 9.3

is pursuing a uniform price policy. D_T is the horizontal summation of D_1 and D_2, and MR_T may be constructed as marginal to D_T or as the horizontal summation of MR_1 and MR_2. M_TC is the *value* of the seller's marginal cost for the equilibrium output OM_T, and the price charged is M_TP. The marginal-cost function itself is not drawn, because doing so involves certain conceptual problems and, as we shall see, it is not necessary to do so. All we need to know is that the marginal cost of output OM_T is M_TC. If absence of this familiar function is disturbing, the reader may assume that BC is a segment of the firm's marginal-cost curve.

At the price $M_TP = M_2P_2 = M_1P_1$ the firm is selling OM_1 of its output in the first market and OM_2 of its output in the second market. At this price the price elasticity of demand in the first market OF/FI is greater than that of the total market OF/FK, and the price elasticity of demand of the second market OF/FL is less than that of the total market. As established in Chapter 4, the price elasticity of demand in the total market is a weighted average of those of the two separate markets. Consequently, as shown in Figure 9.3, the marginal revenue received in the first market is greater than the marginal cost of the output being sold, whereas marginal revenue in the second market is less than marginal cost.

In essence the seller in pursuing a single-price policy is being guided by the price elasticity of the total demand for his output. On this basis he has made the profit-maximizing decision with respect to price and output. In any instance, however, in which the respective elasticities of demand are not the same in both markets, it will be true that marginal revenue in the more elastic market will be greater than marginal cost, while marginal revenue in the less elastic market will be less than marginal cost.

Thus the effect is the same as though the seller had simultaneously experienced an increase and a decrease in demand elasticity in two previously isoelastic markets. *If he can do so* he will react as the previous analysis suggests. In the market in which the demand is more elastic he will increase output from BH_1 (OM_1) to BG_1, lowering the price from M_1P_1 to that price on D_1 directly above G_1. In the market in which the demand is less elastic he will reduce his output from BH_2 (OM_2) to BG_2 and raise his price from M_2P_2 to that price on D_2 directly above G_2. By these adjustments marginal revenues will have been equated in each market and will also be equal to marginal cost.

But how do we know, in a situation such as that portrayed by Figure 9.3, that *total* output has not changed and therefore that the magnitude of marginal cost has not changed as a result of the decision to adopt a differential pricing policy? In short, how do we know that the amount by which output was reduced in the second market (H_2G_2) is exactly the quantity (H_1G_1) by which output was increased in the first market? Our reason is that $BH_1 + BH_2 = BC$ *and* $BG_1 + BG_2 = BC$. Since both statements

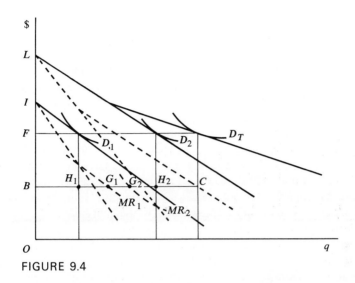

FIGURE 9.4

are true, H_2G_2 must equal H_1G_1. Thus the marginal-cost curve passing through C in Figure 9.3 could be horizontal, could be upward sloping, or could even be downward sloping (as long as it wasn't more steeply sloped than MR_T). The magnitude of the firm's marginal cost cannot change unless total output changes, and total output will be unaffected by a decision to pursue a differential price policy in cases in which the demand functions are linear.

While many of the relevant discussions in the literature on transportation implicitly or explicitly assume that total output is necessarily greater under price discrimination than it would be under a single-price policy, actually the condition under which this would be the case is quite precise. In Figure 9.4 the straight-line demand functions of Figure 9.3 have become construction lines tangent to three convex demand functions. The effect of convexity in the first or more elastic market is to move G_1 to the right. The effect of convexity in the less elastic market is to move G_2 to the left. Thus the amount by which output will be increased in the more elastic market (if the firm deserts the uniform price policy) has been increased, as has the amount by which output will be decreased in the less elastic market. Thus whether or not total output is affected by desertion of the uniform price policy depends upon the degree of convexity in moving from P_1 *down* D_1 relative to that in moving from P_2 *upward* on D_2. Thus, only if the more elastic demand D_1 is also more convex (downward) than is the less elastic demand D_2 (upward) will total output increase.[13]

---

[13] For a mathematical discussion of the point see Joan Robinson, *The Economics of Imperfect Competition* (London: Collier-Macmillan, Ltd., 1933), pp. 193–94 n.

If this condition is met, so that total output is increased by the decision to engage in price discrimination, a rising marginal-cost curve (upward sloping through point C in Figures 9.3 and 9.4) decreases the magnitude of the increase in output but cannot altogether prevent an increase in output. After all, only if some increase in output occurs can the marginal cost be greater. Similarly, a downward-sloping marginal-cost curve increases the magnitude of the increase in output but cannot, without the necessary convexities, occasion an increase in output.

Conceivably the marginal-cost curve can be so negatively sloped that the prices in both markets are lower under price discrimination than under a single-price policy. This result, sometimes advanced in transportation literature as general, can only occur if the demand function in the more elastic market is also more convex *and* if the marginal-cost function is sufficiently negatively sloped. While the marginal-cost functions of railroads are generally thought to be negatively sloped (over a large range of output), this is far from sufficient ground for a conclusion that price discrimination results in greater output and lower rates than would a uniform price policy.

Different Products, Different Costs, and Interrelatedness of Costs

The equilibrium condition for profit maximization is not altered if the price discriminator sells different products (or services) to his different customer groups. Profit is still maximized by setting prices in the several markets such that marginal cost and marginal revenue are equal in each market. If the marginal costs in the several markets are different but *independent*, the validity of the equilibrium condition is immediately apparent, for maximizing the profit in any one market cannot affect the profitability of any other. If, however, the marginal cost of one product depends not only upon the output of that product but also upon the output of the other products (that is, if the marginal costs are interrelated), the validity of the equilibrium condition may not be so obvious. The assumption of an initial position of disequilibrium and the describing of the equilibrating process temporally in terms of discrete changes (two time-honored pedagogical devices) may make it apparent that the rationale of price discrimination is not altered by its extension to the sale of different products (or services) even when the marginal costs of producing these products (or services) are interrelated.

Assume that two products, the marginal costs of which are interrelated, are being produced and that an additional dollar is spent in producing more of one product while, simultaneously, one dollar less is spent in the production of the other. If this should cause the revenue from the sale of the first product to rise by more than the fall in the revenue received from the sale of the second product, total profit would be increased. Total profit would be increased by *any* excess of the rise over the fall, for no *net* additional money has been spent by the firm. The transfer of production from one market to the other would thus continue until there was no further opportunity to increase the revenue received by the firm for the given expenditure.

When the rise in revenue in one market becomes equal to the fall in revenue in the other market, the additional revenue (yielded by the quantity that could be produced for one dollar) in each market is equal and the transfer between markets ceases. If then by incurring a *net additional* expense of one dollar the firm could still receive more than one dollar in revenue from producing more of either product, the dollar would be spent, output increased, and production again transferred between markets until the revenue rise in one market equalled the fall in the other. The process would continue until the incurring of a net additional dollar of expense in order to increase output would no longer yield more than one dollar in additional revenue, and the transferring of production between markets would no longer affect the total revenue received. At this point the marginal cost in each market would equal the marginal revenue in that market, the price in each market would be adjusted to the elasticity of demand in that market, and profit would be maximized. Thus the basic rationale of price discrimination is unaffected by the existence of more than one product, by differences in the marginal costs of producing different products, and by interrelatedness of marginal costs.

Determinants of the Elasticity of Demand for Motor Transport Services

The price elasticity of the demand for the output of any firm is determined, in part, by the actual and potential alternatives open to the customer. Given the economic characteristics of motor trucking, price discrimination could not be a continuing or pervasive characteristic of motor-carrier rate structures (in the absence of economic regulation) because the elasticity of the demand for the services of an individual firm would be extremely high in each of its markets. The degree of monopoly in any market would be very small. In still other terms, since the demand for transport is a derived demand, the first determinant of derived-demand elasticity (Chapter 8) would overshadow all other determinants, and the elasticity of the demand for the services of a particular firm would be very great in each of the markets it served.

To the extent that governmental regulation succeeds in controlling entry and in securing collusion in rate setting, however, demand elasticities other than that for the output of the individual firm become relevant and price discrimination becomes feasible. If firms serving the same markets are grouped, for rate-making purposes, and entry is restricted, the elasticity of the demand for their services *as a group* becomes relevant. This elasticity (Chapter 4) will, of course, be much smaller than that of the demands for their individual services, and (assuming no offsetting changes in the costs of the carriers) rates will be correspondingly increased. Further, the rates can be *differentially* increased in accordance with the differential effects of the other determinants of derived-demand elasticity in the various markets served by this group of carriers.

Thus, firms purchasing the services of this group of carriers will be confronted, in the markets for their own outputs, by differing demand elasticities. Other things being equal, firms possessing lower elasticities of demand for their products will, in turn, have lower elasticities of demand for the services of this group of carriers (Chapter 8). Similarly, the elasticity of the demand for the services of this group of carriers will be affected by the different supply elasticities of the other inputs used by the various customer firms (Chapter 8). Most widely recognized in transportation literature, however, is the influence of the third determinant of derived-demand elasticity—"the importance of being unimportant," or the ratio of transportation cost to the total cost of the product (Chapter 8). In transportation literature this determinant is usually called the "value-of-service" principle, although the term is sometimes broadened to include one or more of the other determinants of derived-demand elasticity.[14] In accordance with this "principle," more valuable commodities can be transported at higher rates "because" the value of the service of transportation to their owners is greater.

Thus the group of motor carriers can expect to meet the prerequisites of price discrimination so long as entry is restricted and pricing is collusive. The maintenance of cartel solidarity is never easy, however, and the individual firms are constantly tempted to cut rates (as such or by an equivalent change in their particular services) in view of the greater elasticity of the demand for their individual services. This is especially the case if control of entry is not complete. Restriction of entry and maintenance of sufficient cartel solidarity are the cornerstones of the economic regulation of motor trucking. That government has at least partially succeeded in its efforts despite the economic characteristics of motor trucking is quite remarkable, and these efforts deserve at least the scrutiny we shall give them in the ensuing sections.

THE CONTROL OF ENTRY INTO MOTOR TRUCKING

A Thumbnail Sketch of the Relevant History

The emergence of, and subsequent developments in, the economic regulation of motor carriers can be understood only in light of the historical

---

[14]Eleanor Heyman, "The Value of the Service: Its Various Meanings and Uses," *The Journal of Land and Public Utility Economics*, vol. IX (Aug. 1933), pp. 252–65.

relationship of motor carriers to the railroads. A key element in this relationship has been product rate discrimination.

At the time of the advent of the motor carriers the railroads were almost classic examples of product rate discriminators. Regulation had limited price discrimination based on the geographical location of customers but actively encouraged price discrimination based on the separation of customers by the products they wished transported. By the time the motor carriers had become an important mode, the primary goal of railroad regulation had become the strengthening of the financial position of rail transport,[15] and it was readily recognized that product rate discrimination (or "value-of-service rate making") contributed to this goal.

A second derivative goal of regulatory policy was the curtailment of "wasteful" (from the standpoint of the industry) competition.[16] Oligopolistic rivalry could be quite intense at times, posed a continual threat to the financial welfare of the railroads, and hampered the technical cooperation between carriers often necessary for through service (such as arrangements for interchange of equipment). Thus it was much better, from the viewpoint of the regulatory authorities, to cartelize this industry and help it to price collusively.

Efforts to maintain cartel solidarity, however, cannot be too rigid without being self-defeating. Cartel members must be free to follow the demand elasticity for their particular services where there is not a significant cross elasticity of demand relative to any other cartel member. But where there are such cross elasticities, the individual cartel member must *not* be free to follow indiscriminately the elasticity of demand for his particular output. Instead, all members must permit the pricing decision to be made on the lower elasticity of the demand for their services as a group. Regulation that is designed to maximize the financial welfare of the cartel members as a group must, therefore, be flexible if it is to succeed and must not be hampered by what appears, legally, to be inconsistency—or, in noneconomic terms, illogic.

Unfortunately (from the standpoint of regulatory authorities and the industry), no amount of success in cartelization can assure profitability or prevent society, in retrospect, from judging an investment as unwise. Inequitable as it may seem to him and his proponents, a monopolist is not assured of a profit. Of course, financial welfare has never been the sole goal of regulatory policy with respect to the railroads, and some of the other goals are diametrically opposed to this one. As the only mode in which the concept of common carrier has retained much of its original meaning, the railroad has often been forced to offer services at a loss and has often been limited

---

[15] Joseph B. Eastman, "Transportation by Rail and Otherwise," *The American Economic Review*, vol. XXII (March 1932), p. 254.

[16] G. Shorey Peterson, "Transport Coordination: Meaning and Purpose," *Journal of Political Economy*, vol. XXVIII (Dec. 1930), p. 671.

in its ability to exploit any monopolistic power it possessed. Nonetheless, regulation had not succeeded in securing for the railroads an "adequate" return on their investments at the advent of the motor carrier, though the return might well have been even smaller in its absence and might well have been more nearly adequate if the early growth of motor carriage had not coincided with the Great Depression.

As it was, the railroads, the regulatory authorities, and most transportation experts reacted with horror at the early growth of the motor carriers.[17] This horror spawned (or resuscitated from an earlier era of railroad-canal controversy) a number of arguments more notable for their longevity and continued currency today than for their internal logic. A major argument was that the goal of regulation must be the achievement of a "coordinated transportation system" in which each mode of transportation would occupy its "appropriate economic sphere." In some versions the argument was so thinly veiled that it was obvious that "appropriate" was a derivative of the anticipated effect upon railroad earnings.[18] Implicit in almost all versions was an assumption of knowledge of the differential impact of future technological changes upon the several modes. Thus spokesmen revised at almost every printing the mileage dimension of the "appropriate economic sphere" of motor trucking, the necessity for revising never seeming to shake their confidence in their ability to define such "appropriate economic spheres."

In still another version, "appropriate economic sphere" was defined in terms of relative costs. In this version the goal of regulation was essentially that of allocating traffic to the low-cost mode. Beyond the objection that costs are affected by technology, this argument suffered further difficulties arising from an implicit assumption of knowledge of the relevant costs, from a confusion of cost and price as an allocating mechanism, and from the fact that price is only one determinant of the desirability (to consumers) of the service rendered.

As we have seen (Chapters 5 and 6), there are a host of production and cost situations affecting the nature of the firm's cost functions and the firm's output decision. If a motor truck is partially loaded and committed for a trip, for example, the relevant marginal cost of an additional shipment is its user cost alone, since the firm is in, essentially, the market period. Despite the multiplicity of cost conditions and their specificity to particular conditions known only to the firm, it was assumed in this version of the "transportation coordination argument" that costs can simply be divided into those that vary with traffic volume and those that do not, and that

---

[17]See, for example, G. Lloyd Wilson, "Discussion," *The American Economic Review,* vol. XXIV (March 1934), p. 68, and Sidney L. Miller, "Discussion," *The American Economic Review,* vol. XXV (March 1935), p. 132.

[18]Cf. C. S. Duncan, "Discussion," *The American Economic Review,* vol. XXX (March 1940), pp. 158–59.

regulatory authorities can then determine these costs and use them as the basis for a determination of "appropriate economic spheres."

Initially, relative costs, and not rates, were at issue in the argument. Though it was not always made explicit, the very difficulty that regulation was to surmount arose because shippers appeared only too willing (other aspects of the service being the same) individually to apportion their traffic on the basis of relative *rates* (or costs *to them*). As the rate structure "deteriorated" under the competitive thrusts of the motor carrier, the distinction became less important.

Finally, the "relative-cost" method of determining "appropriate economic spheres" suffered from the "drawback" that even if the relative costs could be determined, there was no guarantee than an allocation of traffic on this basis would yield the result desired (by regulatory authorities), since it would inevitably be altered by the relative desirability to shippers of aspects of service other than price (such as speed, flexibility, and so on). Thus, a final version of the argument was in terms of the "inherent natural advantages" of each mode. While this suffered from all of the deficiencies of the other versions if attempts were made to define it objectively, it was sufficiently vague to call forth fewer attempts to do so, and to render it less obvious that only particular shippers and transportation firms at particular times and places could ever, by their collective actions, actually erect a transportation system in accordance with the "inherent natural advantages" of each mode.

Buttressed by this and other arguments, regulatory authorities, the railroads, and some of the motor-carrier firms turned to Congress for assistance. Earlier attempts by the states (except Delaware) had not succeeded in controlling entry into motor trucking even though (except in West Virginia and Kentucky) control of entry was given to the same body that had jurisdiction over railroads.[19]

Thwarting the efforts of the state regulatory bodies was product rate discrimination, and in large measure the villain was recognized only indirectly. The fact that railroad rates were determined in a significant degree by the "value-of-service" principle, or product rate discrimination, meant that the motor carrier could compete with the railroad on much more traffic than would otherwise have been possible. Regulatory authorities recognized this, indirectly, as evidenced by their contention that the motor truck was pirating traffic that the railroad could have best handled. Many of the products transported by trucks could probably have been carried by the railroad at less cost. As long as rail rates on such products were determined by the "value-of-service" principle, however, the lowest cost *to the public* was incurred by shipping such products by motor truck.

---

[19]Henry R. Trumbower, "The Regulation of the Common Carrier Motor Vehicle with Respect to its Competitive Aspects," *The American Economic Review*, vol. XIX (March 1929), pp. 231–34.

The railroads by their practice of product rate discrimination intensified the competitive pressure of motor trucks. The states, by more or less forcing motor common carriers to adopt rate tariffs modeled after that of the railroad, and by forcing these carriers in other ways to follow the example of the railroad, found themselves with the same problem on their hands once more. Protecting the railroad against the motor common carrier meant that the latter, in turn, would have to be zealously guarded against the contract carrier, for the continued presence of product rate discrimination was a tremendous stimulant to contract carriers. Only so much pressure could be exerted on contract carriers, however, before this pressure escaped in the form of private carriage.[20]

Thus, simple restrictions upon entry that concentrated upon entry into the industry (rather than specific markets) and upon entry as a common carrier were ineffectual as long as the entrants utilized basically the same system of pricing that had so magnified the pressure for their entry. This same pressure was given expression by the entrance of contract and private carriers who could not be so easily controlled by a system of regulation designed for an industry in which large natural barriers to entry existed. A system of regulation was "needed" (*given the goals of regulation*) that could more efficiently erect unnatural barriers to entry.

The "Grandfather" Clause

By the Motor Carrier Act of 1935 federal regulatory authority over motor carriers was vested in the Interstate Commerce Commission. Among the provisions of the act was a "grandfather clause" designed to sanction bona fide operations as of June 1, 1935. Within the designated period of 120 days of the effective date of the act the I.C.C. was swamped by approximately 90,000 applications for operating authority based on this provision.

Faced with this avalanche of applications (which took many years to process) and realizing that control of entry was the cornerstone of "effective" regulation, the I.C.C. interpreted this provision much more stringently than Congress had intended (as indicated by congressional testimony).[21] Though periodically rebuffed by the courts, the I.C.C. required detailed evidence for each article transported, and inability to prove that any commodity had

---

[20] For purposes of economic regulation, motor carriers are classified as common carriers, contract carriers, exempt carriers, and private carriers. Whatever service a common carrier is authorized to provide he may offer to the public generally. The contract carrier must enter into specific agreements (contracts) with particular shippers to provide the authorized service and may not actively solicit traffic from the public. The exempt carrier is a for-hire carrier hauling certain commodities the transportation of which is exempt from economic regulation (but not safety regulation). The private carrier is engaged in transporting the goods of its owner and it, also, is not subject to economic regulation.

[21] U.S., Congress, Senate, *Restrictions Upon Motor and Water Carriers,* Senate Document 78, 79th Cong., 1st Sess. (Washington, D.C.: U.S.G.P.O., 1945), pp. 218–19.

been transported on the "grandfather" date and continuously from that time, on that route, and in "substantial" quantities resulted in the striking of that commodity and/or route from the certificate (for common carriers) or permit (for contract carriers).[22]

In administering the "grandfather clause" the I.C.C. set the pattern that was to characterize its later efforts. In *economic terms* its actions were quite consistent with its view of the goals of regulation. Control of entry had to be strict if these goals were to be achieved. Since the commission was dealing with essentially an economic question, consistency in economic terms could not be sacrificed to consistency in terms of legal canons. Thus the legal profession began, in this area, a long period of bafflement. For example, complete satisfaction of the nominal grounds upon which a previous favorable decision was rendered was to become no assurance of a favorable decision in a current case, and factors held irrelevant in prior cases could be the nominal grounds for an unfavorable decision in a present case.

Public Convenience and Necessity

Unless granted in a "grandfather" proceeding, a common carrier can secure a "certificate of convenience and necessity" that will permit the carrier to operate or to extend its operations territorially or commoditywise only if the applicant can

> ... affirmatively establish that its proposed operation will serve a useful public service, responsive to a public demand or need; that this purpose cannot or will not be served as well by existing carriers; and that granting of the application will not endanger or impair the operations of existing carriers contrary to the public interest.[23]

This principle has been followed so strictly as to make it very difficult for a new carrier to enter the field or for an old carrier to extend its operations. All the burden of proof is upon the applicant, while little or no proof of their contentions is required of those carriers or others objecting to the proposed authorization. The attempt to prove "affirmatively" that existing services are inadequate and that there is a need for the proposed service must leave no suspicion that supporting shippers are interested primarily in lower rates, for the level of rates is a matter "not properly in issue" in a

---

[22]The "operating authority" of a motor carrier refers, roughly, to the scope of the carrier's legal authority with respect to the goods that may be transported, the routes over which the goods may be transported, the areas, points, or shippers that may be served, and so on. The "license" of a common carrier is its certificate of convenience and necessity, which specifies the carrier's "operating authority." The similar "license" for contract carriers is called a "permit."

[23]*Home Transfer and Storage Co., Extension—Frozen Foods*, 63 MCC 709, 726 (1955), and *Zero Refrigerated Lines, Extension—Galveston*, 95 MCC 40, 48 (1964).

public-convenience-and-necessity proceeding.[24] Furthermore, the objections of other carriers are not rendered irrelevant by the fact that they cannot or do not wish to perform the proposed service themselves.[25]

The supporting shipper must "affirmatively demonstrate" that there is a "real need" and not a "mere desire" for the proposed service. Despite tragic lists of difficulties arising from the existing service the commission can readily hold that there is ". . . . no more than a desire, and not a need, for the proposed service . . . ."[26] The supporting shipper must have made a "thorough" investigation of the adequacy of existing services and this investigation can be held insufficient in the face of uncontested evidence of all manner of shortcomings.[27] The investigation must also have been recent.[28]

In proving the services of existing carriers to be inadequate the applicant must also show that existing carriers are *unable or unwilling* to provide "adequate" service.[29] And where existing service has been improved because of an application for new service, the commission has quieted fears of shippers that the existing service will sink back to its old level if the new temporary service is not made permanent by holding that ". . . the record affords no reasonable basis for such a conclusion."[30]

Perhaps the best basis for a plea of operating authority as a common carrier is a contention that if such authority is not granted, the traffic will be handled by contract carriers. Though the bulk of the regulation of contract carriers is designed to prevent these carriers from serving more than a limited number of shippers, and though the commission does not attempt to force motor common carriers to serve shippers or points that they do not wish to serve, common carriers are readily permitted to begin operations competitive with contract carriers "because" the latter cannot be *forced* to serve all shippers in the area.[31]

Consistent with the Public Interest

For new operating authority as a contract carrier the applicant must show that he is "fit, willing and able to perform such service" and that the proposed service is "consistent with the public interest and national trans-

---

[24] *Malone Freight Lines, Inc., Extension—Textiles,* 61 MCC 501, 502, 507 (1952).

[25] *Inland Petroleum Transportation Co., Inc., Extension—Oregon,* 61 MCC 726, 729 (1953). See also *Donald Jule La Tulip Contract Carrier Application,* 64 MCC 397, 398–399 (1955).

[26] *Transcon Lines Common Carrier Application,* 63 MCC 7, 23 (1954).

[27] *Miller, Extension—Poughkeepsie, New York,* 61 MCC 631 (1953).

[28] *Home Transfer and Storage Co., Extension—Frozen Foods,* 63 MCC 709, 718 (1955).

[29] *Ibid.,* p. 726, and *Zero Refrigerated Lines, Extension—Galveston, loc. cit.*

[30] *Southern Express, Inc. Common Carrier Application,* 62 MCC 35, 43 (1953).

[31] *Quality Milk Service, Inc., Extension—Molasses,* 64 MCC 5, 7 (1955). See also *Navajo Freight Lines, Inc., Extension—Silver,* 95 MCC 551, 558–559 (1964).

portation policy." Though contrary to the general consensus among legislators at the time of passage of the Motor Carrier Act, the I.C.C. has made it at least as difficult, if not more so, to secure a permit for contract carriage as a certificate for common carriage and has narrowly circumscribed the operations of contract carriers.[32]

To secure a permit to enter the industry as a contract carrier or to extend the operations of an existing contract carrier it must be shown that the existing *common*-carrier service is inadequate.[33] As a matter of practicality, existing common-carrier service cannot be shown inadequate unless the commission desires this result.

The typical request is for a permit for an extension of authority that will permit the contract carrier to serve its supporting shipper more effectively. When the supporting shipper's organization and sales territory grow, he may wish the services of the contract carrier to be available in his expanded territory or modified in other ways to accommodate these services to his growth. He generally seeks to show that only interline motor common-carrier service is available, that the transit times of these carriers and the railroad are too long to permit him to develop the new territory effectively, that he has used the existing common-carrier service and that it resulted in extensive damage to his product, that many of his customers have no rail sidings and the existing motor common carriers are not authorized to serve them, that having the contract carrier on call will give him flexibility necessary to meet competition, as will the ability to control routing and divert shipments, that congestion at loading docks and interruptions of production are prevented by contract-carrier service, and other similar advantages.

Despite such unchallenged contentions, the commission will often deny the extension.[34] In some instances it will note, apparently in justification, that the supporting shipper's competitors *suffer under a similar deficiency of existing service.*

Alternate Routes

As a result of the construction of new highways or the improvement of existing highways or for other reasons, carriers often seek authority to travel over alternate routes.

---

[32] *Restrictions Upon Motor and Water Carriers, op. cit.,* pp. 211–12.

[33] See, for example, *Walter C. Benson Co., Extension—New York, New Jersey and Pennsylvania,* 61 MCC 128, 130 (1952). In 1961 the Supreme Court admonished the I.C.C. to consider the "distinct" need of the shipper that a contract carrier's service is designed to meet, thus somewhat softening this criterion (*Interstate Commerce Commission* vs. *J-T Transport Co.,* 368 U.S. 81).

[34] See, for example, *Clyde R. Sauers, Extension—East Cambridge, Massachusetts,* 61 MCC 65 (1952); *Robert T. Wilson and G. Bennett Wilson, Extension—Dairy Products,* 61 MCC 51 (1952); and *Atkinson, Inc., Extension—Twisted Paper,* 61 MCC 390 (1952).

Two basic principles are involved in dealing with such requests. By one or the other (or both) of these principles the carrier must show that he really doesn't need the new authorization if he is to get it! The first principle is that a request for alternate-route authority will not be granted if "improved service" will result.[35] What this means is that if, in the commission's opinion, the alternate-route authority will cause diversion of traffic from the railroads or from other common carriers, it will not be granted. The second principle is that the applicant must already be an "effective competitor" between the points for which the alternate route is sought.[36] If the applicant is not now transporting a "substantial" portion of the traffic, the alternate-route authority will not be granted. In perhaps no other single aspect of its actions are the efforts of the I.C.C. to shelter markets from competitors more apparent.

Return-Haul Restrictions

Return-haul authority is technically separate from primary-direction authority. Nonetheless, larger carriers typically possess broader return-haul authority than do smaller carriers, general-commodity carriers have greater return-haul authority than special-commodity carriers, regular-route carriers have greater return-haul authority than irregular-route carriers, and contract carriers have much less than common carriers.[37]

Applications for return-haul authority where none exists, or for greater authority if some is already possessed, must meet essentially the same tests of public convenience and necessity or public interest applied to requests for other types of operating authority.

The Agricultural Exemption

Motor carriers of livestock and agricultural products were exempted from economic regulation by the Motor Carrier Act of 1935. Not even the I.C.C. has contended that regulated carriers could or would provide better services than those currently provided by exempt agricultural carriers (to their customers) or that they would do so at so low a price. Nevertheless the commission apparently views the exemption as a regrettable failure of Congress to subject a large portion of the motor trucking industry to the proper regulation. Consequently, the I.C.C. has interpreted the exemption

---

[35] *Watson Bros. Transportation Co., Inc., Extension—Alternate Routes*, 64 MCC 405, 433. See also *Best Way of Indiana, Extension—Alternate Route*, 95 MCC 263, 265 (1964).

[36] *Guy Spaulding, Extension—Alternate Routes*, 64 MCC 135, 139 (1955). Also *Best Way of Indiana, Extension—Alternate Route, op. cit.*

[37] *Restrictions Upon Motor and Water Carriers, op. cit.*, pp. 127–33.

as narrowly as possible, engaging in repeated skirmishes with the courts and the Agricultural Department as a result. In its struggle the I.C.C. has held that *washed* spinach, *dressed* poultry, *redried* leaf tobacco, gladiolus and gladiolus bulbs, *beheaded* shrimp, and so on were not exempt products and could therefore be transported only by regulated carriers.[38] The commission's struggle has been characterized by perseverance and resilience, achieving a singular victory with passage of the National Transportation Act of 1958, which accepted the I.C.C.'s list of exempt commodities.

Commodity Restrictions

The authority to haul general commodities is highly prized by motor carriers; as a general practice the commission ceased granting it after the first two or three years of regulation. When authorization other than general commodities is granted, commodity classes or specific commodities may be designated. In either event, numerous cases arise requiring the commission to interpret commodity authorizations to determine whether or not certain items are included therein. The commission seems to interpret commodity authorizations as rigidly as it thinks the courts will permit, and quite often is forced by adverse court decisions to yield authority that it had previously denied.

The Keystone and Allied Restrictions upon Contract Carriers

Though the commission realizes that rigid regulation of contract carriage increases private carriage, it has developed over the years many special regulatory devices to be employed against contract carriers. One of these is the Keystone restriction, which limits a contract carrier to a particular class of shippers, a restriction explicitly designed to protect common carriers against contract carriers.[39] The restriction makes the contract carrier particularly vulnerable to change, for if his principal shipper fails, or purchases motor trucks, the contract carrier is often forced to go out of business because of his legal inability to negotiate contracts with other shippers in the area.

In a series of cases the I.C.C. has held that a contract carrier cannot interchange with other carriers—common or contract, that he cannot actively solicit traffic, that he cannot render a through service by "tacking" or combining operating rights, and that he must have the traffic of only one

---

[38]See *Interstate Commerce Commission* vs. *Dunn*, 186 F.2d 116 (1946); *Monark Egg Corporation Contract Carrier Application*, 44 MCC 15 (1944); and *Determination of Exempted Agricultural Commodities*, 52 MCC 511 (1951).

[39]*Keystone Transportation Co. Contract Carrier Application*, 19 MCC 475 (1939).

shipper in the same truck at the same time. As the commission summed it up in the *Craig Contract Carrier* case, "It is intended that all over-the-road truckers shall, whenever possible, fall within the description of common carriers."[40]

Control of Entry in the Future

Given the difficulties they had to surmount, the regulatory authorities have done a truly remarkable job of erecting artificial barriers to entry in motor trucking. In a dynamic economy the passage of time brings change, and change leads to even greater control of entry and reduction in the number of carriers. With the disappearance of old products and the rise of new ones, with changes in the highways, with the growth of shippers and their relocation, and with many of the other concomitants of change, the regulatory preening of motor-carrier firms will continue.

As the process continues and contract carriers are largely emasculated, larger shippers will continue to turn to private carriage. Meanwhile, mergers will increase concentration in motor common carriage in order to take advantage of regulatory economies of size and to carve out better-isolated market positions that will increase monopoly power. A social cost that may not be so obvious as a larger transport bill is that entry into industry generally will become more difficult. New firms will have to rely upon the common carriers unless they can enter at such a size as to make private carriage feasible. Thus barriers to entry in the economy as a whole will be increased.

RATE REGULATION

As a leading student of transportation has noted, "The truth of the matter is that freight rates are neither fixed nor are they loose. They range, in fact, over the entire span from tightly controlled charges to virtual anarchy."[41]

Regulated carriers are grouped, for rate-making purposes, into rate bureaus and conferences, these organizations being exempted by the Reed-Bulwinkle Act from prosecution under the antitrust laws. Through these organizations the vast majority of rates are established and changed without the necessity of commission action. The freight rate structure, as the above quotation suggests, is sufficiently flexible to permit individual carriers normally to exercise considerable autonomy in setting rates in markets in accord with the elasticities of the demand for their services in those markets. Where

---

[40] *Craig Contract Carrier Application*, 31 MCC 705, 712 (1941).

[41] L. L. Waters, "Competition in Freight Transport," in *Essays on Transport Problems in the 1960's*, George M. Smerk, ed. (Bloomington, Ind.: Bureau of Business Research, 1967), p. 54.

cross elasticities of demand *with other regulated carriers* are low, the individual carrier can to a considerable extent "tailor-make" his rates—in accord, for example, with actual or potential competition from private carriage or the other factors determining the elasticity of the demand for his particular services. *But*, where cross elasticities of demand *with other regulated carriers* are *high*, the "need" arises for rate regulation to maximize the profitability of these carriers as a group by forcing observance of the elasticity of demand for the group's services rather than that for the output of the individual carrier. The basic purpose of rate regulation is thus to assure collusion in pricing in markets where there are high cross elasticities of demand for the services of regulated carriers.

In motor trucking, rate regulation is supplemental to control of entry. Control of entry stakes out certain traffic as more or less the sole province of the individual regulated motor carrier and concerning which he has considerable freedom in pricing. Other traffic is more or less isolated from other regulated carriers but not from private carriage (actual or potential). Still other traffic, however, must be shared with other regulated carriers. Rate regulation is most prominent in connection with the latter type of traffic and constitutes a method of enforcing cartel solidarity for a group of carriers of the same mode, and a method of arbitrating disputes between cartels.

It should perhaps be pointed out that regulatory authorities are not nefarious schemers deliberately plotting a misallocation of resources and an uneconomical and discriminatory rate structure. The regulatory authorities are interested primarily in the financial condition of the common carriers (as were perhaps the congressmen who passed the legislation that guides them). A rate structure determined to a large extent by the "value-of-service" principle will maximize profits (or minimize losses) for groups of carriers only if there is sufficient collusion between carriers to make maintenance of the rate structure feasible. The effect of rate regulation is to encourage that collusion.

The Rate-Making Procedure

Any common carrier, or groups of common carriers through their rate bureau or conference, desiring to initiate a new rate or to change an existing rate, must publish the tariff or supplement containing that rate and file it with the I.C.C. If no objection is raised, the new rate takes effect thirty days after notice has been given to the commission and to the public, or in less than thirty days if the commission so directs. For the vast majority of rates this is all that is involved in their establishment.

Any interested party may, however, protest the new rate, or change in the existing rate. In most cases the proposed rate is protested by the rate bureau or conference or competing carriers, who generally allege that the proposed rate is unreasonably low. In a few instances shippers may protest on the grounds that the proposed rate is unreasonably high or unjustly discriminatory. Also, infrequently, the I.C.C. may protest the proposed rate.

After hearings the commission may find the proposed rate lawful, and allow it to take effect, or it may find the proposed rate unlawful and leave the original rate in effect, or it may find the proposed rate unlawful and determine the lawful rate.

In the case of contract carriers the procedure is essentially the same except that the contract carrier's *minimum* rate is involved. In setting the contract carrier's minimum rate, the commission is directed by law to see that no advantage is given to a contract carrier over a common carrier that would be inconsistent with the national transportation policy.

A very important provision of law is that in determining the lawfulness of a proposed new rate, or a proposed change in an existing rate (if either is contested), *the burden of proof rests not upon the protesting parties but upon those proposing the new or changed rate.* In regulatory law, because of the lack of objective criteria, the question of who has the burden of proof is crucial.

In complaints against *existing* rates the burden of proof rests with those bringing the complaint. Legally anyone can bring a complaint to the commission. The commission can then dispose of the complaint, after hearings, in basically the same ways as indicated above for new rates. Complaints against existing rates, however, are not numerous because of the burden of proof. Of those that do occur, a significant proportion are brought by the commission itself.

Suspended Rate Reductions

The overwhelming majority of motor-carrier rate cases involve suspended rate reductions. There are several reasons for their preponderance. Rate increases often occur as blanket increases for an area of the country or the country as a whole. As individual carriers find these higher rates untenable with respect to particular commodities because of such factors as competition by private carriers or railroads, they attempt to readjust their rates in accordance with the varying elasticities in the product-delineated markets for their services. Pressure for selective rate reductions need not, of course, arise only after a general rate increase. Given the influence of the value-of-service principle throughout the rate structure, private-carrier competition is a recurring threat, and railroad rate decreases may drive not only individual carriers but whole groups of motor carriers to seek rate reductions upon particular traffic.

The two basic *nominal* criteria that must be met for approval of a rate reduction are that it is necessary to meet competition and that it is "compensatory." In finding that a rate reduction is necessary to meet competition the commission often finds the railroad to have a competitive advantage over the motor carrier. Frequently there has been a previous decrease by the railroad of the rate applicable to this traffic, with the result that the motor-carrier rate exceeds the rail rate by a greater amount than it formerly did. The railroads will plead that this great a disparity in rates is necessary because of the inherent advantages *of motor trucks* over railroads. But the commission, despite a legal prohibition against its allocating traffic between modes,[42] believes that each type of carrier must be given a "fair opportunity to compete" for traffic and will permit the rate reduction if it is thought necessary to achieve this result. Ordinarily the motor carrier must show that the existing differential is in excess of that necessary to permit both the railroad and the motor carrier to share in the traffic and that as a consequence it has suffered a diversion of traffic to the railroad or has been precluded from competing for this particular traffic. Basically the same "share of the pie" argument must be made convincing if a rate reduction is to be granted on grounds of competitive necessity vis-à-vis other regulated motor carriers.

While nominally a separate criterion, the question of whether or not a rate is "compensatory" is foreclosed if the lower rate has been found competitively necessary. If the lower rate is competitively necessary it will be found "compensatory." The "basis" for a "finding" that the proposed rate is "compensatory" may be that the revenue received on the traffic at the lower rate compares favorably with some measure of the carrier's overall costs, most frequently the "system-average" costs,[43] or the "system-average" costs of other motor carriers in the area. Or the anticipated revenue may be compared with the average revenue on all traffic transported or that on certain other specific commodities. Another alternative basis for a "finding" that the lower rate is "compensatory" is by comparison with other rates on the same commodity or on commodities deemed to have similar transportation characteristics.

In a large proportion of approved rate reductions the commission also notes that those carriers objecting to the rate reduction would not be affected by the rate reduction, since they had not in the past attempted to share in the traffic and were not at present attempting to do so. In short, the competitive relationship between regulated carriers would not be affected by the rate reduction.

The majority of suspended rate reductions, however, are *disapproved.* The grounds for disapproval are, nominally, that the criteria for the reduction have not been met *or* that it has not been *shown* that they have been

---

[42] *Interstate Commerce Commission* vs. *Mechling*, 330 U.S. 567.

[43] "System-average" costs are the total costs of the carrier in a preceding period divided by the number of miles of operation.

met. For example, the commission will either find that no competitive necessity exists for the rate reduction *or* that no competitive necessity has been *shown* to exist. If the carrier proposing the lower rate and the complaining carrier were both sharing in the traffic at the old rate, the new lower rate won't be granted. And if the commission concludes that there is not a competitive necessity for the rate, it is likely also to find the proposed rate "noncompensatory" and a threat to the existing competitive relationship between carriers.

In finding that a rate is *not* "compensatory" the commission may again use such bases as "system-average" costs, revenue comparisons, and rate comparisons as mentioned above. But in finding that a proposed lower rate has not been *shown* compensatory the commission may quite accurately point out the deficiencies in each of these measures and conclude that they cannot be used to prove that a rate is compensatory. Always available if needed are criticisms concerning the method used to allocate fixed costs among the products transported, since there is no method of allocating such expenses on other than purely arbitrary grounds—despite the fact that when it wishes to *approve* a lower rate as "compensatory" the commission may do so even though the proponent has submitted no cost data.[44]

In finding that a proposed lower rate would disturb the existing competitive relationship between regulated carriers the commission may hold that it would disrupt the rate structure, constitute unfair and destructive competition, or be lower than necessary to meet the competition. The commission may add that diversion of traffic to the proponent would result from the decreased rate.

Suspended Proposed Rate Increases

Rate increases ordinarily occur as blanket increases for all regulated motor carriers in a given area of the country. Relative to the ponderous machinery set in motion by a proposed rate reduction, the grounds for justifying a proposed general rate increase are fantastically simple. Essentially they consist of statements that expenses of operation have been rising and that the "operating ratio"[45] for the average carrier is considerably above some norm, usually 93. Railroads usually testify in favor of the increase.

---

[44] *Drugs or Medicines from Elkhart, Indiana, to Topeka, Kansas,* 64 MCC 761 (1955).

[45] The ratio of total expense to total revenue, for some past period. The use of operating ratios has occasioned qualms within the commission itself. Changes in operating ratios imply little about changes in motor-carrier profitability. Minimizing the operating ratio means that production is halted where marginal cost is equal to the product of the ratio of total cost to total revenue and marginal revenue, a clearly nonsensical result that implies (when the ratio is less than unity) needless loss of profit and avoidable underutilization of capacity.

Other Types of Rate Cases

Complaints against existing rates are few, owing to possession by the complainant of the burden of proof. Nonetheless, shippers may complain that a rate is too high, or other carriers may complain that the rate is too low. Cases may sometimes arise concerning pickup, delivery, or other ancillary charges. The commission itself may initiate rate hearings. Finally, cases arise concerning product classification. In all except the last of these types of cases the commission's philosophy and rules are consistent with those evident in suspended-rate cases. In the last type, however, the commission appears to approach the question of which rate applies to a given commodity completely apart from its general consideration for the financial welfare of the common carriers and other general regulatory goals. Despite the fact that the shipper always wishes his commodity classified in such a way as to make applicable the lower rate, the commission appears to display no particular bias for, or against, this result.

Cases involving product classification are particularly interesting for the view they give of product rate discrimination at work. It is to be expected, for example, that essentially the same commodity will be transported at different rates if there are different uses or functions to which it may be put. If purchasers differentiate between essentially the same products, there will be demands of different elasticities for the product in each of its uses and consequently different elasticities of derived demand for its transportation. The rate setter can exploit these differences by setting different rates. Similarly, in cases in which a product undergoes processing that leaves unaffected the cost of transporting it but that reduces the elasticity of demand for its transportation, the rate charged under product rate discrimination will be accordingly increased.

Goals of Rate Regulation

Motor-carrier rate regulation is primarily concerned with preventing reductions in transport rates where such reductions threaten the general level of rates or their stability. Rate reductions (when contested) are normally permitted only if the commission is convinced that the reduction is necessary to permit the carrier or group of carriers to meet competition and if the reduction will have negligible repercussions on the competitive relationship between carriers. Nominally important is the compensatory nature of the rate, but in practice this criterion has little independent existence, serving primarily to reinforce findings arrived at on other bases.

Rate regulation imposes few restraints upon the efforts of carriers collusively to raise their rates. The major restraint is the rather inconsistent proviso that the rates on all commodities be raised simultaneously. This limits the ability of the carriers to practice product rate discrimination and gives rise—after every rate increase—to a host of litigations by which individual carriers or groups of carriers try to reduce their rates on specific commodities.

A major goal of rate regulation is to reconcile three different demand elasticities. An individual motor common carrier, harassed by the threat of private carriage, may view the demand for the transportation of some particular product as highly elastic, while the cartel of which he is a member may view the demand for the transportation of that commodity as much less elastic. In turn the elasticity may appear even smaller to the commission, for it must view rates from the standpoint of their ability to maximize the return of all common carriers. The commission undoubtedly realizes the anomalous fact (though in other terms) that in the cartel arrangement which it heads the subsidiary units must be restricted in their ability to practice separately product rate discrimination, for the attempts of all firms to follow the elasticities of the demand that they separately face might well lead to a lessened ability of any of them to discriminate. Completely independent product rate discrimination by individual firms would constitute the path to a more competitive organization of the industry, in which the ability to follow this practice would be greatly reduced. Thus, as long as the primary goal of regulation is to safeguard the financial position of selected transport firms, the regulatory authorities must see to it that these firms together follow a principle that they are not completely free to follow separately.

SUMMARY AND CONCLUSIONS

In order to engage in price discrimination a firm must be able to separate its customers into different groups and must possess different degrees of monopoly power in selling to these groups. Motor-carrier firms can readily separate their customers on the basis of commodities they wish transported. Furthermore, the market separation involved is subject to little "leakage" because the customer cannot readily switch markets (so as to buy always in the low-priced market) or act as a seller in the high-priced market (having purchased in the low-priced market). Given the economic characteristics of motor trucking, however, it would appear that the monopoly power prerequisite could not be met and that price discrimination could not be a prominent pricing practice in this industry.

The monopoly-power prerequisite is met, for a large portion of the industry, by a system of governmental regulation, the effect of which is to create artificial barriers to entry and encourage cartelization and collusive pricing. To a truly remarkable extent this system of regulation has succeeded in overcoming the natural economic characteristics of motor carriers so that price discrimination, or product rate discrimination, can be a prominent feature of pricing in a large portion of the industry.

Price discrimination is, of course, not confined to transportation. This form of pricing is found throughout the economy, from the differential markups and discounts of retailers and the pricing practices of multiproduct firms to the charges levied for household utilities. Undoubtedly more firms engage in some form of price discrimination than pursue a uniform price policy. The one-good, one-price firm is confined largely to our textbooks. Even so, an understanding of price discrimination in the forms that it takes in transportation is particularly important. There can be little sophisticated evaluation of governmental policy in this major area of the economy without a thorough understanding of the theory of price discrimination. In its absence we are reduced to attempts to understand economic realities as though the tools and concepts for doing so had not progressed beyond the medieval concept of the "just" price. And since this major area of the economy is perhaps more closely related to the government than any other (in which the government itself is not the major buyer or producer), an ability to evaluate governmental policy in this area is all the more important.

SELECTED REFERENCES

ADAMS, WALTER, and H. M. GRAY, *Monopoly in America* (New York: The Macmillan Company, 1955).

LOCKLIN, D. PHILIP, *Economics of Transportation* (Homewood, Ill.: Richard D. Irwin, Inc., 1960).

MAXWELL, W. DAVID, "The Regulation of Motor-Carrier Rates by the Interstate Commerce Commission," *Land Economics*, vol. XXVI (Feb. 1960), pp. 79–91.

————, "Product Rate Discrimination in Motor Trucking," *The Southern Economic Journal*, vol. XXVII (April 1961), pp. 305–19.

U.S., Congress, Senate, *Restrictions Upon Motor and Water Carriers*, Senate Document 78, 79th Cong., 1st Sess. (Washington, D.C.: U.S.G.P.O., 1945).

WILLIAMS, ERNEST W., JR., *The Regulation of Rail-Motor Rate Competition* (New York: Harper & Row, Publishers, 1956).

production theory and
production management

Up to this point we have conceived of the firm as a single decision-making unit. In firms of sufficient size and complexity, however, specialization exists within the management function itself. In this chapter we are concerned with selected aspects of that part of the management function known as "production management" and some of the decision making that is the primary responsibility of the "production manager." In the words of a leading student of this area:

> Production managers conceive of their field as consisting of the development and operation of a process for *getting work done*. In their opinion, the organization has entrusted them with the responsibility of transforming *input* resources into a desired set of *outputs*. The transformation *process* is to be accomplished in a manner that is most compatible with the company's objectives. The production manager interprets this to mean that the outputs should be of some assured level of quality produced at minimum cost.[1]

At the center of production management is the concept of the *production process*, the system by which inputs are converted or transformed into

---

[1] Martin K. Starr, *Production Management: Systems and Synthesis* (Englewood Cliffs, N.J.: Prentice-Hall, Inc., 1964), p. 43.

outputs. The analogy to the production function of Chapter 5 is immediately apparent. But, like most analogies, this one can be misleading. The production function of Chapter 5 is merely a statement of the quantitative relationship between inputs and output. As such, it implicitly assumes that much of the production manager's job has already been done. By assuming a given "state of the arts," or technology, the traditional economic discussion of the production function assumes that the choice of the production process and the selection of inputs has already been made. Yet a major responsibility of the production manager is the technical design of a production process that will yield most economically the range of desired outputs.

Similarly, the relationship between inputs and output in the economist's concept of the production function is *invariant*: a_1 of input A, and b_1 of input B, if used, yield automatically the maximum output X_1. Yet much of the production manager's responsibility is to so organize and control inputs and the production process that a_1 of input A and b_1 of input B do, in fact, yield the maximum output X_1. Thus, in terms of the production surface of Chapter 5, the economist somewhat blithely assumes that matters have been so arranged that the firm always operates *on* the surface itself, whereas much of the production manager's responsibility is to see to it that the outputs constituting the surface actually result from the input coordinates indicated. The production manager is only too well aware that in the absence of efforts to secure them such optimal results need not occur.[2]

The production manager also objects to the assumption, implicit in the drawing of an isoquant, that there exists an infinity of different combinations of the quantities of given inputs that would yield the same (maximum) output. In most real-world firms, he would aver, there are at best only a few combinations of the quantities of the given inputs that could yield the same (maximum) output. Only a few points on a given isoquant, in other words, are effective alternatives.

Finally, the production manager treats *time* more overtly than does the economist. In Chapters 5 and 6 it was stressed that factor services are yielded through time, that production occurs through time, and that these facts lead to a classification of production situations into the market period, the short run, and the long run. More direct treatment of the problem of time, as it relates to production, is deferred by economists to a body of thought known as capital theory. But the production manager can have no such easy recourse to this mental compartmentalization; thus a more prominent feature of his analysis of production problems is the thought that "time is money." In order to minimize costs he must attack time directly. He must, subject to other constraints, minimize the time spent by a unit of raw

---

[2] In fact, it may well be the case that the best the production manager can do is to maximize the *probability* (given certain constraints) that optimal results will occur.

material in inventory, and he must also minimize the time required by the production process itself. Because time enters into the production manager's analysis more directly, opportunity cost is a more immediate and pressing concern for him than traditional economic analysis would suggest, despite the fact that the concept of opportunity cost is the cornerstone of the economist's theory of costs.

Nonetheless, much of the analysis of Chapters 5 and 6 can be related to the decision-making processes of the production manager. While we cannot readily relate the analysis of Chapters 5 and 6 to that portion of the production manager's function that lies, by analogy, beneath the production surface, many points of agreement or essential similarity still remain, and others can be yielded by modification and extension of the analysis of these earlier chapters.

First of all, the view of the nature of inputs and that of constraints is almost immediately transferable into production management. The distinction between factors of production and factor services is mirrored in production management by distinctions such as those between labor and labor hours and between machines and machine hours.[3] Similarly, the very manner in which constraints are defined in production management, as so many hours of machine time or so many man hours of labor, implies that less than these maxima may be used, thus implying the distinction between divisibility in acquisition and divisibility in use (as do such concepts as "slack").

The production manager desires to produce any of the outputs that he is asked to produce and can produce in a given situation at minimum cost, other aspects of output (quality, time required, and so on) being the same. Again neglecting that portion of his duties lying beneath the production surface (and also ignoring any problems arising from lack of continuity), we find that the concept of the output-expansion path and its associated cost functions become immediately descriptive of the production manager's decision making, for the output-expansion path (if unique) is a locus of the least-cost combinations of inputs that can be used to produce the outputs that the firm can produce in the given situation. Thus, the economist's short-run decision, for example, that the least-cost combination is a_1 of the variable input (in acquisition and in use) together with b_1 of the available services of the fixed input, is also the decision of the production manager, assuming further that the production manager also sees to it that combining a_1 and b_1 does yield the maximum possible output from this combination and that this point on the output-expansion path actually exists.

---

[3]Timms speaks of the input of labor *skills* through time, and of *inventories* of labor skills. The services of machinery and other facilities are treated at the same level of abstraction. See Howard L. Timms, *The Production Function in Business*, rev. ed. (Homewood, Ill.: Richard D. Irwin, Inc., 1966), chap. 1.

Finally, by relaxing such assumptions as that of no intertemporal substitution of factor services and no alternative use for factor services, we can modify the analysis of Chapters 5 and 6 to reflect more closely the production manager's greater emphasis upon time and his more pressing concern with opportunity costs.

The basic plan of the chapter is to revisit the market period, the short run, and the long run, modifying the assumptions in terms of which these situations were bounded in a manner that will permit description of more of the production manager's decision making. In addition, some of the more obvious relationships between the analysis of Chapters 5 and 6 and linear programming will be pointed out. Relating parts of one system of thought to parts of another is at best a difficult task, and we shall be content with modest results. At least, our facility in conjoining different assumptions should be increased. At best, we may perceive a degree of interrelatedness beyond that which is explicitly constructed.

A MORE COMPLEX MARKET PERIOD

It will be recalled that in the logical "situation" or "arena of action" called the "market period" in Chapters 5 and 6 it was assumed that the firm had already purchased all of its inputs. It was also assumed that there was no alternative to the present use in production of the factor services purchased other than nonuse—that is, factor services not used in production in this period, in this particular process, were simply lost. Thus, so long as there was no intertemporal substitution of factor services, no user costs, and no possibility of the firm's acting as a *seller* of factor services, there was no unique output-expansion path (although there was a maximum output as a terminus of the output-expansion path), and the firm's average total cost was synonymous with its average fixed cost.

Let Figure 10.1 represent a somewhat similar situation. In anticipation that he would be asked to produce the output I_1, and in view of the costs of labor services and the services yielded by machines, the production manager in some previous long-run situation decided that the optimal combination of these two inputs was a_1 of the services of his machines and b_1 of direct labor services. Accordingly, a quantity of machinery was purchased, or set aside for this process, such that, *at its optimal rate of operation*, it could yield the quantity of factor services a_1 *during a standard eight-hour shift*. The constraint on this input is thus less stringent than in the earlier market-period analysis, for (over some range of input) this quantity of machines can yield greater quantities of factor services by operation at a higher-than-optimal rate and/or by operation for a greater proportion of the day. Operation at a higher-than-optimal rate necessarily entails such drawbacks as greater-than-optimal wear and tear on the machinery and a higher

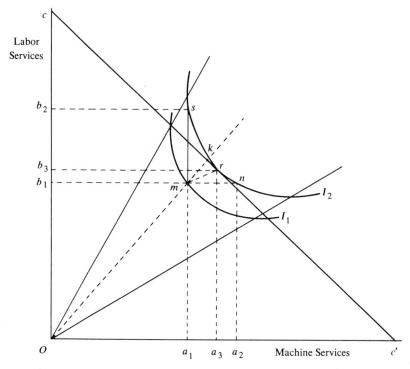

FIGURE 10.1

percentage of rejects (or both), and operation for a larger portion of the day necessarily requires some increase in the input of labor services. Delivery into the process of less than a_1 units of factor services can be accomplished by operating the machines at less than the optimal rate and/or by diverting some of them into idleness or to some other productive process. By the definition of optimality, and by the nature of returns to proportion, however, less-than-proportionate increases in output and greater-than-proportionate decreases in output result from such changes in the quantity of machine services, for a given quantity of labor services.

Similarly, the constraint upon labor services is more flexible than in the earlier analysis. The quantity of labor services b_1 is the quantity of direct labor services delivered into the productive process *during the eight-hour day*, assuming that an optimal allocation of the firm's supervisory and quality-control personnel (indirect labor services) to all productive processes has been made. Thus (over some range of input) a quantity of direct labor services larger than b_1 can be yielded (from a given quantity of labor) into the production of output of acceptable quality by overtime and/or by increasing the proportion of the firm's total labor input that is devoted to the supervision and quality control of this particular process. A decrease in the quantity of direct labor services yielded by the given quantity of labor can be accomplished by a decrease in supervisory and quality-control personnel devoted to this particular process and/or diversion of some of the labor services yielded by the given quantity of direct labor into idleness or to some other productive process.

Thus the constraints in this more complex market-period situation are less firm (at least upward) than in Chapters 5 and 6, and the decision making of the production manager is correspondingly more complex. While the production manager has only a given quantity of direct labor available for this process, there is some variability of the quantity of labor services entering into production (upward as well as downward variability), and the same is true of the services of machines.

If all goes in the firm as anticipated, the production manager will be asked to produce the output I_1 and will do so by the combination of inputs corresponding to m (Figure 10.1). If, however, he is asked to produce the larger output represented by I_2, several options may be open to him. It may be possible to produce the desired larger output by increasing the machines' rate of operation. If so, point n on I_2 is an effective alternative. Quite often it will be true, however, that little increase in output can be achieved by this stratagem. The line of which $b_1 m$ is a segment, in other words, may well intersect the lower ridge line before intersecting I_2. Similarly, it may often be true that point s does not occur, that the line of which $a_1 m$ is a segment does not intersect I_2 before it reaches the upper ridge line. Point s can occur only if the desired increase in output can be secured by diversion of more supervisory and/or quality-control effort to this particular process (without simultaneously increasing the quantity of machine services going into production).

Even if s and n exist, they are apt to be uneconomical alternatives. Proceeding from m to n, output increases less than proportionately to increases in machine services, with decreasing returns to proportion being fully reflected in rising marginal costs. Operation at a rate higher than the optimal is also likely to increase machine maintenance costs and "down" time due to machine malfunctions, also contributing to the rise in marginal costs. Similarly, movement from m to s is entirely characterized by returns to proportion (a declining marginal productivity of labor services), and marginal costs also are apt to rise because of the opportunity cost of diverting more supervisory and quality-control personnel time and effort to this particular process.

Other strategies for increasing output require simultaneous increases in both inputs. Thus the combination $b_3 a_3$ may be an effective alternative, and it may be secured by an increase in supervisory and quality-control effort and a concomitant increase in machine speed. Alternatively, the same combination may be secured by overtime, perhaps the cheapest way of securing additional *non*labor input. In part, overtime permits utilization of nonlabor factor services that would simply be lost. In part, overtime permits utilization in this period of nonlabor factor services that would otherwise be used only in some subsequent period. To the extent that a machine depreciates with use, overtime shortens its useful life and shifts factor services from the *end* of its useful life to the present. But these particular factor services are, from the standpoint of the present, the least costly factor services that the machine yields. This intertemporal substitution of factor services is the least costly because the present value of machine services otherwise available only toward the end of the machine's useful life is less than that of any other of its services. Nonetheless, this opportunity cost rises with increasing diversion of future services to the present.

In general, overtime requires a premium payment for labor services that more than compensates for any reduction in the cost of additional non-labor inputs. If the long-run output-expansion path is that of which *omk* is a segment, production at *r* must be more costly than if the production manager had correctly anticipated a call for I_2 output and had selected the input coordinates that yield *k*. Of course, *k* may still be an effective alternative if the production manager incorrectly anticipated a call for I_1 (and in some process characterized by fixed coefficients it could even be the only effective alternative), but, even so, attainment of *k* (when one has initially chosen *m*) must be more costly than an original choice of *k* that would have required no overtime and/or no additional supervisory and quality-control effort coupled with an increase in machine speed. Otherwise *k* could not have been a point on the original long-run output-expansion path. Thus the additional cost of the additional output $I_2 - I_1$ must be greater than if I_2 had been correctly anticipated, and the market-period marginal-cost function for outputs greater than that anticipated can be expected, in general, to be an upward-sloping function (assuming the long-run marginal-cost function to be constant). The production manager in this situation will produce the required extra output by the strategy that occasions the least increase in total cost (assuming there to be more than one effective alternative strategy for producing the desired increase in output).

It should be noted that all effective alternatives must lie on that portion of I_2 bounded by *s* and *n*. A choice of any point on I_2 above *s* would mean not only a needless expenditure for some labor services but a simultaneous exclusion from present production of machine services possessing a positive marginal productivity (unless the point lies on the line of which *ms* is a segment, in which case the point would lie above the upper ridge line, implying a negative marginal productivity for labor services). Similarly, choice of a point on I_2 below *n* would imply operation of the machines at a rate more nonoptimal than at *n*, simultaneously excluding from production some already purchased labor services possessing a positive marginal productivity.

Starting at m, the problem is that of finding the least costly strategy for moving to I_2. Whether additional labor services are secured from the given stock of direct labor by overtime, by increasing the proportion of supervisory and quality-control effort, or both, additional labor services can be secured only at a greater cost per unit. Similarly, additional machine services can be secured only at a greater unit cost. These two costs provide a set of isocost lines (such as cc' in Figure 10.1) independent of those that determined the selection of the long-run output-expansion path, so that a market-period expansion path such as mr results, yielding the coordinates of point r as the least costly method of producing the larger output in this situation.

Figure 10.2 depicts a market-period situation in which the production manager has *overestimated* the output he would be asked to produce. Again he has acquired a quantity of labor such that (together with the optimal quantity of supervisory and quality-control personnel) it could yield b_1 of labor services in a standard eight-hour day and a quantity of machines such that they could yield the quantity of machine services a_1 at the optimal rate of operation during an eight-hour day. Instead of I_1 the production manager is asked to produce I_3.

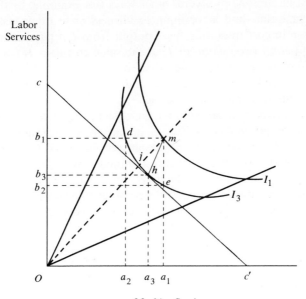

FIGURE 10.2

If d occurs, one effective alternative may be to reduce machine speed, thus in effect transferring some of the services of machines to subsequent periods. Similarly, if e occurs, the production manager may decrease the output of acceptable quality by transferring supervisory and quality-control personnel to some other process. Neither strategy can reduce total cost to the level at which it would have been if the production manager had initially chosen the coordinates of point j. The present value of future services cannot be as great as that of those utilized currently, and the contribution to other processes of the transferred supervisory and quality-control personnel cannot be as large as the contribution they would have made to this particular process if m had been the "correct" output. Thus the production manager cannot fully compensate for his erroneous choice of outputs by either of these two strategies.

The effective alternatives lie on the portion of I_3 bounded by d and e, if these points occur, or by the upper and lower ridge lines, if they do not. The relative "offsets" received by diversion of the two inputs would, in effect, establish a set of isocost curves independent of those determining the long-run output-expansion path, and this new set of isocost curves (together with I_3) would determine the least costly strategy for producing I_3 in this situation (h in Figure 10.2). The point h may reflect an effective alternative attained by diversion of some supervisory and quality-control personnel to other processes while simultaneously decreasing machine speed, or it may be attained in any one of several other ways (for example, by diversion of some machine time and labor input to idleness or to other tasks). Again, the decrease in cost in cutting back output from I_1 to I_3 cannot be great enough to permit production of I_3 at the same cost as if I_3 had been correctly anticipated. Even if j is the logical or only feasible choice, alternative uses for the "slack" in labor services and machine time cannot fully compensate for the fact that "slack" exists.

Thus, for outputs larger than the design output to which m refers, market-period marginal costs must be greater than long-run marginal cost, and for outputs smaller than the design output, market-period marginal costs must be smaller than long-run marginal cost. As output is reduced, there is probably some limit to the diversion of inputs to other present uses and to reductions in machine speed. Before reaching such a limit marginal costs would continue to decline as output is reduced by reason of the declining present value of the additional units of machine services diverted to future periods and diversion of inputs to less productive alternatives. These factors, acting to decrease marginal cost as output decreases, could well be reinforced by increases in the per-unit cost of other inputs (such as raw materials), arising from the firm's inability to maintain the "economic order quantity" or economic lot size for the purchase of inputs (Figure 10.3).

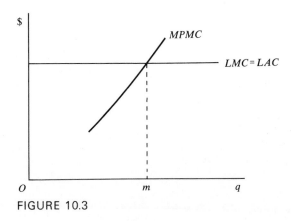

FIGURE 10.3

A MORE COMPLEX SHORT RUN

In the short run at least one input is fixed or indivisible and at least one input is variable or divisible. In Chapter 5 it was argued that the most realistic view of the short run is that the services of the variable factor are divisible in use and in acquisition, whereas the services of the fixed factor are divisible in use (up to a constraint) but indivisible in acquisition.

That this view of the short run and the nature of the constraint upon the fixed input is more relevant to production management (rather than the traditional view, in which the services of the fixed factor are fixed in *use* as well as in acquisition) is evident from abundant references implying, directly or indirectly, that all of the services that a fixed factor can yield need not be combined with all quantities of other inputs. Factories do not have to operate 24 hours of the day, and even within an eight-hour day some machines may be left idle or diverted to other processes. That such diversion of inputs (to idleness or to other uses) can occur despite indivisibilities in acquisition indicates that factor services may well be divisible in use even if indivisible in acquisition.

In Figure 10.4 the services of labor are assumed to be divisible in acquisition and in use, and it is assumed also that the firm has already acquired a stock of machines such that, at the optimal rate of operation, there is available for production during an eight-hour day a_1 of machine services. In some previous long-run period (given the factor-service prices) the process was designed for the anticipated output I_1 by the use of the combination of inputs a_1 and b_1. Again it is assumed that the anticipated output is incorrect and the production manager is actually requested to produce the larger output I_2.

If the point s occurs, one strategy to achieve the desired increase in

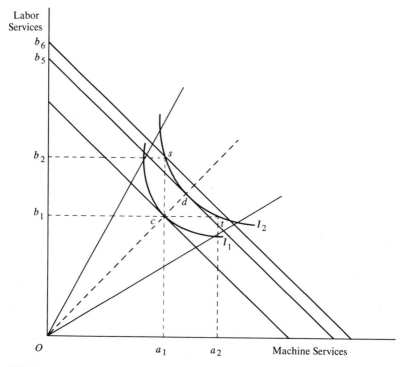

FIGURE 10.4

output is to increase the *acquisition* and use of labor services. In contrast to the market-period situation of the previous section, the larger input of labor services is accomplished not by increasing the proportion of supervisory and quality-control services to direct labor services but primarily by an increase in direct labor services (the proportion of supervisory and quality-control services to direct labor services may, in fact, decline). Thus, while short-run marginal costs will increase as a result of the decreasing marginal productivity of labor services as output increases along the path cs (assuming no change in the price of direct labor services), the short-run marginal cost of producing I_2 by the input combination $a_1 b_2$ is less than if the same point occurred under market-period conditions. The short-run marginal cost of producing I_2 at s will, of course, be larger than if the output I_2 had been anticipated. The penalty for being wrong, or the difference in the total cost of producing I_2 at s rather than at a correctly anticipated d, is $b_6 - b_5$ multiplied by the price of labor services (assuming this price to be constant). On the other hand, if t occurs and this strategy (of increasing machine speed) is selected, the penalty for being wrong is the same as under market-period conditions, and the increase in marginal costs (market-period and short run) is the same.

If strategy t can be, and is, adopted, however, the penalty for being wrong can*not* be calculated in the same manner as for strategy s. If a_1 reflects operation of the given stock of machines at the optimal rate, the additional machine services $a_2 - a_1$ can be secured from the same quantity of machines only at a higher cost per unit than for a_1. Securing additional machine services by exceeding the optimal rate of operation is thus analytically equivalent to securing additional labor services from a given stock of labor by the payment of overtime premium wages. Thus the penalty for being wrong for strategy t would have to be depicted by an isocost line passing through t, possessing a greater (absolute) slope than those shown, and calculated by multiplying the difference between the labor-services intercept (greater than b_5) and b_5 by the price of labor services (assuming this price to be constant).

Assuming that s and t occur, strategy t is as unlikely to be the most economical way of securing the desired increase in output as it was in the market-period situation of the previous section. Strategy s, while more likely than it was in the market period (since overtime need not be paid and since the stock of direct labor is not fixed), is still improbable because diminishing returns to labor services combined with a_1 machine services could be offset to some extent by increasing machine speed. The set of possible strategies lies on the st portion of I_2, if s and t occur, or on that portion of I_2 within the ridge lines if they do not. As in the market period, the desired higher output I_2 cannot be produced at as low a total cost as if it had been correctly anticipated. Even if d is selected, operation of the given stock of machines at rates higher than their optimum means that the isocost line passing through d would have a higher labor-services intercept than b_5. With the exception of t, however, any short-run strategy selected will permit production of the increase in output $I_2 - I_1$ at a smaller additional cost than the corresponding market-period strategy. Since additional machine services are more expensive, relative to direct labor services, for outputs greater than I_1 (assuming the price of labor services not to have changed), the short-run output-expansion path will proceed from c to a point on I_2 that lies between points d and s.

Figure 10.5 depicts a short-run situation in which the production manager has *overestimated* the output that he would be asked to produce. Anticipating an output of I_1, he had, in some previous long run, designed a process that could most economically produce this output by the combination a_1 of machine services and b_1 of labor services.

Again, one possible strategy is to change the labor-services input, leaving the other input unchanged. If g occurs, the desired lower output can be achieved by reducing the use, *and acquisition*, of labor services. Since this does not require the nonoptimal use of the same stock of direct labor (as it would in the market period), the reduction in costs accompanying

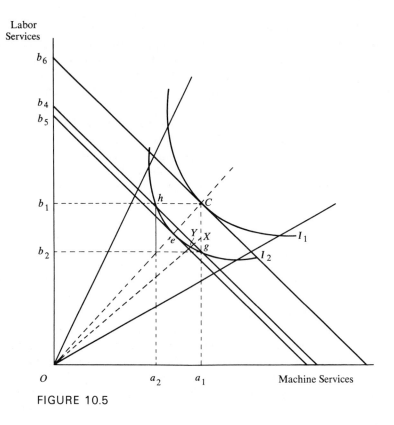

FIGURE 10.5

the decrease in output will be larger than if the corresponding strategy had been employed in the market-period situation. The reduction will not be sufficiently large, however, to compensate for the error in the selection of the output, as indicated by the fact that $b_6 - b_4 < b_6 - b_5$. Strategy g is not likely to be the most economical alternative. The reduction in labor services with no reduction in machine services has lowered the marginal productivity of machine services in this process at this time, providing an incentive to use these services in some other process and/or in some future period. These considerations, and others, establish a user cost for machine services which, together with the price of labor services, determines a short-run output-expansion path such as OXC according to which reductions in output would occur. Thus in this situation a determinate combination (the coordinates of point Y) would be used to produce the lower output I_2 at the least possible cost. Unless the short-run output-expansion path happens to be OhC, the reduction in cost accompanying the decrease in output will be greater than that available by any alternative in the market period but not so great as if the lower output had been selected initially.

Thus, as shown in Figure 10.6, short-run marginal costs are greater than long-run marginal costs for outputs larger than that for which the process was designed but not so great as market-period marginal costs.

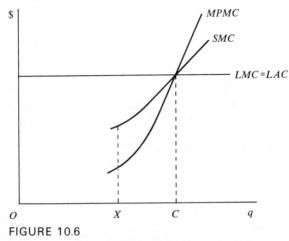

FIGURE 10.6

For smaller outputs, short-run marginal costs are greater than market-period marginal costs but not so great as long-run marginal costs. As output decreases from C to X, marginal costs fall because of returns to proportion. As output is further reduced, marginal costs will probably continue to decline over some range despite the linearity of this portion of the short-run output-expansion path—owing to decreasing "offsets" in the form of alternative uses of machine services in other processes and/or to the declining present value of larger quantities of machine services diverted to the future. Moreover, as output is reduced, there may well be an inability to maintain the economic order quantity in the purchase of all inputs.

THE SEMI-LONG RUN: THE PROBLEM OF PROCESS DESIGN

In the market period it was assumed that all inputs were constrained, although these constraints have been somewhat more flexible in the present chapter than in earlier chapters. In the short run it was assumed that at least one input was constrained while at least one other input was divisible in acquisition as well as in use. Here again the constraint was somewhat more flexible in the present chapter than in earlier chapters.

The obvious progression from all inputs constrained is to no inputs constrained, but proceeding directly from the short run to this form of the long run requires omission of an unnecessarily large proportion of the production manager's tasks. Given limits upon other inputs that do not infringe upon those under consideration, we can still analyze a situation in which the inputs *under consideration* are variable in acquisition and in use but require no appreciable alterations in the acquisition of other inputs. For example, in a multiproduct, multiprocess plant the production manager is asked to select the best combination of machines and labor to produce a given output of a particular product, it being assumed that production of this product will require no capital expenditure for buildings and no appreciable changes in the expenditures for the various necessary service systems (water, heat, light, and so on). "Slack" is in some sense assumed for inputs other than those under consideration, together with no appreciable user cost for alterations in the magnitude of this slack.

Thus in the background there are factors in terms of which this analysis is a short run, but also in terms of which there is excess capacity available to this process at no cost. If the process under consideration requires no additional building space (or diversion from other uses), building services may be available to it on the same terms as air. For any quantity of the inputs that *do* involve cost we must ensure combination of this quantity with that quantity of the "free" inputs at which the marginal productivity of the latter is zero. Except for this (sometimes critical) consideration, we may ignore these "background" inputs in the analysis.

Ignoring the feedbacks and interrelationships with *product* design, the problem posed is most closely related to what the production manager terms "process design" (although much that is involved in process design cannot be related to the analysis).[4] Having been given the product specifications and the desired output, the production manager's task is to design a process that will yield the desired output most economically, in terms of the required labor services and machine services.

A major initial question for the production manager concerns the firmness of the estimate of the desired output. If it is very firm, he may be able to design a relatively *unadaptable* or inflexible process that can produce at the required rate but only with great difficulty, if at all, at higher rates— except by using more of both inputs. Similarly this relatively unadaptable process may not be capable of any but the smallest decreases in its rate of output, if at all, except by diversion from this process of both men and machines. But this process may be significantly less expensive than alternative, more adaptable, processes.

Adaptability is thus concerned with the relative ease with which the proportion between inputs can be altered. More specifically, adaptability can be defined in terms of the relative rate of change of the marginal product of one input with respect to variation in that input from the design quan-

---

[4]Timms, *The Production Function in Business*, pp. 287–91.

tity.[5] A completely unadaptable process would thus require utilization of inputs in a fixed proportion. Adding more than the design quantity of labor services to the design quantity of machine services would result in no increase in output. The same would be true of the addition of machine services to the design quantity of labor services. Similarly, a process more adaptable than another would be one in which separate variation of inputs from their design quantities would result in less rapidly declining marginal products of the two inputs. One process could, of course, be more adaptable than a second with respect to one input and less adaptable with respect to another.

Geometrically, a more adaptable process may be represented by a larger angle formed by the ridge lines with the origin. Thus in Figure 10.7 the solid ridge lines could represent a more adaptable process than that represented by the dotted lines. A fixed-proportions, or completely unadaptable, process would thus be one in which the two rays, in effect, converged into a single ray from the origin passing through the design output m.

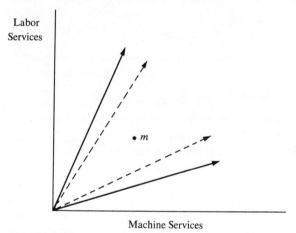

FIGURE 10.7

Assuming that the cost of greater versus lesser adaptability has been weighed against such factors as the probability of variation from the design output, inventory cost, and so on (if a choice of relative adaptability existed), the analysis of Chapters 5 and 6 becomes directly descriptive of the production manager's selection of the appropriate input quantities. Though the price of labor services and that of machine services may well not be known with the degree of precision that the analysis assumes, within this limitation the rational production manager would seek equality in the respective ratios

[5]Cf. Eirik G. Furubotn, "Investment Alternatives and the Supply Schedule of the Firm," *The Southern Economic Journal*, vol. XXXI (July 1964), p. 21, n. 1.

of marginal productivity to input price or tangency of the isocost curve and the isoquant (assuming further that sufficient points on the isoquant exist). The least costly combination to use in the production of the design output I_1 in Figure 10.8 is thus $a_1 b_1$. To say that the production manager follows this rationale is, of course, not to say that he does so consciously or that he employs the terminology and tools of this analysis.

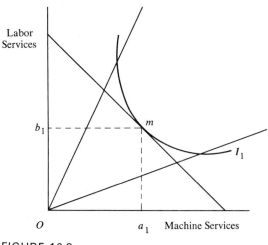

FIGURE 10.8

In the choice of the design output, consideration must have been given to the effect of variation in output upon cost. Given the usual assumptions of a linear homogeneous production function, constant input prices, and so on, the output-expansion path would be linear, and marginal and average cost equal and constant. It is very unlikely, however, that the price of a unit of factor *services* will be constant at all inputs. A machine that costs twice as much as another is apt to be capable of yielding into production more than twice as large a quantity of machine services, causing the cost per unit of these services to decline at greater outputs. Similarly, hiring twice as many men may permit (by specialization of function, division of operations, and the like) more than twice as large a quantity of labor services to enter production. Consequently, over a considerable range of output marginal and average costs may decline as output increases, in the semi-long run.

PRODUCTION THEORY AND LINEAR PROGRAMMING

Familiar to most readers is the mathematical technique of linear programming, a tool of widespread usefulness in production management. The present section, using problems familiar to production management, relates this technique to the production theory and the context of Chapter 5.

When applied to production problems, linear programming assumes a linear, homogeneous production function—the type for which we argued in Chapter 5. Also assumed is the type of input constraint that in Chapter 5 was concluded to be most realistic: any fixed input is fixed only in the sense that no quantity *larger than* the stipulated quantity may enter into production. Any fixed input is thus indivisible in acquisition but divisible in use, up to the constraint of the maximum quantity available.

A fundamental difference in assumptions, however, is that in the linear programming approach the production *surface* is not smooth. Instead it is assumed that there are a discrete number of *completely unadaptable* processes. Thus there can only be returns to scale, and the only way in which the proportion between inputs can be altered is by choosing a different process. All of the output that is produced by a given process requires the combining of inputs in the same proportion. Nonetheless, the relationship *between* processes is consistent with what would be expected from the law of variable proportions—that is, less of one input must be accompanied by more of another if the same output is to be produced by two different "admissible"[6] processes.

Figure 10.9 is an attempt to portray these assumptions more clearly. *OA* and *OB* represent two completely unadaptable processes. In effect they

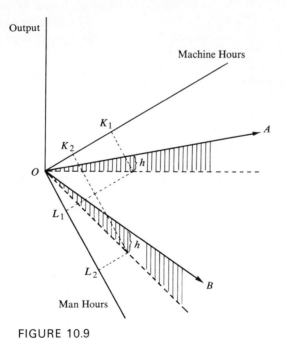

FIGURE 10.9

---

[6]A process that requires more of *both* inputs (per unit of output) is, by the assumption of rationality, an "inadmissible" process.

constitute two vertical slices through the production surface. The options open to the firm are to produce its output by process OA, or by process OB, or some by one and the remainder by another. The output h can be produced by using OK_1 machine hours together with OL_1 man hours, and this same output can also be produced by a combination of OK_2 machine hours with OL_2 man hours. Producing this output by process OB thus requires less machine hours and more man hours. It is assumed that all points on the top of the slices exist; that is, any output shown by OA or OB can be produced by the inputs comprising its coordinates—the rays OA and OB are continuous. OA and OB are thus similar to the returns-to-scale output-expansion paths of Chapter 5, except that they are dictated by the necessity of combining inputs in a given proportion rather than by tangency of isocost lines and isoquants, and except that there are more than one of them.[7]

As indicated previously, all output can be produced by process OA, or all by OB, or part by one process and the remainder by the other. Assume that the production manager is in a situation analogous to the market-period situation of Chapter 5. He has available to him OK_1 machine hours (Figure 10.10), OL_2 man hours, and the two processes OA and OB. The rays are scaled in terms of the outputs that he can produce so that if he uses only process OA he can produce an output of OA_1 by using all of his machine hours and OL_1 of the available OL_2 man hours. *In terms of output,* $OB_1 = OA_1$, so that he has an alternative of producing the same output by utilizing all of his available man hours but only OK_2 of the available OK_1

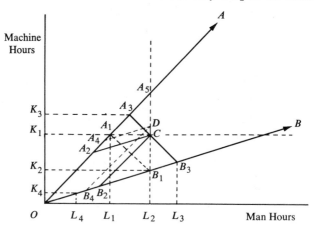

FIGURE 10.10

[7]Another difference is that the processes OA and OB could also refer to the production of two different products rather than to two different processes for producing a single product. Finally, as the statement in the text implies, OA and OB also differ from output-expansion paths in that they do not necessarily indicate the cost-minimizing inputs that can be used in producing the indicated outputs.

machine hours. By assumption there is no user cost and no intertemporal substitution of factor services, so that machine hours or man hours not utilized are simply lost. We next ask whether or not the production manager could secure a larger output by dividing his already acquired stocks of input, devoting a portion to output by one process and the remainder to the other.

The solution (without proof) is presented in Figure 10.10. From the point C at which the constraints intersect, CA_2 is constructed parallel to OB and CB_2 is constructed parallel to OA. By producing OA_2 of the output by process OA and OB_2 of the output by process OB, we obtain a total output larger than OA_1 or OB_1 (the two are equal in terms of output). To produce this larger output entirely by process OA would require OK_3 machine hours—more than are available. Similarly, to produce this larger output entirely by process OB would require OL_3 man hours—also more than are available. But the larger output can be produced by dividing production between the two processes. Further, the solution portrayed in Figure 10.10 indicates the maximum output that can be secured and utilizes all of the available man hours and machine hours.[8]

While lines such as A_3B_3 and A_1B_1 are not isoquants, they do have many of the same properties. While point C does not lie on any output-expansion path, it does indicate a set of input requirements that could be used to produce the output OA_3 or OB_3 just as do the coordinates of points A_3 and B_3. Similarly, the coordinates of any point on A_1B_1 indicate the input combinations that can be used to produce the same output, even though all points other than A_1 and B_1 would require production to be divided between the two processes OA and OB.

As in the market-period situation of Chapter 5, there is no unique output-expansion path. Outputs larger than OA_1 or OB_1 would require some division of production between the two processes, but a unique division would be necessary only to produce the maximum output OA_3 (or OB_3). The combination of inputs used to produce any of the possible outputs, however, would have to lie within OA_1CB_1O. Also as in the market-period situation of Chapter 5, the firm's average fixed costs would be the same as its average total costs.

Figure 10.10 may also be used to portray a situation analogous to the short-run situation of Chapter 5. Assume, again, that the production manager has available a stock of OL_2 man hours but that machine hours are available to him only at a cost (perhaps the opportunity cost of their use in still other processes or the cost of using machines in the present rather than in the future). There is, however, no relevant physical constraint upon the quantity of machine hours devoted to production in the processes OA and OB.

---

[8] For the proof of the solution presented in Figure 10.10 see William J. Baumol, *Economic Theory and Operations Analysis,* 2nd ed. (Englewood Cliffs, N.J.: Prentice-Hall, Inc., 1965), p 278, n. 5.

Since a cost is associated with machine hours but not with labor hours (up to the constraint OL_2), the production manager will wish to maximize the output that he can secure from any given input of machine hours, or he will wish to minimize the machine-hour requirement for any output—for outputs equal to and less than OB_1. Thus machine-hour inputs less than OK_2 are combined with less than all of the available man hours (OL_2), yielding an output-expansion path (O, B_2, B_1) for outputs less than OB_1. OK_4 of machine hours are combined with OL_4 of the available man hours, for example, leaving $OL_2 - OL_4$ man hours idle. The portion O, B_2, B_1 of the firm's output-expansion path is thus analogous to the returns-to-scale part of the basic short-run output-expansion path of Chapter 5. (There is no reason to assume in Figure 10.10, however, that the ray OB corresponds to a ridge line of the surface as it did in Chapter 5.)

Because of the assumption of completely unadaptable processes, there can be no returns to proportion from combining more than OK_2 machine hours with OL_2 man hours, *in the manner in which this was done in Chapter 5*. Nonetheless, outputs larger than OB_1 (or OA_1) can be secured by combining OL_2 man hours with more than OK_2 machine hours by utilizing both processes—that is, by dividing the inputs between the two processes in the manner indicated for the market-period situation above. In the present situation OA is, of course, the more costly process, since it requires a higher proportion of machine hours to man hours than does process OB. Thus, larger and larger outputs (than OB_1) can be secured (up to OA_5) by the use of larger and larger (than OK_2) quantities of machine hours along with OL_2 man hours, provided that the inputs are divided between the two processes in the manner previously described. Thus an output equal to OA_3 can be produced by using OK_1 machine hours and OL_2 man hours, provided that OB_2 of the output is produced by process OB and OA_2 by process OA. Similarly, a still larger output can be produced by the input combination represented by point D. Note, however, that in order to produce this larger output, increased reliance must be placed on the more costly process. Only OB_4 of this larger output would be produced by process OB while OA_4 would be produced by process OA. Production of the maximum output OA_5 would require sole dependence upon the more costly process.

Thus, if properly interpreted, B_1A_5 can be considered the remainder of the short-run output-expansion path, so that the output-expansion path OB_1A_5 becomes quite similar to the basic short-run output-expansion path of Chapter 5. Further, while outputs equal to or less than OB_1 would be produced at constant marginal costs (assuming the cost per unit of machine hours to be constant), marginal costs would increase for outputs larger than OB_1, reflecting the increasing proportion of larger outputs that would have to be produced by the more costly process.

Finally, if there are no relevant physical constraints upon either input but a cost is associated with each, we have a linear programming situation analogous to the basic long-run situation of Chapter 5 and to the semi-long-run situation of the preceding section. The production manager's problem is the selection of the best process, given several completely unadaptable processes and given also the input costs. In Figure 10.11 the rays OA, OB, and OC represent the alternative processes and the isocost line has the same meaning as in Chapter 5 (depicting the various combinations of the inputs that could be secured for a given expenditure, given also the input costs). Line segments such as $A_1 B_1$ and $B_1 C_1$ indicate *input* combinations that could yield the same output by the use of the adjacent processes (processes OA and OB for the line segment $A_1 B_1$ and processes OB and OC for the line segment $B_1 C_1$). Thus, with the reservations expressed earlier, $A_1 B_1 C_1$ may be thought of as a linear approximation of an isoquant, as may $A_2 B_2 C_2$.

In the situation depicted by Figure 10.11 the production manager would select process OB. While production of the same output could be accomplished by either of the other processes alone or by combinations of any adjacent processes, the cost of doing so by any alternative other than process OB alone would require a larger total expenditure on inputs. For this output the total cost of input requirements is minimized by selection of process OB. Assuming that at other expenditure levels the cost per unit of labor *services* and machine *services* remained the same, the output-expansion path would be $OB_1 B_2$, and so on, and average and marginal costs would be constant. If the isocost lines coincided with line segments such as $B_1 C_1$, $B_2 C_2$, and so on, the production manager could select process OB, process OC, or any combination indicated by the line segments without affecting his costs. Thus, in this event there would be no unique output-

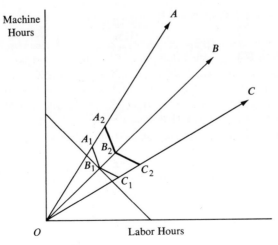

FIGURE 10.11

expansion path, although any path selected would have to lie within the rays OB and OC.

SUMMARY AND CONCLUSIONS

Production management can be related to the production and cost theory of Chapters 5 and 6. The concept of the production process, basic to the production-management area of business administration, is similar to the economist's concept of the production function, although there are marked differences in the two concepts.

The logical "situations" or decision classifications of the market period, the short run, and the long run have analogies in the situations confronted by the production manager and can be used, with some modifications, as explanations of his decision-making process. Many of his decisions cannot be analyzed by modification or extension of the economist's heuristic devices, however, because of basic differences in concepts and assumptions. A major difference is the economist's implicit assumption that production always occurs *on* the production surface, whereas much of the production manager's efforts are directed to achieving this result.

A particularly fortunate matching of assumptions occurs between the production theory of Chapter 5 and a major tool of production management— linear programming. The particular type of production function argued for in Chapter 5 turns out to be the type of production function that must be assumed if this tool is to be used. Similarly the type of constraint defended in Chapter 5 as most realistic is the type of constraint assumed when linear programming is used in production management. Finally, the output-expansion paths of Chapters 5 and 6 have analogies under the assumptions of linear programming, although substantial alterations in the meaning of this concept often occur.

SELECTED REFERENCES

BAUMOL, WILLIAM J., *Economic Theory and Operations Analysis*, 2nd ed. (Englewood Cliffs, N.J.: Prentice-Hall, Inc., 1965), chaps. 5 and 12.

DORFMAN, ROBERT, PAUL SAMUELSON, and ROBERT SOLOW, *Linear Programming and Economic Analysis* (New York: McGraw-Hill Book Company, 1958).

STARR, MARVIN K., *Production Management: Systems and Synthesis* (Englewood Cliffs, N.J.: Prentice-Hall, Inc., 1964).

TIMMS, HOWARD L., *The Production Function in Business*, rev. ed. (Homewood, Ill.: Richard D. Irwin, Inc., 1966).

WU, YUAN-LI, and CHING-WEN KWANG, "An Analytical and Graphical Comparison of Marginal Analysis and Mathematical Programming in the Theory of the Firm," in Kenneth E. Boulding and Allen W. Spivey, eds., *Linear Programming and the Theory of the Firm* (New York: The Macmillan Company, 1960).

the marketing theory of the firm and the balance of marketing instruments

While not unique to this area of business administration, literature in the field of marketing reflects a theory of the firm that (not surprisingly) is more complex and realistic but less manageable and cohesive than that sketched in Part I. Our immediate objective in this chapter is to summarize the essential points of the marketing theory of the firm—to portray "the" situation confronting "the" firm, as viewed by scholars in this area. The second section then considers the reactions of the firm to certain aspects of this situation—more specifically, the question of the "balance" of marketing instruments. This question is treated first in terms of the conditions that must be met if a balance is to exist, and then in terms of the presumed behavior of marketing instruments—that is, sales response functions. Finally, the concept of balance is grafted onto the notion of the product life cycle to illuminate the problem of maintaining a balance of marketing instruments through time.

THE MARKETING THEORY OF THE FIRM

Consumer Wants

Despite discussions of such subjects as product differentiation and price discrimination, economists tend to think of the consumer's wants implicitly as belonging in a classification coincident with that of economic

245

goods. The consumer has a want: it is met by a good that the consumer purchases. That want is met by that good: other wants are met by other goods. In marketing, consumers are viewed as a far more heterogeneous group, possessing wants at the same time more basic than those fulfilled by a particular good and also incapable of placement in a classification coincident with a classification of goods.[1] In marketing, a particular consumer has a basic want that is met, imperfectly and partially, by the acquisition of a particular good from a particular source (or at least he thinks it will be met by this acquisition). At a particular point in time the want of the consumer is more nearly met by purchasing this good from this source than by purchase of the same or other good from any other source. But the chances are that this purchase does not exactly meet the want of this consumer at this point in time. Even if it did, of few of the firm's customers would this be true, and it might well not be true of this customer at other points in time.

Thus, for many of the firm's customers, purchase of its wares is a compromise. Owing to the tremendous diversity of consumers, the compromise is inescapable. This is true even apart from the consumer's evaluation of the merits of the product, for more is involved in the consumer's decision to buy from a particular source than his evaluation of the product.

This view of consumers' wants, as something more basic and yet more changeable than a particular product or service, leads to greater emphasis upon alterations in the product or service, upon the rise of new products and the decline of old ones, upon factors other than product or service that may affect the decision to purchase, and upon the multitude of other variables that the firm must consider in any attempt to maximize its profits. Partially from this view of consumers' wants there arises a concept of the firm as constantly seeking a more satisfactory adjustment to the desires of the consumer, these desires themselves often being only vaguely definable (even by the consumers) and subject to change both by the actions of the firm and also independently.

The Firm's Limited Scope of Discretionary Action

From consideration of the firm's relationships to its customers, to other firms, and to the economy as a whole, there emerges a picture of the typical firm as buffeted by some forces to which it can only react, and as affected by some that it reacts to and also can influence to some degree— leaving a single category of forces to a considerable degree under the control of the firm. Thus Allison suggests a classification of the factors affecting

---

[1] Philip Kotler, *Marketing Management: Analysis, Planning, and Control* (Englewood Cliffs, N.J.: Prentice-Hall, Inc., 1967), pp. 68–69.

the firm's revenue and selling costs:[2] *outside factors, firm-influenced factors,* and *firm-controlled factors.*

Outside factors, in this classification, are factors that the firm cannot control or influence but that affect the relative effectiveness of the firm-controlled factors. Outside factors include the level of economic activity (and buyers' expectations concerning future levels), the demand for complementary items and items of which the firm's product is a component, government actions, and population characteristics (income distribution, ethnic composition, age distribution, and so on). Firm-influenced factors, which also affect the relative effectiveness of firm-controlled factors, include employee efficiency, customer reactions, technology specific to the firm's products, number of competitors, the firm's relationship with independent channel agencies that sell the product or products, and the actions of producers of substitute and complementary products.[3]

Firm-controlled factors, in Allison's classification, are interrelated and include such things as advertising, distribution channels, the particular group of customers to whom the firm is seeking to appeal, location, pricing, product quality and design, and sales promotion.[4] The exercise of the firm's control over these factors is limited, however, by restrictions imposed by the firm itself (such as nonprofit goals) or imposed externally (such as industry practices arising from market structure and historical experience).[5]

The same basic concept of the firm as possessing limited control over a group of variables, factors, or instruments—the limitations of the degree of control stemming from the firm itself as well as from the external environment—is reflected in the following quotation from Verdoorn:

> . . . an enterprise has at its disposal certain possibilities, each of which, however, is subject to certain limitations. In addition, the enterprise strives for a plurality of objectives, the most important of which is the maximization of present profits. In this, the other objectives act as so many side conditions. Both the possibilities and these side conditions represent certain boundary conditions which, in the process of maximizing present profits, must not be exceeded. Finally, with regard to its marketing policy, the enterprise can utilize a number of instruments for the purpose of realizing both its main and its auxiliary objectives.[6]

Finally, the same basic idea is found in Kotler's discussion of *decision*

---

[2] Selling costs is a term for the outlays of the firm that affect its revenue as well as its costs. Thus an improvement in product quality may well affect revenue and cost.

[3] Harry Allison, "Framework for Marketing Strategy," *California Management Review,* vol. IV, no. 1 (Fall 1961), pp. 79–81.

[4] *Ibid.,* p. 80.

[5] *Ibid.,* pp. 76–78.

[6] P. J. Verdoorn, "Marketing From the Producer's Point of View," *The Journal of Marketing,* vol. XX, no. 3 (Jan. 1956), p. 227.

variables versus *environmental* variables[7] and in the following classification of the "demand" variables that affect the firm's sales volume (output):

> *Customer variables.* Company sales are affected by the number of buyers in the market and by their incomes, motives, needs, attitudes, and purchasing habits. A company can do very little to alter these customer variables. Its task is to use market analysis and forecasting to learn how to make the most profitable adaptation to them.
>
> *Environmental variables.* Company sales are affected by environmental variables which transcend particular markets, such as the level of economic activity, the character and course of legislation, and the pattern of weather. These variables are also beyond the control of individual companies, and the task is again one of profitable adaptation through careful forecasting and planning.
>
> *Competitive variables.* Company sales are affected by the policies of other companies producing similar and substitute products. Although a company generally has little control over the actions of competitors, it can seek to anticipate them and to plan accordingly.
>
> *Marketing decision variables.* Company sales are affected by product quality, price, promotion, and distribution. Given customer characteristics, environmental characteristics, and the actions of competitors, the final level of company sales will depend upon the company's marketing program.[8]

Of most relevance for the purposes of the present chapter is that group of forces over which the firm has a significant degree of control--Allison's "firm-controlled factors," Ferber and Verdoorn's "marketing instruments," and Kotler's "marketing decision variables." Emphasis upon these variables permits a more complete answer (than that provided by Part I) to the question, "What determines the quantity that the firm can sell?" It also permits construction of an analysis to explain the allocation of the firm's marketing effort among the various marketing instruments that can affect the quantity the firm can sell.

Marketing Instruments and the Demand for the Firm's Output

In Chapter 4 the concept of the demand for the output of the individual firm was developed, but it was in no way indicated that the firm, itself, could affect the quantity sold by means other than alterations in its price. In Chapters 5 and 6 the determinants of the firm's costs were discussed, but it was in no way indicated that the firm might have costs other than those incurred in production. But, as the previous discussion has indicated, the firm (in the marketing theory of the firm) has a limited ability to affect quantity sold by means other than price changes and, quite obviously, changes in quantity occasioned by such means will affect the firm's costs.

---

[7] Kotler, *Marketing Management*, p. 26.

[8] Philip Kotler, *Marketing Management: Analysis, Planning, and Control*, p. 264. © 1967. Reprinted by permission of Prentice-Hall, Inc., Englewood Cliffs, N.J.

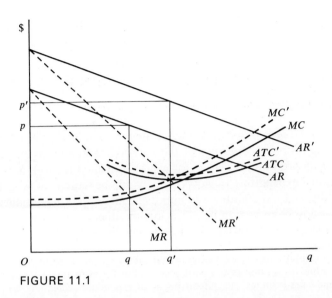

FIGURE 11.1

Economists, however, have not been entirely insensitive to these considerations, and much of the marketing theory of the firm rests upon their contributions.[9] Basically the effect of marketing instruments (other than price) has been analyzed as a simultaneous increase in the demand for the firm's output and in the firm's costs. Such instruments as advertising are employed to raise the demand curve and render it less elastic (by, say, increasing customer loyalty).[10] So long as the firm's total revenue is increased by more than the increase in costs occasioned by advertising, the firm's profits are increased. While the firm's price may well be other than it would be if advertising were not employed, the change in price is a *result* of adjustment to the effect of advertising rather than an independent change.

Figure 11.1 indicates the effects of a change in advertising expenditures. AR is replaced by AR' (the two need not be parallel), MR by MR', MC by MC', p by p', and q by q'. Comparison of the profit rectangles (the difference between average total cost and average revenue at the optimum outputs multiplied by the respective outputs) indicates whether or not the increase in advertising occasioned an increase in profit. So long as it did so, expenditures upon advertising would be increased.

While an analysis such as the above can be generalized to all nonprice instruments, it suffers from a number of shortcomings, including an inability to make direct comparisons of the relative effectiveness of the various

---

[9] For the work of a pioneer in this area, see E. H. Chamberlin, *The Theory of Monopolistic Competition* (Cambridge, Mass.: Harvard University Press, 1933).

[10] At a given price.

marketing instruments. In the second section of the present chapter, this and related questions are considered in greater detail by an alternative approach.

THE BALANCE OF MARKETING INSTRUMENTS

Conditions for a Balance of Marketing Instruments

A basic question in marketing strategy is whether or not the firm is making the proper *relative* use of the various marketing instruments that can affect its profitability. How, for example, is the firm to know whether an additional expenditure on advertising would be more profitable than the same additional expenditure on improvement of product quality? And, might not a price reduction be preferable to either? One answer is that the various instrument variables will be properly "balanced" if

> ... the additional sales [volume] obtained by a small increase in unit costs are the same for all non-price instruments and at the same time equal to the additional sales [volume] accompanying a corresponding decrease in unit prices.[11]

Why these are the conditions for a balance of marketing instruments can be explained geometrically, algebraically, or in terms of the calculus.

Figure 11.2 depicts an increase in the demand for the output of the firm, this increase being occasioned by an increase in per-unit marketing expenditures attributable to a change in one of the (nonprice) marketing instruments. Advertising expenditures may have been increased, for example, by 10 cents per unit, resulting in the larger sales volume $(q + \Delta q)$ at the original price (p).

One of the interesting things about marketing expenditures is that they affect both cost and revenue. But a cost is a negative revenue, insofar as its effect upon profitability is concerned. Thus, we can get the *net* average revenue of the larger sales volume merely by subtracting the increase in per-unit marketing expenditures from the price. In effect, we adjust the upward shift of the demand curve to compensate for the fact that this upward shift was occasioned by an increase in cost. Having done so, we need only compare the result with the original demand function. If AR_N lies above D (as shown), increases in marketing expenditures per unit on the marketing instrument in question are more profitable than would be equal decreases in price ($\Delta S < \Delta p$, where ΔS represents the change in unit marketing expenditures). Similarly, if AR_N lies below D, a decrease in unit marketing expenditures upon this instrument is called for. If the net average revenue (AR_N) coincides with the original demand function, this means that

---

[11]Robert Ferber and P. J. Verdoorn, *Research Methods in Economics and Business* (New York: The Macmillan Company, 1962), p. 535.

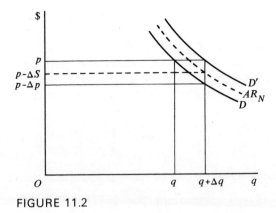

FIGURE 11.2

price and the nonprice instrument are perfectly balanced. In terms of our example, lowering the price by 10 cents (Δp) would have exactly the same effect upon sales volume (and profitability) as would an increase of 10 cents per unit in advertising expenditures.

Turning the argument around, price and this nonprice instrument will be in balance when equal (opposite) changes occasion the same change in sales volume. A balance of price with all nonprice instruments would require this same condition of each of them, thus necessarily implying that a given change in the marketing expenditure per unit on any nonprice instrument would occasion the same change in sales volume.

Let us define the elasticity of a particular marketing instrument as

$$\eta_s = \frac{S}{q} \frac{\Delta q}{\Delta S}$$

(where S = unit expenditure on this instrument). When the price and the nonprice instrument are in balance,

$$\eta_s = -\frac{S}{q} \frac{\Delta q}{\Delta p},$$

$$\frac{p}{S} \eta_s = \eta_p,$$

$$\frac{p}{S} = \frac{\eta_p}{\eta_s}.$$

That is, when the price and the nonprice instrument are in balance, the ratio of price to the marketing expenditure per unit on the nonprice instrument will equal the ratio of their respective demand elasticities. Further, since a balance between all instruments implies that $\Delta q/\Delta s$ is the same for all nonprice instruments, the ratio of any two nonprice demand elasticities must be the same as the ratio of the unit expenditure upon each. Finally, the ratios of all nonprice elasticities to the unit expenditures on the respective instruments are equal and also equal to the ratio of price elasticity to price.

$$\frac{\eta_{s_1}}{\eta_{s_2}} = \frac{S_1}{S_2}, \qquad \text{thus} \qquad \frac{\eta_p}{p} = \frac{\eta_{s_1}}{S_1} = \frac{\eta_{s_2}}{S_2}.$$

The same conclusions can be reached algebraically. Let

S = marketing expenditure per unit upon a particular nonprice instrument,

C = production (variable) cost per unit (assumed constant),

π_1 = profit derived by strategy one (variation of marketing expenditure per unit),

π_2 = profit derived by strategy two (price variation),

p = price,

q = quantity.

Then the change in profit by strategy one is

$$\Delta\pi_1 = p\,\Delta q - [\Delta S(q + \Delta q) + \Delta q(C + S)]$$

$$= p\,\Delta q - \Delta S(q + \Delta q) - \Delta q(C + S),$$

and the change in profit by strategy two is

$$\Delta\pi_2 = [\Delta q(p - \Delta p) - q\,\Delta p] - \Delta q(C + S)$$

$$= p\,\Delta q - q\,\Delta p - \Delta p\,\Delta q - \Delta q(C + S).$$

If the strategies are equal in their effects upon profitability, then

$$\Delta\pi_1 = \Delta\pi_2,$$

$$p\,\Delta q - \Delta S(q + \Delta q) - \Delta q(C + S) = p\,\Delta q - q\,\Delta p - \Delta p\,\Delta q - \Delta q(C + S),$$

$$-\Delta S(q + \Delta q) = -\Delta p(q + \Delta q).$$

Thus, if the changes in quantity resulting from the two strategies are the same, the change in unit marketing expenditure is the same as the change in price. Conversely, the two strategies will be in balance if equal (opposite) changes in price and unit marketing expenditure occasion the same change in quantity sold. The elasticity relationships, of course, follow as before, since $\Delta q/\Delta S = -\Delta q/\Delta p$.

In terms of the calculus:[12] let

F = the fixed costs of the firm, all other symbols retaining the same meaning,

$q = f(p, S)$,

$\pi = q(p - C - S) - F$.

If the two strategies are to have the same effect upon the firm's profit (for opposite changes), then

$$-\frac{\partial \pi}{\partial p} = \frac{\partial \pi}{\partial S},$$

$$-\frac{\partial \pi}{\partial p} = -(p - C - S)\frac{\partial q}{\partial p} - q,$$

$$\frac{\partial \pi}{\partial S} = (p - C - S)\frac{\partial q}{\partial S} - q,$$

$$-(p - C - S)\frac{\partial q}{\partial p} = (p - C - S)\frac{\partial q}{\partial S},$$

$$\therefore \quad -\frac{\partial q}{\partial p} = \frac{\partial q}{\partial S}.$$

Since

$$\eta_s = \frac{S}{q}\frac{\partial q}{\partial S},$$

the equality

$$-\frac{\partial q}{\partial p} = \frac{\partial q}{\partial S}$$

---

[12]This treatment is similar to that of Ferber and Verdoorn (*Research Methods*, pp. 543–44) except that herein the conditions of *balance* are treated separately from those for full equilibrium. This makes it more readily apparent that the elasticity relationships follow from the conditions of *balance* and do not necessarily presume full equilibrium.

implies that

$$\eta_s = \frac{S}{q}\left(-\frac{\partial q}{\partial p}\right),$$

$$\frac{P}{S}\eta_s = \frac{P}{q}\left(-\frac{\partial q}{\partial p}\right) = \eta_p,$$

$$\therefore \quad \frac{\eta_p}{\eta_s} = \frac{P}{S}.$$

(Since $\partial q/\partial S$ and $\partial q/\partial p$ in this approach are equivalent to $\Delta q/\Delta S$ and $\Delta q/\Delta p$, respectively, in the first approach, the other elasticity relationships again follow in the same way.)

For full equilibrium there must be not only a balance in the use of all marketing instruments but also maximum profit. Nonetheless, since balance is a necessary (though not sufficient) condition for the maximum-profit position, the maximum profit relative to any one instrument is the maximum profit relative to all instruments. Put otherwise, profit maximization with respect to any one of any number of balanced instruments is automatically maximization with respect to all others.

Thus, geometrically, *if each price change is balanced against alternative marketing instruments*, then D in Figure 11.2 corresponds throughout with AR_N, and the equilibrium output is determined simply by the equating of marginal revenue and marginal cost (assuming second-order conditions to be met).[13] It would not be possible, at this output, to secure a net average revenue greater than the price by a reallocation of marketing expenditures among the various nonprice instruments or by an increase in such expenditures.

Algebraically, full equilibrium requires that $\Delta\pi_1 = \Delta\pi_2 = 0$. Meeting this condition with respect to one strategy automatically means that it is met for all others—a conclusion we can reach mathematically as follows. If $\Delta\pi_1 = 0$, then

$$p\,\Delta q - \Delta S(q + \Delta q) - \Delta q(C + S) = 0 \qquad \text{(from the algebraic treatment above),}$$

$$\Delta q(p - \Delta S) - \Delta q\left(q\frac{\Delta S}{\Delta q}\right) = \Delta q(C + S),$$

$$p - \Delta S - q\frac{\Delta S}{\Delta q} = C + S,$$

---

[13] Note that the balance conditions must be met if the statement is to be correct.

$$\frac{\Delta q}{\Delta S} = \frac{q}{p - C - S - \Delta S}.$$

If $\Delta \pi_2 = 0,$

$$p \, \Delta q - q \, \Delta p - \Delta p \, \Delta q - \Delta q (C + S) = 0 \qquad \text{(from the algebraic treatment above),}$$

$$\Delta q(p - \Delta p) - \Delta q \left(q \frac{\Delta p}{\Delta q} \right) = \Delta q(C + S),$$

$$p - \Delta p - q \frac{\Delta p}{\Delta q} = C + S,$$

$$\frac{\Delta q}{\Delta p} = \frac{q}{p - C - S - \Delta p}.$$

As earlier established, balance alone establishes the equality of $-\Delta q / \Delta p$ and $\Delta q / \Delta S$. Thus, if $\Delta \pi_1 = 0$ and the strategies are balanced, $\Delta \pi_2 = 0$ also.

In terms of the calculus (and again assuming second-order conditions to be met) profit maximization requires that (in terms of the previous discussion):[14]

$$-\frac{\partial \pi}{\partial p} = \frac{\partial \pi}{\partial S} = 0.$$

If $-\partial \pi / \partial p = 0,$

$$-(p - C - S) \frac{\partial q}{\partial p} - q = 0,$$

$$-\frac{\partial q}{\partial p} = \frac{q}{p - C - S}.$$

Similarly, $\partial \pi / \partial S = 0$ implies this same condition (and is implied by it):

$$(p - C - S) \frac{\partial q}{\partial S} - q = 0,$$

$$\frac{\partial q}{\partial S} = \frac{q}{p - C - S}.$$

---

[14] No equivalent of Δp in the corresponding algebraic treatment occurs in this treatment, because finite changes are not involved.

These apparently nonsensical conditions are actually quite familiar relationships in an unfamiliar form. Multiplying the "price condition" by p/q,

$$-\frac{p}{q}\frac{\partial q}{\partial p} = \frac{p}{q}\frac{q}{p - C - S},$$

or

$$\eta_p = \frac{p}{p - (C + S)}.$$

Since we know from Part I that

$$\eta_p = \frac{\text{price}}{\text{price} - \text{marginal revenue}},$$

and since C and S are constant per unit, marginal cost $= C + S$.

Thus, this equilibrium condition reduces to the familiar condition that marginal cost equal marginal revenue. Generalizing over all marketing instruments, in equilibrium the marginal revenue received from each instrument is equal and also equal to marginal cost.

Sales Response Functions and the Balance of Marketing Instruments

In the previous subsection the conditions necessary for a balance of marketing instruments were stipulated. A more thorough analysis of how such a balance among nonprice variables is achieved, conceptually, requires consideration of the presumed form of the relationship between nonprice marketing instruments and sales (total revenue). Put otherwise, the previous subsection indicates the conditions that must be met if a balance is to *exist*. By analogy, the simple price-discrimination model of Part I contains the *condition* that marginal revenue be equal in each market, but this condition, per se, does not specify how marginal revenue is presumed to vary with output. Similarly, the previous subsection does not specify the *behavior* of the instruments that must be brought into balance. In the present subsection the relationship between expenditures upon marketing instruments and sales revenue, as usually described in the marketing literature, is converted into a form that is more familiar (to economists), permitting discussion of the behavior involved and the concept of balance, itself, in terms analogous to those employed in Part I.

The fundamental assumption with respect to the relationship between expenditure upon a nonprice marketing instrument and sales (total revenue)

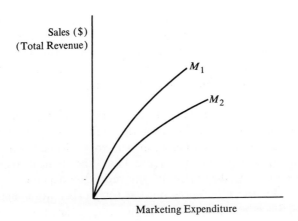

FIGURE 11.3

is that, at any time, such expenditures are subject to "diminishing returns." More precisely, it is assumed that (at least in the relevant range) sales (total revenue, *price constant*) increase at a decreasing rate as the marketing expenditure upon a given marketing instrument increases. While this general relationship is assumed to be true of all nonprice marketing instruments, it is also assumed that the rates of increase may well be different for different instruments. These assumptions, when portrayed geometrically, yield the *sales response* curves of Figure 11.3.[15] In Figure 11.2 it is assumed that increasing the firm's expenditure upon market instrument number one (M_1) would increase sales (total revenue) at a less rapidly decreasing rate than would be the case for marketing instrument number two (M_2).

Actually, the sales response curve is a very general tool in the marketing theory of the firm; by no means is it confined to the context in which we have placed it. Thus M_1 and M_2 in Figure 11.3 could represent the sales response functions for expenditures upon the same marketing instrument (such as advertising) in two territorially different markets, or they could represent the results of varying the expenditures upon two different aspects of product quality, upon two advertising media, upon the sales forces in two different markets (territorially or in terms of products), and so on. Whatever the context, the basic assumptions (decreasing but possibly different rates of increase) are the same—yielding analytically the problem of achieving a balance in the allocation of any given total expenditure between the alternatives posed. Any firmwide balance, however, presumes balances at less aggregative levels. A balance of expenditures upon all marketing instruments presumes that funds allocated, say, to advertising, are in turn allocated optimally among the various media, that the funds allocated to a

---

[15] Philip Kotler, *Marketing Management: Analysis, Planning, and Control,* p. 276. © 1967. Reprinted by permission of Prentice-Hall, Inc., Englewood Cliffs, N.J.

particular medium are in turn allocated optimally among the various products, that the funds allocated to a particular medium and to a particular product are optimally allocated territorially, and so on. The fact that the logic of achieving the balance is the same in any context should not obscure the fact that a host of interrelated decision processes of this type are occurring.

Thus, returning to the context of the firm as a whole, the problem is that of achieving an optimal allocation of the firm's total marketing expenditure among the various marketing instruments. The geometrical solution to the problem is presented in Figure 11.4. The vertical axis represents expenditures upon M_1, the horizontal axis represents expenditures upon M_2, and the straight line CD represents the total expenditure upon the two instruments. Since both axes are stated in terms of the same units, the angle formed by CD and the horizontal axis (angle 1) is necessarily 45°.

Implied by the assumptions made concerning the sales response curves (if an allocation problem exists) is a family of convex (to the origin) iso-revenue curves such as R_1, showing the various combinations of expenditures upon M_1 and M_2 that would occasion a given level of sales (total revenue). At point A on R_1, withdrawal of a unit of expenditure upon M_1 could be compensated by a relatively small increase in expenditures upon M_2, since at A expenditures upon M_1 would be relatively large and those upon M_2 relatively small. At point A the negative change in total revenue occasioned by withdrawal of a unit of expenditure upon M_1 could be easily offset by the positive change in total revenue occasioned by a relatively small increase in the expenditures upon M_2. At point B, however, a unit withdrawal in the expenditures upon M_1 would require a relatively large increase in expenditures upon M_2—if total revenue is not to change—since at B the expenditures upon M_2 are large relative to those upon A. Thus, going down

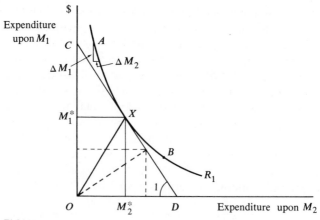

FIGURE 11.4

any isorevenue curve the ratio $-\Delta M_1/\Delta M_2$ declines, or the curve is convex (to the origin).

In considering an expenditure "mix" such as that indicated by point A, the firm would conclude not only that the total expenditure involved exceeds the budget but also that the amount by which it does so could be reduced (without affecting sales) by reducing the expenditure upon M_1 while increasing the expenditure upon M_2 by a lesser amount. The same reasoning would dictate opposite adjustment for combinations on R_1 to the right of the tangency (such as point B). Thus, given the total expenditure to be made upon the two instruments, the firm could attain the level of sales R_1 only by allocating OM_1^* to M_1 and OM_2^* to M_2. This allocation and only this allocation would maximize sales (total revenue) relative to the total expenditure constraint.[16]

At the tangency, of course, the slopes of CD and R_1 are the same (-1). At this point $-\Delta M_1/\Delta M_2 = 1$, and a small change in the expenditure upon M_1 would cause sales to change by the same amount, as would the same small change in the expenditure upon M_2. The two instruments are thus in balance. Generalizing for all marketing instruments, the condition of balance is characterized by[17]

$$\frac{\Delta R}{\Delta M_1} = \frac{\Delta R}{\Delta M_2} = \frac{\Delta R}{\Delta M_3} = \cdots .$$

Mathematically (since at any point on R_1, $dR = 0$), at the tangency

$$\frac{\partial R}{\partial M_1} dM_1 + \frac{\partial R}{\partial M_2} dM_2 = 0,$$

$$-\frac{dM_1}{dM_2} = \frac{\dfrac{\partial R}{\partial M_2}}{\dfrac{\partial R}{\partial M_1}} .$$

Since $-dM_1/dM_2 = 1$, generalizing,

$$\frac{\partial R}{\partial M_1} = \frac{\partial R}{\partial M_2} = \frac{\partial R}{\partial M_3} = \cdots ,$$

---

[16]The dotted lines in Fig. 11.4 indicate the (equal) allocation (of the total expenditure) that would occur if the two instruments were equally effective. The point X would occur, in this case, where the dotted lines meet the budget line. If M_2 were the more effective instrument, the point X would occur even further down the budget line.

[17]This condition is equivalent to the balance condition of the previous subsection. Since price is constant, revenue changes only because quantity changes.

or the *marginal sales response* $\partial R/\partial M$ must be equal for each instrument.

The conclusion reached is analogous to one reached in the treatment of simple third-degree price discrimination in Part I. There, output must be so allocated among markets that the marginal revenue in each market is equal (a necessary but not a sufficient condition for profit maximization). Similarly, to attain a balance of marketing instruments, we must allocate any expenditure upon these instruments so that the marginal sales response for each instrument is equal (again a necessary but not a sufficient condition for profit maximization). Finally, the condition of balance of marketing instruments is strictly analogous to the principle of rational consumer's expenditure in demand theory and to the condition in the theory of production that the ratio of marginal products to prices of inputs must be equal (the "prices" in the problem of balance are, of course, equal).

The analysis can readily be extended to yield the analytical counterparts of other tools familiar from Part I. For example, since in the analysis yielding Figure 11.4 price is presumed constant, division of R_1 and all iso-revenue curves by the price would yield a family of isoquants, each showing the various combinations of expenditures upon M_1 and M_2 that would yield the same sales *volume* or output. The budget line in Figure 11.4 would be unaffected, and the answer to the question of how best to allocate a given total expenditure upon the two instruments would be the same (OM_1^* upon M_1 and OM_2^* upon M_2). The condition of balance would then be

$$\frac{\partial q}{\partial M_1} = \frac{\partial q}{\partial M_2} = \frac{\partial q}{\partial M_3} = \cdots.$$

Thus, mechanically, all that would be involved is the substitution of q_1 for R_1 in Figure 11.2. Then a vertical section of the surface taken parallel to one axis at a given value of expenditure upon the other instrument would yield a curve of the same form as the sales response curve, the only difference being a substitution of quantity for the vertical axis rather than sales (total revenue). Reversing the axes would then yield a total-variable-cost curve with respect to expenditures upon this instrument. This curve, in turn, would yield (by the methods of Part I) the "variable-proportions" marginal-cost and average-variable-cost curves for this instrument. Diagrammatically, the derivation is illustrated by Figures 11.5–11.8.[18]

Though not always explicit in the relevant literature, it is perhaps fair to say that the sales response curve for increases in the *total* expenditure upon market instruments (as a whole) is presumed to increase at a decreasing

---

[18]The analysis could be readily extended to become analogous to the treatment of price discrimination in Part I (utilizing the various marginal-cost functions for the various instruments and showing that any marketing expenditure must be so allocated that the marginal costs of these instruments are equal).

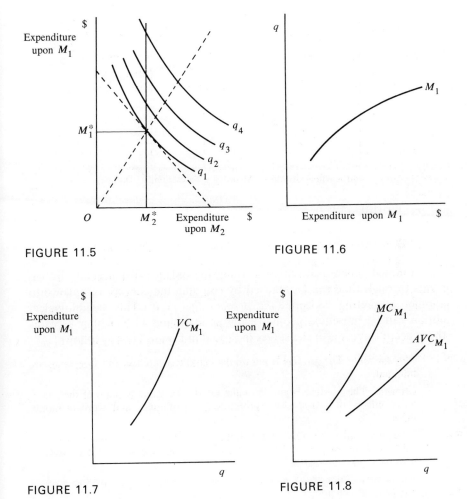

FIGURE 11.5   FIGURE 11.6

FIGURE 11.7   FIGURE 11.8

rate (perhaps after an initial range of increase at an increasing rate), even
if each total expenditure is optimally allocated among instruments. Converting to a quantity basis by dividing by the price, taking a vertical section
of the surface along the line on which O and X are points (Figure 11.5) would
again yield a curve similar to that of Figure 11.6.[19] Completing the steps
indicated by Figures 11.7 and 11.8 would thus yield upward-sloping "returns-
to-scale" marginal-cost and average-cost curves for balanced expenditures
upon all nonprice marketing instruments.

---

[19] In Figure 11.5, successively higher isoquants represent equal increases in output.
The greater spaces between successive isoquants reflect the assumption of decreasing "returns
to scale."

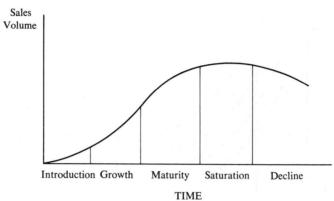

Sales Volume

Introduction   Growth   Maturity   Saturation   Decline

TIME

FIGURE 11.9

The Product Life Cycle and the Balance of Marketing Instruments

Limited generalizations concerning the balance of marketing instruments through time can be reached by coupling the concept of balance to another marketing concept—*the product life cycle*. This semibiological notion can be presented geometrically as in Figure 11.9. Kotler explains the concept (in terms of the stages indicated in Figure 11.9) as follows:

Introduction. The product is put on the market; awareness and acceptance are minimal.

Growth. The product begins to make rapid sales gains because of the cumulative effects of introductory promotion, distribution, and word-of-mouth influence.

Maturity. Sales growth continues but at a declining rate because of the diminishing number of potential customers who remain unaware of the product or who have taken no action.

Saturation. Sales reach and remain on a plateau marked by the level of replacement demand.

Decline. Sales begin to decline absolutely as the product is gradually edged out by better products or substitutes.[20]

Quite obviously, the concept of the product life cycle is very general. Its length and that of its component stages would vary with the rapidity of technological change, the form of market organization in the industry of which the firm is a part, the ease of entry into the industry, the relative durability of the product, and many other considerations. More important for present purposes, however, is the evident fact that even for the specific product of a specific firm, the duration of the product life cycle and of its

---

[20]Philip Kotler, *Marketing Management: Analysis, Planning, and Control*, p. 291. © 1967. Reprinted by permission of Prentice-Hall, Inc., Englewood Cliffs, N.J.

component stages would be affected by changes in the various market instruments. Thus, if we had such a cycle for one level of expenditure for one non-price marketing instrument, and for one distribution of this expenditure through time, other cycles would result if the magnitude or the temporal distribution of this expenditure were altered. Similarly, a different price or a different temporal distribution of prices would yield a different curve. What is involved is a large number of parameters, so that (in the absence of further definition) we have not one but a large family of product-life-cycle curves (if the product life cycle is indeed an analytical concept rather than merely a historical description).

But clearly the product-life-cycle concept does presume some alterations in the various marketing instruments. The concept is seldom, if ever, defined as of one value and one temporal distribution of the expenditures for each marketing instrument. Thus, if we wish to speak of the product life cycle while permitting variation in expenditures upon market instruments, we must specify a *principle* of variation such that a unique cycle (conceptually) results. In short, we must define the concept more precisely.

One method is to couple the concept of balance to that of the product life cycle so as to yield the *balanced* product life cycle. This gives a unique curve for a given total marketing budget. A unique curve also results if profit maximization is assumed (though each of the two conditions might give a different curve). Either assumption implies at each point in time an allocation of marketing expenditures and selection of price such that there is a balance of marketing instruments. In this view the concept of the product life cycle provides a rationale for very different allocations of expenditures and different reliance upon price changes at different points of time—either to maximize profit or optimally allocate marketing expenditures. For example, price reductions may have to play a larger role in the saturation stage than in the growth stage, while the opposite may be true of promotional expenditures.

The problem of a balanced product life cycle is complicated by the explicit introduction of time into the analysis. To achieve a balance of marketing instruments at any point in time, we must take into consideration the effect upon *future* sales volume of a *present* change in the expenditures upon those instruments. Thus some form of discounting to the present is involved in striking the balance at any given time. This difficulty does not alter the basic principle, but it severely handicaps any attempt to make the principle operational (or to ascertain whether or not it has been followed in a particular case).

For all but the single-product firm, a balance of marketing instruments at a given time requires not only their balance for any one product but also a simultaneous balance of any one instrument across all products. A matrix could be constructed showing the equality conditions for the balance for any particular instrument, perhaps, by its rows

$$\frac{\partial q_1}{\partial M_j} = \cdots = \frac{\partial q_n}{\partial M_j}$$

(where M_j is the expenditure upon the instrument and there are n products), and the equality conditions for the balance for any particular *product* by its columns

$$\frac{\partial q_i}{\partial M_1} = \cdots = \frac{\partial q_i}{\partial M_e}$$

(where q_i is the quantity of the product and there are e marketing instruments). Such a matrix would be a complicated but more precise way of saying that, for example, an additional dollar of expenditure upon the advertising outlays devoted to any single product must have the same effect upon profitability as an additional dollar spent upon that part of the product-quality expenditures devoted to any other product.

Finally, the balanced product life cycles for a multiproduct firm would be interdependent. At any point in the life cycle of a particular product, what would constitute a balance of market instruments would depend not only upon the stage it had reached but also upon the stages that the firm's other products had reached. One firm, confronted with impending saturation with respect to a particular product, might wisely react by improving its quality so as to achieve the balance. Another, with a higher proportion of its other products in the earlier stages, might just as rationally react to the same situation by decreasing the quality of this product. Yet both reactions could have been dictated by considerations of balance.

SUMMARY AND CONCLUSIONS

Marketing is a fertile field for the application of microeconomic tools. The reason is not that these tools are immediately transferable but that they can be altered and expanded without departure from their essential logic. The perceptive student of microeconomics will recognize, in their altered forms, tools familiar to him in his own field—and he may also appreciate the increased explanatory value in marketing yielded by their alteration.

The present chapter has considered only a few of the marketing topics that are related to microeconomics. Detailed consideration of other topics, such as market segmentation, would have yielded far more links to subjects such as the theory of price discrimination. Nonetheless, even the limited applications made may have given the reader some increased appreciation of the versatility and meaningfulness of these tools.

In the marketing theory of the firm, the firm's customers are reifications of the consumers in traditional economic theory. Rather than one simple abstraction, the firm's customers are regarded as a heterogeneous lot, explicitly differing in age, habits, location, income, custom, and a host of other respects. The consumer's wants are viewed as more basic than products, and the consumer is regarded as responding to the total circumstances of a purchase rather than simply to the product. Partly for this reason, the firm is viewed as making the best adjustment it can to many of the forces affecting its well-being, while retaining a limited scope of action with respect to other factors affecting it. "Marketing instruments" can be used by the firm—within limits—to affect the quantity sold, so that this variable, quantity, becomes dependent not only upon price but also upon such other factors as advertising, product quality, distribution channels, and sales force.

While marketing instruments can be analyzed simply in terms of shifts in the demand for the firm's output (and changes in its elasticity) simultaneous with increases in the firm's costs, a more thorough analysis considers the proper allocation of marketing effort among them. (The somewhat ambiguous term "marketing effort" reflects the substitutability of price and nonprice instruments.) This question of the "balance" of marketing instruments can be treated, first, in terms of the conditions necessary for the proper relationship between the instruments (including price) at a given level of expenditures upon these instruments and at full equilibrium. Second, the question of balance (among nonprice instruments) can be treated in a manner that takes into consideration the nature of the relationship assumed between expenditures on these instruments and sales revenue. Isorevenue curves, the optimum allocation of expenditures among instruments, isoquants, and cost functions for marketing expenditures can thus be developed. Finally, by coupling the concept of balance to that of the product life cycle, we can make a few generalizations concerning the question of the balance of marketing instruments through time.

SELECTED REFERENCES

ALLISON, HARRY, "Framework for Marketing Strategy," *California Management Review*, vol. IV, no. 1 (Fall 1961), pp. 75–94.

CHAMBERLIN, E. H., *The Theory of Monopolistic Competition* (Cambridge, Mass.: Harvard University Press, 1933).

DORFMAN, ROBERT, and P. O. STEINER, "Optimal Advertising and Optimal Quality," *The American Economic Review*, vol. XLIV (Dec. 1954), pp. 826–36.

FERBER, ROBERT, and P. J. VERDOORN, *Research Methods in Economics and Business* (New York: The Macmillan Company, 1962).

index